Student Learning Guide to Accompany

Economics
Third Edition

Student Learning Guide to Accompany

Economics
Third Edition

by Lewis C. Solmon

Thomas J. Pierce
and
Richard L. Moss
**California State College
San Bernardino**

Addison-Wesley Publishing Company
Reading, Massachusetts
Menlo Park, California
London
Amsterdam
Don Mills, Ontario
Sydney

This book is in the Addison-Wesley Series in Economics

This text is also available in split paperback volumes: *Student Learning Guide to Accompany Macroeconomics, Third Edition* and *Student Learning Guide to Accompany Microeconomics, Third Edition.*

ISBN 0-201-07637-3
ABCDEFGHIJ-HA-89876543210

To the Instructor

This **Student Learning Guide** has been designed to help students review and study the material in **ECONOMICS, Third Edition**.

The workbook takes into consideration three difficulties students may encounter. First, they may not recognize in the text all the points and concepts with which they should be familiar. To help students identify and review the major points, *Learning Objectives* and a complete *Outline* have been included for each chapter of the text.

The second difficulty students may encounter is being able to evaluate how much they have or have not learned before taking an examination. To help them evaluate mastery of the material, there is a *Concepts and Definitions* section for each chapter which consists of fill-in and multiple-choice questions. The answers to all questions are printed at the end of each chapter.

Finally, because students may have difficulty interrelating and applying various concepts within a chapter, or from chapter to chapter, Application questions have been included for each chapter. The answers to these questions are also found at the ends of the chapters.

To the Student

This **Student Learning Guide** has been designed to help you understand and review the material in **ECONOMICS, Third Edition**.

After you have read a chapter in the text, you may use this workbook in any of several ways to review and test your understanding of the material, and to further your understanding of how various points in the text are related to one another or to your own economic environment.

Each workbook chapter (which corresponds to a chapter in the text) is divided into parts: (1) *Learning Objectives*; (2) a complete review *Outline*; (3) a self-test review of *Concepts and Definitions*; and (4) *Application* questions. Each of these parts is described below, with suggestions on how to use them.

LEARNING OBJECTIVES

The *Learning Objectives* alert you to the major points to be learned in each chapter.

OUTLINE

The *Outline* lists and briefly explains the topics covered in the chapter. Read through the outline, and as you do, question yourself about each item. Do you remember it? Can you develop an explanation of the point, theory, or concept? Can you think of situations or illustrations to which it might apply? If you cannot, go back to the text and reread the section covering that item. If you find terms or concepts you do not understand, look them up in the glossary at the back of the text. If you do not fully understand a definition, return to the place in the chapter where the term is introduced and explained more fully.

CONCEPTS AND DEFINITIONS

Tests contain questions in a variety of forms. You may be asked to fill in sentences, to choose from several possible answers, or to match terms with their definitions. The *Concepts and Definitions* review questions are designed to help you determine how well you have learned the material in each chapter.

To aid you in your review, we have printed the answers at the end of each chapter in the **Student Learning Guide**. Write down your answers first, either in the space provided or on a separate sheet of paper. Then check your answers with those at the end of the chapter. If any of your answers are incorrect, return to the text and review the material related to that question.

If you go through each of these study and review aids after you read each text chapter, and review each point that you find you do not fully understand, you will be better prepared to apply what you have learned to the following chapters. Also, your reviews for examinations will be faster and easier. The review outline and the study questions will again help you in preparing for exams; at that time, you might want to skim the outline and check points that are not yet clear.

APPLICATIONS

Each of the *Applications* pulls together several points made in the chapter or in several chapters. Developing answers to these questions will help you understand better how various concepts and theories are interrelated, how they may be applied to study new situations, and how they relate to your own economic environment.

Contents

Chapter 1

Introduction to the Study of Economics

LEARNING OBJECTIVES

The purpose of this chapter is to give an overview of the study of economics: to describe the scope of economic inquiry, the strengths and limitations of economics as a social science, and to introduce the methods of analysis used by economists. It establishes a framework for the descriptive and analytical material which follows in the text.

After reading Chapter 1, you should be able to:

1. define economics and discuss the purpose and scope of economic analysis;

2. describe the major problems confronted by economists (and other social scientists) in their study and analysis of human behavior;

3. discuss why economists (and others) rely on models in their analysis of human behavior;

4. describe the kinds of problems economists must be aware of when using models to represent reality.

CHAPTER OUTLINE

I. Economics is the study of people's behavior as they deal with the problem of scarcity.

   A. Because the supply of nearly all resources is limited, individuals must make choices regarding how to use their time, money, or other resources to achieve satisfaction.

   B. Economic decisions are made by all individuals in virtually every activity they undertake.

   C. The social science of economics studies the choices made by individuals in an attempt to detect systematic patterns of behavior.

   D. Generalizations drawn from the study of people's behavior in the past are used to help understand other behavior, to predict outcomes, and to draw conclusions about the effects of certain behavior in the present and the future.

II. Economists gather and analyze data regarding the economic activities undertaken by people.
    A. Although individual behavior is difficult to predict, economists are usually successful in drawing conclusions about the behavior of large groups of people, and in describing the implications of certain government policy changes.
    B. Because people's economic, and social behavior varies over time and is not, in most instances, suited to laboratory control procedures, the predictions made by economists will not always be entirely accurate.
    C. Because social conditions change over time, policy predictions which are accurate for one time period may not be valid in another.
    D. Conclusions which may be accurate for small groups are often inaccurate when extended to larger groups. In logic, this is known as the fallacy of composition and may occur when microeconomic conclusions are applied to macroeconomic problems.
III. Economists follow the scientific method in their analysis of human behavior.
    A. Models which incorporate economic concepts are formulated to describe expected outcomes.
    B. Because models are a simplification of reality, essential elements are sometimes unintentionally omitted. These omissions may result in inaccurate theories and predictions.
    C. Data are gathered and analyzed to confirm or refute the hypotheses or theories embodied in the economic models.
    D. Mathematical and graphical analysis are central to most forms of economic analysis and the presentation of economic data.

KEY TERMS

You should be familiar with the meaning of the terms listed below. For definition of these terms, please refer to the glossary at the end of your textbook and to the appropriate section in this chapter.

economics	model
economic good	fallacy of composition
free good	macroeconomics
opportunity cost	microeconomics
marginal unit	

CONCEPTS AND DEFINITIONS

Fill-in Questions

Complete each sentence by writing in the blank the most appropriate word or words from the terms listed below or by circling the word in parentheses that is correct.

model(s)   empirical
economics   fallacy of composition
opportunity cost   economics
marginal

1. (Economic/Free) goods are both scarce and desirable so that people are willing to give something up to obtain them; (economic/free) goods on the other hand, are available in unlimited supply without any sacrifice by consumers.

2. Generalizations used to help organize data are known as _Model_ _____.

3. _Economics_ is the discipline that deals most directly with the problem of scarcity.

4. Information about the economic activities of people which has been collected through observation and experience is known as _Empirical_ data.

5. A (social/physical) science is concerned with human behavior while a (social/physical) science deals primarily with inanimate matter or energy.

6. The _Oppt. cst_ is a measure of what must be sacrificed or given up to obtain (economic/free) goods.

7. A (model/concept) or theory is a framework for analyzing and predicting various outcomes.

8. If only one person stood up at a ball game, that individual would be able to see better. The conclusion that if all people stood up they would therefore see better is an example of _Falley. of Comp._.

9. If after studying economics for six hours I decide to study one *additional* hour, that seventh hour is known to economists as a(n) _Margin l._ hour.

10. The existence of a relationship between two variables is known as (correlation/causation). Even if we find (correlation/causation) between two variables, that does not imply (correlation/causation).

11. "Micro" is a prefix meaning small and "macro," a prefix meaning large; thus, (microeconomics/macroeconomics) is the study of the entire economy or of a major component within it, while the study of a single market or industry within an economy would be within the scope of (microeconomic/macroeconomic) analysis.

12. A single unit added to or subtracted from a series is called a(n) _____ _Marginal_ unit.

Multiple Choice Questions

Circle the correct answer.

1. Generalizations that guide the way information is perceived and understood

and that provide a means for relating many seemingly diverse facts are known as

    a. the scientific method.

    b. theories.

    c. observations.

    d. concepts.

2. Economic goods are those items which are

    a. desirable and scarce.

    b. desirable and available in unlimited supply.

    c. available only to people with money.

    d. produced as a result of economic analysis.

3. If a good is a free good, it is available

    a. only to those on welfare.

    b. only to those on welfare and other forms of government aid.

    c. to everyone in unlimited amounts without cost.

    d. to those who purchase at least one unit of the item.

4. The problem of scarcity

    a. is a basic dilemma of human existence.

    b. is a condition which concerns only philosophers and theologians.

    c. results from the greed of a few individuals.

    d. applies only to the current petroleum situation.

5. Modern economics is considered a social science

    a. because it deals only with social problems.

    b. because it deals with human behavior and applies principles of the scientific method to its subject matter.

    c. because of the influence of socialist thought on its conclusions and predictions.

    d. because it seeks to explain the social basis for actions.

6. One of the most important elements of the scientific method is

    a. ensuring that empirical data fit the theory.

    b. keeping careful and complete records of observations and work in progress.

    c. maintaining an objective and emotionally neutral attitude.

    d. ensuring that no one else has performed similar research.

7. The opportunity cost of a good is

    a. the satisfaction derived from the purchase of the good.

b. the alternatives that must be sacrificed in order to obtain the good.

c. the depreciated value of a good.

d. the amount of an individual's equity in the good.

8. The study of economics is concerned primarily with

a. the production and accumulation of material possessions.

b. the behavior of individuals who save regularly.

c. stock-exchange transactions and other aspects of the stock market.

d. choice in the presence of scarcity.

9. Marginal analysis is a method of investigation used

a. when precise answers are not terribly important.

b. as a last resort when data cannot be analyzed in any other fashion.

c. when concern is with small changes in a series.

d. all of the above.

ANSWERS

Fill-in Questions

1.	economic; free	7.	model
2.	models	8.	the fallacy of composition
3.	economics	9.	marginal
4.	empirical	10.	correlation; correlation; causation
5.	social; physical	11.	macroeconomics; microeconomic
6.	opportunity cost; economic	12.	marginal

Multiple Choice Questions

1.	d	6.	c
2.	a	7.	b
3.	c	8.	d
4.	a	9.	c
5.	b		

Chapter 2

Utilization of Economic Resources

LEARNING OBJECTIVES

The purpose of this chapter is to identify some of the basic characteristics of economic systems in which individuals have unlimited desires for economic goods but only limited resources with which to fulfill them. Following the approach outlined in Chapter 1, economists have formulated models of consumer behavior which include various economic concepts. These models and the conclusions drawn from them are the cornerstones of modern economic theory and serve as the basis for the theoretical and practical material that is presented in the chapters that follow.

After reading Chapter 2, you should be able to:

1. describe what is meant by the economist's notion of unlimited desires for economic goods and services;

2. distinguish between economic necessities and luxury items;

3. explain how scarcity of economic resources may exist even when they seem to be abundant and discuss the implications of scarce resources for an economic system;

4. describe how a desire to obtain maximum satisfaction from limited resources influences decisions regarding where, how, and for what purposes economic resources will be used;

5. demonstrate an understanding of the concept of opportunity cost as it relates to individual choice and to the choices faced by an economy as illustrated by a production possibilities curve.

CHAPTER OUTLINE

I.   A fundamental assumption in economics is that of the existence of unlimited desires or a never-ending demand for consumer goods and services.
A. Consumer goods, material or otherwise, satisfy human demands.

    B. Although for any individual the desire for some items such as television sets may be limited, the individual's desire for all goods is regarded as unlimited.

    C. Economists distinguish between the desire for physical necessities (food, clothing, and shelter) and the desire for luxuries (goods that are not absolute necessities, such as a dishwasher).

II. A second fundamental assumption in economics is that all economic resources used to create and provide goods and services are limited or scarce.

    A. In economics, four basic categories of economic resources—known as factors of production—are identified: land, labor, capital, and entrepreneurship. Occasionally, technology is included in the list of economic resources.

       1. The term land refers to all natural resources that might be used to produce goods and services.

       2. Labor is used to describe the human effort needed to turn raw materials into useful goods and services. The amount of labor available may be increased by population growth or by programs that increase the number of hours that a person can perform a job and the skill or speed with which he or she performs it.

       3. Capital is the term used by economists to describe those resources (machines, buildings, equipment) which may be used to produce other goods. It does not refer to money since money cannot *directly* produce any goods for consumers. Characteristics of people who are productive (such as knowledge and skills) are often referred to as human capital.

       4. Entrepreneurship refers to a collection of skills (including managerial ability and a willingness to take risks) that are essential to the efficient production of economic goods and services and to economic growth.

       5. Technology is the application of industrial science to production and distribution. It is the means by which economic systems can increase their productivity without increasing the use of resources.

    B. An economy must utilize all productive resources fully and efficiently to obtain maximum satisfaction.

       1. Resources may be wasted through unemployment or used inefficiently through underemployment.

       2. Production of goods can be made more efficient and less costly through economies of scale.

III. Economic choices involve opportunity costs.

    A. Because economic resources are scarce, all desires cannot be satisfied simultaneously. Therefore it is necessary to choose between competing alternatives.

    B. Because resources are scarce, society is always forced to make choices. To produce more of any one good that society wants means giving up certain amounts of other goods. The amount of other goods and services that must be sacrificed to obtain more of any one good is called the opportunity cost of that good.

    C. The notion of scarce resources and the problem of choice confronting an economy is illustrated by the production-possibilities concept. Production possibilities indicate the various combinations of goods an economy can produce when it is fully and efficiently employing its resources.

1. At any point in time, points on the production-possibilities curve describe the maximum production capability of an economy.
2. A movement from one point to another along the production-possibilities curve describes an increase in the production of some goods and a decrease in the production of others. The opportunity cost of obtaining additional amounts of some good (for example, bread) is measured in terms of the loss of production of other goods (for example, shoes).
3. Points on the production-possibilities curve indicate full employment and efficient production. Points inside the curve indicate inefficient use or unemployed resources. Production at a point outside the curve is not possible given available resources.
4. Changes in the stock (quantity and/or quality) of economic resources or improvements in the methods of production will shift the production-possibility curve reflecting economic growth.
5. Most economists assume that the production curve will reflect a situation of costs that is to obtain additional units of one good an economy will have to sacrifice ever-increasing amounts of other goods. Such increasing costs are due to the law of diminishing returns and to diseconomies of scale.

KEY TERMS

You should be familiar with the meaning of the following terms. For definition of these terms, please refer to the glossary at the end of your textbook and to the appropriate section in this chapter.

consumer goods and services
luxuries
factors of production
land
labor
capital
entrepreneurship (business enterprise)
technology
underemployment of resources

economies of scale
opportunity costs
production possibilities
increasing costs
law of diminishing returns
diseconomies of scale
marginal product
short run
long run

CONCEPTS AND DEFINITIONS

Fill-in Questions

Complete each sentence by writing in the blank the most appropriate word or words from the terms listed below or by circling the word in parentheses that is correct.

luxuries	entrepreneurship
diseconomies of scale	consumer goods and services
factors of production	labor
unemployed	underemployment
capital	diminishing returns
land	economies of scale
	marginal product

1. A business firm has grown so large that it has become less efficient and has higher costs than when it was smaller. This is an example of _diseconomies of scale_.

2. An economy's _production possibilities curve_ describes the various combinations of goods and services that could be produced if all resources were fully and efficiently used.

3. _Capital_ is the term used by economists to refer to resources that may be used to produce other goods.

4. Economists argue that people spend an increasing proportion of their income on _luxuries_ as incomes rise.

5. The expressions productive inputs and _factors of production_ mean the same thing and refer to resources used to produce goods and services.

6. A person without a job but actively seeking work is said to be _unemployed_.

7. _Entrepreneurship_ is the set of skills and abilities used to combine land, labor, and capital in efficient and innovative ways.

8. The four factors of production identified in economic analysis are: _land_, _cap_, _labor_, _entreprnrshp_, and _____.

9. The production-possibilities curve reflects a situation of (increasing/decreasing) costs.

10. The law of _diminishing returns_ states that beyond a certain point, the addition of successive equal amounts of a variable input to a fixed input will result in smaller and smaller additions to output.

11. All natural resources used in production are classified by economists as _land_.

12. The portion of output that is used to satisfy human desires is known as _consumer goods & services_.

13. _Capital_ goods are goods that have been produced already and now can be used to make other goods.

14. The wasteful and inefficient use of human and nonhuman resources is known as _underemployment_.

15. When a business firm's costs are reduced as a result of growth in size of the operation, the savings may be attributed to _economies of scale_.

16. The additional output resulting from a business firm's use of additional resources is known as the _marginal . product_ of resources.

17. The (long/short) run is a production period when a business firm may change the amount of all resources used in production while in the (long/short) run the amounts used of only certain resources may be changed.

Multiple Choice Questions

Circle the correct answer

1. A country's decision to increase its stock of capital means that it wants to

    a. increase its money supply and the availability of credit to businesses.

    b. increase the ratio of savings to spending.

    c. increase government expenditures on consumer goods and services.

    d. increase production of goods used to produce other goods and services.

2. If an economy is operating at full employment, an increase in the production of one good will result in

    a. a reduction in the amount of production of some other goods or services.

    b. overemployment of human and capital resources.

    c. diminishing returns in production.

    d. a shift of the production-possibilities curve to a new higher level.

3. A central reason for the worsening position of the United States in international trade is

    a. a lack of technology and entrepreneurship in the United States.

    b. high levels of taxation on imports and exports.

    c. an outmoded stock of capital relative to countries in Europe and the far east.

    d. the extensive investment in United States industry by OPEC countries.

4. A business firm is able to produce more and more goods without increasing the amount of raw materials used. Which of the following statements indicates how this might be possible?

    a. The productivity of the firm has increased.

    b. The firm is subject to the law of increasing costs.

    c. The firm has experienced economies of scale.

    d. The rate of taxation on business has changed.

5. If an economy is producing at full employment

   a. all capital must be used to capacity and each worker must have a full-time job.

   b. each productive input must be used to capacity and technological developments must be occurring rapidly.

   c. every worker must have a full-time job although other resources may be underutilized.

   d. there may be unemployment but it must be voluntary.

6. The phrase "underemployment of human resources" means

   a. people are employed in subordinate positions.

   b. some people are working less than full time.

   c. resources are not being used in their most efficient manner.

   d. people cannot find jobs although they want to work.

7. If unit costs of a product drop as a firm increases the size of its operations, it may be concluded that the firm has taken advantage of

   a. economies of scale.

   b. factors of production.

   c. diminishing marginal returns.

   d. marginal productivity.

8. In constructing a production-possibilities curve for an economy, it is assumed that

   a. economies of scale for producers are present.

   b. only one good for consumers may be produced.

   c. all resources are being fully and efficiently used.

   d. equal amounts of all goods are made available to consumers.

9. An economy's failure to produce the maximum amount of output is illustrated by

   a. a shift of the production-possibilities curve.

   b. a point inside the production-possibilities curve.

   c. the horizontal and vertical intercepts of the production-possibilities curve.

   d. a point beyond the boundary of the production-possibilities curve.

10. The production-possibilities curve is bowed out because of

   a. the law of decreasing costs.

   b. the laws of supply and demand.

c. the laws of the land.

d. the law of increasing costs.

11. If production is subject to the law of diminishing returns, that means that

   a. total output is getting smaller and smaller.

   b. additional inputs are unproductive.

   c. further production is just barely worthwhile and should be curtailed.

   d. each additional unit of variable input will yield smaller and smaller increases in output when applied to a fixed input.

12. If the opportunity cost of any one good increases at an increasing rate as more units are produced by even larger firms, that is an indication of

   a. increasing marginal returns.

   b. diminished factors of production.

   c. diseconomies of scale.

   d. increasing marginal product.

APPLICATIONS

1. Assume that labor in combination with capital and other factors of production is used to produce an output as shown below. (Output is measured in bushels per day.)

Number of workers	Total amount of output produced	Marginal Product
1	10 bushels	
2	25 bushels	
3	35 bushels	
4	40 bushels	
5	42 bushels	

   a. Compute the marginal product of the second, third, fourth, and fifth workers and enter those values in the space provided.

   b. At what point do diminishing returns set in? _____

   c. Assume output sells for $5.00 per bushel, and each worker must be paid $15.00 per day. Is it worthwhile to hire the fifth worker? What about the fourth worker? Why? (Support your decision in both cases).

2. An economy may use its resources to produce public or private goods as shown by the production-possibilities curve below.

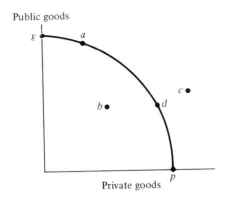

The following questions refer to the production-possibilities curve shown above. Determine whether the statements are true or false, and circle the appropriate response.

a. Point *b* represents less than full employment or inefficient use of available resources.   True False

b. Points *a* and *b* are on the production-possibilities curve.   True False

c. Although the economy cannot produce Point *c* at this time, technological change or newly discovered resources might permit the economy to operate at Point *c*.   True False

d. Since every economy is confronted with the problem of scarcity, it would not be possible to increase output of both public and private goods if the economy were at Point *b*.   True False

e. The shape of the production-possibilities curve demonstrates the law of increasing costs.   True False

3. Show how the curve shown in problem 2 would change if the resources available for production remained unchanged but technological developments in the private sector (only) increased the economy's prviate production capability.

4. The choices for an economy producing apples and shoes are represented by the curve below.

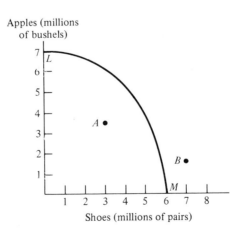

The following questions refer to the production-possibilities curve shown above. Determine whether the following statements are true or false, and circle the appropriate response.

a. At full employment, this economy can produce 7 million bushels of apples and 6 million pairs of shoes.   True   False

b. At point L, resources would be unemployed since no shoes are being produced.   True   False

c. At point B, resources are unemployed.   True   False

d. It is not possible for the economy to produce at point A.   True   False

e. The opportunity cost of producing more apples in this economy would be measured in terms of lost shoe production.   True   False

f. The shape of the production-possibilities curve shows that shoe production is less efficient than apple production since fewer shoes than apples can be produced.   True   False

g. An increase in the economy's production capabilities for both apples and shoes would be shown by shifting the production possibilities curve closer to the origin of the graph.   True   False

ANSWERS

Fill-in Questions

1. diseconomies of scale
2. production-possibilities curve
3. capital
4. luxuries
5. factors of production
6. unemployed
7. entrepreneurship
8. land, labor, capital, and entrepreneurship
9. increasing
10. diminishing returns
11. land
12. consumer goods and services
13. capital
14. underemployment
15. economies of scale
16. marginal product
17. long; short

Multiple Choice Questions

1.	d	7.	a
2.	a	8.	c
3.	c	9.	b
4.	a	10.	d
5.	d	11.	d
6.	c	12.	c

APPLICATIONS

1. a. 15; 10; 5; 2

    b. third worker

    c. No. Hiring the fifth worker results in an increase in output worth $10.00 (two bushels at $5.00 per bushel). The cost to the firm of hiring the fifth worker is $15.00, or $5.00 more than the value of his or her output. The fourth worker adds five bushels of output worth $25.00. Since the wage cost is less than the value of additional output, that worker should be hired.

2. a. true   b. true   c. true   d. false   e. true

3. The technological change referred to in the problem would result in a shift of the production possibility curve from *GP* to *GE* as shown below.

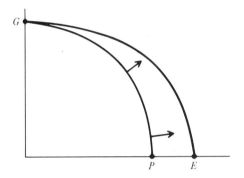

4. a. false   b. false   c. false   d. false   e. true   f. false   g. false

Chapter 3

The Laws of Demand and Supply

LEARNING OBJECTIVES

The basic model of demand and supply is introduced in this chapter. As indicated in Chapter 2, because resources are scarce and consumer wants are unlimited, individuals and societies must make choices about how to use their resources to produce goods and services. This chapter will examine the mechanism by which an economy chooses what will be produced, the method of production, how much, and for whom. In a predominantly free-market economy, supply and demand play a central role in providing the required answers.

After reading Chapter 3, you should:

1. understand the economic basis of exchange and the circumstances under which exchange takes place;

2. be fluent with the economic terms demand, demand schedule, and demand curve. In addition, you should be able to derive individual and market demand schedules and curves from empirical data;

3. understand the assumptions made when deriving a demand schedule or demand curve and be able to identify and distinguish between factors that cause a change in demand and factors that cause a change in quantity demanded;

4. be fluent with the economic terms supply, supply schedule, and supply curve. In addition, you should be able to derive individual and market supply schedules and curves from empirical data;

5. understand the assumptions made when deriving a supply schedule or supply curve, and be able to identify and distinguish between factors that cause a change in supply and factors that cause a change in quantity supplied;

6. be able to describe how the interaction of market demand and supply determines an equilibrium price and quantity, and how the equilibrium price and quantity may change over time in response to market forces;

7. be familiar with the economic causes of shortages and surpluses, and the economic forces that lead to the establishment of black markets.

CHAPTER OUTLINE

I. In order to obtain economic goods, exchange is usually necessary.
    A. In a barter economy, goods are exchanged for goods. This system of exchange may be difficult or cumbersome since everyone willing to trade does not necessarily want to trade for the goods that are available.
    B. The development of money, any item widely accepted as a medium of exchange, facilitates exchange transactions between buyers and sellers.
    C. Exchange can take place only when individuals participating in transactions have differing valuations of the economic goods to be traded.
        1. The price of a commodity is the amount of other goods an individual is willing to give up to obtain a desired commodity.
    D. The value an individual places on additional units of a good is influenced by personal tastes and by the amount of the good the person already possesses.
II. Demand is the quantity of a good or service that individuals are willing and able to buy at each and every price in some specified period of time.
    A. The law of demand states that there is an inverse relationship between price and quantity demanded. As price increases, a smaller quantity will be demanded than at lower prices, and vice versa.
    B. A demand schedule shows the amounts of a good or service people are able and willing to buy at various prices per some unit of time.
    C. A demand curve is a graph of the demand schedule. (N.B. It may be a straight or curved line; in either case, it is called a curve.) When plotting a demand curve, price is shown on the vertical axis and quantity per unit of time is on the horizontal axis.
    D. A demand schedule or demand curve is derived under the assumption that everything that affects demand *except the price of the good itself* is unchanged.
        1. Once a demand curve is obtained, changes in the price of the good will result in *a change in quantity* demanded; that is, a movement along the demand curve.
        2. If the assumption that everything is constant except price is relaxed, and if one or more of the factors held constant is changed, a *change in demand* will occur. This causes the entire demand curve to shift.
            a. The determinants of *individual demand* include, but are not limited to, the price of the good itself, income, prices of other goods, expectations, and individual tastes and preferences.
            b. In addition to the items listed above, the determinants of *market demand* would include the size of the population, level of income, and income distribution.
    E. The market demand for a commodity is the sum of individual demands for the commodity.
III. Supply is the quantity of a good or service that firms are willing and able to provide at each and every price in some specified period of time.

A. The law of supply states that there is a direct relationship between price and quantity supplied. As price is increased, a larger quantity will be supplied than at lower prices, and vice versa.

B. A supply schedule shows the amounts of a good or service firms are able and willing to sell at various prices per some unit of time.

C. A supply curve is a graph of the supply schedule. (N.B. It may be a straight or a curved line; in either case, it is called a curve.) When plotting a supply curve, price is shown on the vertical axis and quantity supplied per unit of time is on the horizontal axis.

D. A supply schedule or supply curve is derived under the assumption that everything that affects supply, *except the price of the good itself*, is unchanged.

　1. Once a supply curve is obtained, changes in the price of the good will result in a *change in quantity supplied*; that is, a movement along the supply curve.

　2. If the assumption that everything except price remains constant is relaxed, and if one or more of the factors held constant is changed, a *change in supply* occurs; that is, the supply curve shifts.

　　a. The determinants of individual supply include, but are not limited to, the price of the good itself, the costs of production, the prices and profitability of related goods, expectations, and technological developments.

IV. The interaction of market demand and market supply establishes an equilibrium price and quantity.

A. At the equilibrium price, the quantity supplied by producers will be equal to the amount demanded by consumers.

B. If the price is above equilibrium, more will be supplied than demanded. This excess supply is called a surplus.

　1. If prices are free to fluctuate, competition among sellers will exert downward pressure on the market price until it reaches a new equilibrium.

　2. If prices are established by law above the equilibrium price, surpluses will persist over time.

C. If the price is below equilibrium, more will be demanded than supplied. This excess demand represents a shortage.

　1. If prices are free to fluctuate, buyers willing to pay more will bid up the market price until the market is in equilibrium at a higher price where quantity demanded is equal to quantity supplied.

　2. If prices are fixed by law below equilibrium, shortages will persist. In this instance, black markets emerge in which goods are bought and sold illegally for more than the legally established price.

KEY TERMS

You should be familiar with the meaning of the terms listed below. For definition of these terms, please refer to the glossary at the end of your textbook and to the appropriate section of this chapter.

market economy	market demand schedule
money	supply
price	product market
market price	resource market
demand	profit
law of demand	law of supply
demand schedule	supply schedule
demand curve	supply curve
"all-other-things-equal" assumption	equilibrium price
normal goods	surplus
inferior goods	shortage
substitutes	black market
complements	

CONCEPTS AND DEFINITIONS

Fill-in Questions

Complete each sentence by writing in the blank the most appropriate word or words from the terms listed below or by circling the word in parentheses that is correct.

demand curve	normal
demand	black market
supply	shortage
substitutes	supply schedule
inferior	market economy
market demand	"all-other-things-equal" assumption
surplus	demand schedule
complements	factor
product	supply curve
equilibrium	

1. The law of ___*demand*___ states that price and quantity are inversely related.

2. In terms of consumption, Pepsi and Coke are regarded to be (sub-stitutes/complements) while hot dogs and mustard are (substitutes/complements) since they are used together.

3. When goods are exchanged at prices above legally established maximum prices, a(n) ___*black mrkt*___ transaction has occurred.

4. As Linda's income increases, she purchases more of a particular good. That good is known as a(n) ___*normal*___ good.

5. A(n) ___*demand curve*___ is a graphical presentation of the information contained in a demand schedule.

6. When market prices are above the equilibrium (or market-clearing) price, a (shortage/surplus) arises. When market prices are below the equilibrium price a (shortage/surplus) arises.

7. A(n) _market economy_ relies substantially on the forces of demand and supply to provide answers to the fundamental questions that arise from scarce resources and unlimited consumer wants.

8. A market for productive inputs is known also as a(n) _factor_ market while one for consumer goods and services is known as a(n) _product_ _____ market.

9. A direct relationship observed between price and quantity would be consistent with the law of _supply_ _____.

10. _Supply_ _____ refers to the amount of a good or service that producers are able and willing to sell at alternative prices per unit time. A graph of this information is known as a(n) _supply curve_ while a table showing the price-quantity relationships is knows as a(n) _supply schedule_

11. As Ron's income increases, he buys less rice. Therefore rice would be classified as a(n) _inferior_ _____ good for Ron.

12. A(n) _demand schedule_ is a table that lists the various quantities of a good or service an individual is able and willing to buy at each and every price per unit of time.

13. A(n) _Market demand_ curve is obtained by adding together the amounts of a good or service that consumers are willing and able to purchase at various prices.

14. When quantity demanded is equal to quantity supplied, the value at which a good is exchanged is known as the _equilibrium_ _____.

15. A shift of the market demand or market supply curve would arise when the _All other things_ _____ is violated.
equal assumption

Multiple Choice Questions

1. Exchange between two individuals can take place only if
   a. each attaches a different value to the goods being exchanged.
   b. one individual has a lot of the good and the other has very little.
   c. money is used as the medium of exchange.
   d. both individuals start out with equivalent amounts of the good.

2. For demand to be effective in the market,
   a. consumers must have both the ability and the willingness to pay for goods and services.

b. the relationship between price and quantity must be known.

c. sellers must make goods and services available in sufficient amounts.

d. people must be willing to pay the same price as others for goods and services.

3. The law of demand establishes

   a. a direct relationship between price and quantity.

   b. an inverse relationship between price and quantity.

   c. a relationship between a person's income and the amount of a good or service that person buys.

   d. rules and regulations for orderly exchange in markets.

4. The demand schedule for any commodity

   a. tells what the market price will be for the commodity.

   b. specifies a direct relationship between price and quantity demanded.

   c. shows that consumption will increase if income increases and vice versa.

   d. is a series of alternative quantities that will be demanded at various prices.

5. A change in people's expectations will result in

   a. a change in demand.

   b. a change in quantity demanded.

   c. a movement along the demand curve.

   d. no effect on demand.

6. If something other than the price of a commodity were to change, this change would result in

   a. a movement along the demand curve.

   b. a change in demand.

   c. either a change in demand or a change in quantity demanded.

   d. a change in quantity demanded.

7. A change in demand could result from

   a. an increase in the price of a commodity.

   b. a decrease in the price of a commodity.

   c. any change in price of a commodity.

   d. a change in the price of some other commodity.

8. An increase in income will cause an increase in the demand for

   a. a public good.

   b. a black market good.

   c. a normal good.

   d. an inferior good.

9. As the price of one good increases
    a. the demand for its substitutes will increase.
    b. the demand for complementary products will increase while the demand for its substitutes and complements will decrease.
    c. the demand for its substitutes and complements will decrease.
    d. the demand for complements will increase while the demand for substitutes decreases.

10. The market supply of a commodity is obtained
    a. by summing the various prices at which firms are willing to supply particular amounts.
    b. by summing the prices and quantities of each and every firm in a market.
    c. by summing the various quantities that firms are willing to supply at various prices.
    d. none of the above.

11. A change in a firm's technology will always result in
    a. a decrease in supply.
    b. an increase in quantity supplied.
    c. a movement down along the supply curve.
    d. a change in supply.

12. The law of supply states that
    a. an increase in supply is always accompanied by an increase in demand.
    b. firms will offer more for sale at high prices than at lower prices.
    c. an increase in supply must drive prices down.
    d. firms will maintain higher prices, even if they cannot sell all of the goods that they want.

13. A shift of the supply curve would definitely be caused by
    a. a change in demand.
    b. a change in quantity supplied.
    c. an increase in the consumer price index.
    d. a change in costs of production.

14. In the United States, the government has established minimum-wage laws. If these laws establish wages below the market-clearing equilibrium for unskilled labor,
    a. a shortage of unskilled labor will result since people want to earn more than the minimum wage.
    b. people will remain voluntarily or involuntarily unemployed.
    c. it will have no effect on the market for unskilled labor.
    d. a surplus of unskilled labor or excess supply will undoubtedly result.

15. The imposition of rent controls where rents would be rolled back to levels below current market-clearing values would cause

a. an increase in demand for rental housing.

b. a change in supply of rental housing.

c. excess demand for rental housing.

d. excess supply of rental housing.

APPLICATIONS

1. The table below shows the demands of three individuals for the commodity dehydrated water. (Prices are in dollars; quantities are in quarts per week.)

Price	Individual X Quantity demanded per week	Individual Y Quantity demanded per week	Individual Z Quantity demanded per week
$10	1	0	0
9	2	0	0
8	3	1	0
7	4	2	5
6	6	5	9
5	6	7	9
4	9	7	10
3	10	8	12
2	11	9	13
1	12	10	14

a. Derive the market demand schedule for dehydrated water for this community of three individuals. (Save your answer since you will need it for a subsequent problem.)

b. Does the market demand schedule derived in part (a) adhere to the law of demand? How do you know?

c. Assume individual Z were to leave the community and that only individuals X and Y remained. What impact would that change have on the market demand curve for dehydrated water?

d. On the basis of the information you have thus far, is it possible to determine the equilibrium price or quantity for this commodity? If yes, explain how you obtained your answer. If no, explain why it is not possible to derive an answer from the information provided.

2. Assume two firms are in the business of producing dehydrated water. Supply data from each of these firms shown below. (Prices are in dollars; quantities are in quarts per week.)

Price	Firm #1 Quantity supplied	Firm #2 Quantity supplied
$10	22	30
9	20	27
8	18	24
7	10	20
6	4	16
5	2	10
4	0	4
3	0	0
2	0	0

a. Derive the market supply schedule for the dehydrated-water industry. (Save your answer since you will need it for a subsequent problem.)

b. Does the market supply schedule derived in part (a) adhere to the law of supply? How do you know?

c. If a third firm were to enter the dehydrated-water industry, what impact would that have on the industry supply curve?

d. On the basis of supply data alone, is it possible to determine the equilibrium price and quantity? If yes, explain how you would derive that information. If no, explain why it is not possible to obtain an answer from supply data alone.

3. Using the supply and demand data from Applications questions 1 and 2, determine the market-clearing equilbrium price and quantity for the commodity dehydrated water.

4. If the government decided that a maximum price of $2.00 should be established by law in order that more people could afford to buy dehydrated water, what impact would that policy have on the market for dehydrated water?

5. If in implementing the policy described in problem 4, the legislative printer made an error and wrote the law such that it established a *minimum* legal price of $2.00 rather than a maximum price of that same amount, what impact, if any, would the printer's error have on this industry?

6. After an active campaign by the dehydrated-water industry lobby, the government decides to establish a minimum legal price of $8.00 for dehydrated water. What impact, if any, would this new price have on the market for this commodity?

ANSWERS

Fill-in Questions

1. demand
2. substitutes; complements
3. black market

9. supply
10. supply; supply curve; supply schedule

4. normal
5. demand curve
6. surplus, shortage
7. market economy
8. factor; product

11. inferior
12. demand schedule
13. market demand
14. equilibrium
15. "all-other-things-equal" assumption

Multiple Choice Questions

1. a	5. a	9. a	13. d
2. a	6. b	10. c	14. c
3. b	7. d	11. c	15. c
4. d	8. c	12. b	

APPLICATIONS

1.

a.
Price	10	9	8	7	6	5	4	3	2	1
Quantity	1	2	4	12	20	22	26	30	33	37

b. Yes. The law of demand postulates an inverse relationship between price and quantity demanded, and the data in the schedule in part (a) illustrates such a relationship.

c. If individual *Z* left the community, the market demand curve would shift to the left. At prices of $7.00 or less, less would be demanded by the remaining individuals.

d. It is not possible to determine the equilibrium price or quantity because the equilibrium is determined by the interaction of both demand and supply. Demand information by itself is not sufficient to arrive at an equilibrium price and quantity.

2.

a.
Price	10	9	8	7	6	5	4	3	2	1
Quantity	52	47	42	30	20	12	4	0	0	0

b. Yes. The law of supply postulates a direct relationship between price and quantity supplied, and the data in part (a) illustrates such a relationship.

c. If a third firm entered the industry, more units would probably be made available to consumers and the market supply curve would shift to the right.

d. The equilibrium price and quantity are determined by the interaction of both demand and supply. Supply information by itself is not sufficient to arrive at an equilibrium price and quantity.

3. The market clears at a price of $6.00 where quantity demanded is equal to quantity supplied (20 quarts per week).

4. While it is true that more dehydrated water would be demanded at a price of $2.00 (33 quarts per week) than at $6.00 (20 quarts per week), no firm is willing to supply the commodity at a price of $2.00. In this situation, a legal maximum price below equilibrium would cause excess demand (or shortage) of 33 quarts per week.

5. The printer's error would have no effect since it is possible for the market to reach (or to remain at) equilibrium.

6. At a minimum price of $8.00, there would be a surplus or excess supply. The quantity demanded at $8.00 is 4 quarts per week, while the quantity supplied is 42 quarts per week. Therefore, at a minimum legal price of $8.00 there would be a surplus of 38 quarts per week.

Chapter 4

The Price System and How It Operates

LEARNING OBJECTIVES

In this chapter we will examine the general features and workings of the price system and see how the demand and supply model introduced in Chapter 3 plays a central role in explaining how the economy allocates scarce resources. In addition, the elements that characterize a competitive free-market economy are discussed as is the relationship of the free-market model to the United States economy.

After reading Chapter 4, you should be able to:

1. describe how resource allocation decisions are made in a market economy;

2. describe the real and money flows that constitute the circular flow of economic activity in a market economy;

3. identify the major characteristics of a competitive market economy and the American economic system;

4. discuss the differences between the economic model of capitalism and the actual features of the United States economy.

CHAPTER OUTLINE

I.   In a market economy, the sum of individual decisions by producers and consumers regarding the use of scarce resources determines market supply and demand schedules for products and services.
   A. In resource markets, firms make purchases (primarily from households) to secure the factors of production that are required to produce goods and services.
   B. Households use the incomes derived from the sale of productive resources to purchase final goods and services that are made available in product markets.
   C. Transactions between households and firms for resources and final goods provide incomes to individuals and receipts to firms so that the exchange process may continue. This is known as the circular flow of economic activity.

II.   Decisions regarding *what* to produce are made by business firms in response to consumer preferences.

    A. A firm's decision to produce a commodity is based on an analysis of expected costs and sales receipts. A firm's costs are determined by forces of demand and supply in resource markets. Sales receipts are determined by demand and supply in product markets. If estimated costs are less than estimated receipts, firms undertake production in anticipation of profits.

    B. Expansion and contraction of industries occurs as resources are shifted into the production of more profitable commodities and away from those which are less profitable or altogether unprofitable.

III. When making decisions about *how* to produce a good a firm compares the relative costs of alternative methods of production and selects the methods that yield the lowest average costs. Many differences in production costs arise because of differences in demand and supply in resource markets.

IV.   The price system also answers the question "*For whom* are goods and services to be produced?" Goods produced by business firms are allocated to consumers who have the desire and income (are willing and able) to purchase them.

    A. Prices paid in product markets are determined by forces of demand and supply.

    B. In a market economy, individuals with the largest incomes and greatest wealth possess the greatest ability to pay for goods and services and, therefore, receive the largest share of production.

V.   In a market economy, it is assumed that people act out of self-interest: producers seek to earn profits; individuals attempt to maximize satisfaction.

    A. In pursuit of self-interest, individuals and business firms generally do not consider society's interests. However, the operation of the price system is such that while pursuing self interest, individuals may actually help promote the goals and welfare of society.

VI.   Another assumption about the operation of the price system is the concept of competition among buyers and sellers in the market.

    A. As a result of competition, economic power is distributed among many buyers and sellers—the model of perfect competition assumes no single buyer or seller can influence the market price.

    B. When competition is absent or weakened, imperfections are introduced into the price system, and resources are not used in the most efficient manner. Government action is sometimes required to deal with market imperfections.

    C. The efficiency of competition directs resources to their most highly valued uses (indicated by market prices).

VII. The United States economy is a capitalist economy. It features the extensive use of capital, the division of labor and specialization, and the private ownership of resources.

VIII. A. In a capitalist economy, free choices are made by individuals pursuing their own self-interest. Consumer choices are registered through dollar votes that ultimately determine what the economy will produce.

B. Although a model of perfect competition is used in analyzing many features of the United States capitalistic free-enterprise economy, it is inaccurate where elements of monopoly and market imperfections occur.

KEY TERMS

You should be familiar with the meaning of the terms listed below. For definition of these terms, please refer to the glossary at the end of your textbook and to the appropriate section in this chapter.

resource markets	perfect competition
product markets	monopoly
circular flow	real flow
price system	money flow
competition	

CONCEPTS AND DEFINITIONS

Fill-in Questions

Complete each sentence by writing in the blank the most appropriate word or words from the terms listed below or by circling the word in parentheses that is correct.

imperfect	real flow
price system	monopoly
circular flow	product
competition	invisible hand
barter	self-interest
resource	perfect competition
money flow	dollar votes

1. The process of households supplying resources to business firms and business firms supplying goods and services to households is known as the _Circular flow_ of economic activity.

2. Business firms make purchases in _resource (factor)_ markets while households buy final goods and services in _product_ markets.

3. One of the assumptions of the competitive model is that people act in their own _self-interest_ and do not consciously look out for the welfare of others.

4. In the inner loop of the circular flow model, physical transactions between households and firms constitute a (real/money) flow.

5. In the outer loop of the circular flow model, no physical goods are exchanged and the inner loop represents a series of (real/money) flow between households and firms.

6. If people were unwilling to accept monetary payments for their economic resources, the circular flow diagram would depict a ___Barter___ economy in which only ___real   flows___ take place.

7. The mechanism used in the American economy to answer the questions: what will be produced, how, and for whom, is known as the ___price system___.

8. The sale of productive resources to business firms will occur in ___resource (factor)___ markets.

9. By making purchases of some goods instead of others, consumers cast ___dollar votes___ which express their preference for one bundle of goods instead of another.

10. When individuals unintentionally promote the interests of society while pursuing their own self-interest the ___invisible hand___ is said to be at work.

11. The rivalry among buyers and sellers in the purchase of resources and products is known as ___Competition___.

12. In ___perfect competition___ there are large numbers of buyers and sellers, no buyer or seller can alter the market price by individual action, and knowledge of all aspects of the market is possessed by every individual.

13. A market in which there is only one producer is a(n) ___monopoly___.

14. The basic elements of a capitalistic economy are: capital is used extensively, ___Competition___ exists among buyers and sellers, and the means of production are owned by private individuals.

15. Misallocation of resources in a market economy is evidence of (perfect/ imperfect) competition.

Multiple Choice Questions

Circle the correct answer.

1. In a market economy, resources are automatically allocated to the production of

    a. the greatest number of goods.

    b. goods for which the market is in equilibrium.

    c. low-cost goods since consumers will demand more at low prices than at high prices.

    d. goods that provide the greatest amount of satisfaction or utility.

2. According to the concept of the circular flow of economic activity,

    a. there is no distinction between real and money flows in an economy.

    b. real and money flows occur between households and firms.

c. firms buy resources from other firms in order to continue the flow of consumer goods.

d. firms sell output in resource markets and buy the factors of production in product markets.

3. In resource and product markets, prices are

a. always in equilibrium as long as the economy is organized along capitalist lines.

b. always in equilibrium if markets are structured to ensure maximum competition between firms.

c. always moving toward but are never in equilibrium because different forces determine quantity demanded and quantity supplied.

d. always found either at an equilibrium level or moving toward an equilibrium where quantity demanded is equal to quantity supplied.

4. A circular flow diagram that contains loops depicting both real and money flows indicate that

a. businesses are organized along competitive lines.

b. business firms are willing to accept only real payment for goods and services.

c. the diagram represents a monetary economy.

d. household spending constitutes income from the sale of resources.

5. In every two-party transaction in competitive markets,

a. both individuals must realize net gains or no exchange will take place.

b. if one person benefits from the transaction, the other part must suffer corresponding losses.

c. both individuals must suffer a loss since each gives up something of value.

d. equity dictates that each individual must gain equally from exchange.

6. A business firm will normally decide in favor of producing a good or service

a. as long as the average costs of production are high enough to ensure a profit.

b. if expected costs of a product are small relative to projected sales receipts.

c. if a majority of customers cast their dollar votes in favor of production of the item.

d. *solely* on the basis of an analysis of expected sales receipts.

7. In markets where individual actions are guided by self-interest,

a. government intervention is never required since the interest of individuals and society coincide.

b. the "invisible hand" forces people to change selfish decisions in favor of those which promote social goals.

    c. society is always worse off than if individuals considered social goals when they made economic decisions.

    d. individuals are often led as if by an invisible hand to promote society's interests.

8. In perfectly competitive markets,

    a. individual firms may find it profitable to raise or lower the market price.

    b. buyers are assumed to have full and immediate knowledge of any changes in production or price.

    c. small differences between products in terms of appearance and quality ensure that consumers will be able to satisfy their individual desires in each market.

    d. it is assumed that all producers make uniform products but charge different prices for them.

9. In a capitalistic economic system, resources are guided to their most efficient use

    a. by individual firms responding to government information regarding consumer demands.

    b. only if firms are large enough to restrict inefficient use of resources by others.

    c. only if competition prevails in resource and product markets.

    d. only as long as technological advances continue to be made by the leading industrial firms.

10. Natural monopolies are firms that

    a. promote the sale and use of natural rather than artificial products.

    b. have secured a patent on the most efficient production methods available.

    c. require a large amount of consumer goods for distribution in the market since they are the only supplier.

    d. follow the guiding signals that are provided by the "invisible hand."

11. The existence of pure competition

    a. ensures that individual firms may determine price and production levels for particular goods and services.

    b. would be unlikely even in a market economy.

    c. is found in any society where decisions are made according to the price system.

    d. insures that consumers will have extensive choice among different brands of each product on the market.

12. In a market economy, the production of specific goods is determined largely by

    a. the structure of the circular flow diagram for that economy.

    b. the choices of individuals pursuing social goals.

    c. the choices of individuals pursuing self-interest.

    d. the extent to which producers have access to resource and product markets.

13. Firms will undertake the production of a product if

    a. sales receipts are expected to be less than the costs of production.

    b. consumer behavior follows the law of demand.

    c. the market for that product is in equilibrium.

    d. market research indicates that sales revenues are expected to exceed production costs.

14. In a market economy, the firm able to pay the highest price for a specific input is the one that

    a. will use only a small quantity of that input in production.

    b. uses a large quantity in producing consumer goods.

    c. is expected to use the resource most efficiently.

    d. is most profitable and therefore can afford to pay the most for resources.

15. Monopoly is the opposite of perfect competition in that

    a. only one supplier controls the market whereas in perfect competition there are many suppliers.

    b. there are few buyers for products produced by a monopoly whereas there are many buyers for products in perfect competition.

    c. several different prices are charged for a monopoly's output, whereas in perfect competition there is a single price which prevails in the market.

    d. true monopolies never exist but pure competition may be found in every free-enterprise economic system.

APPLICATIONS

1. In the spaces provided below, describe the activities that correspond to each labeled segment in the diagram on p. 36. Remember, the outer loop represents money flows while the inner loop represents real flows.

    a. _____

    _____

    b. _____

    _____

    c. _____

    _____

    d. _____

    _____

Product market

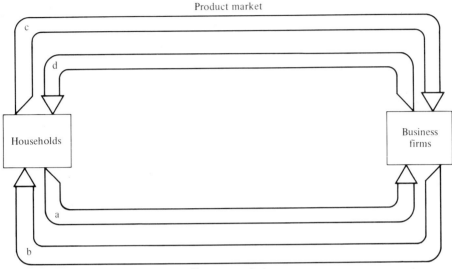

Resource market

2. Many people are concerned that energy problems facing the United States may become more serious in the future, and if available supplies of crude oil fall at least 20 percent below current levels, the president has authority to propose rationing plans to Congress. Such an action would represent an administrative response to the problems of what to produce, how to produce, and who should receive what is produced. For the purposes of this problem, we will assume that from each 42-gallon barrel of crude oil, it would be possible to produce *only* the following commodities: heating fuel, diesel fuel, gasoline, and jet fuel. We will also assume that refining and distribution operations are competitive and that there are no government regulations on the production and distribution of crude oil or refined products.

   a. Assume that every crude-oil producer brings oil to a central market where it can be purchased by refiners. How does the market determine who will get the oil that is available? (Since supplies are assumed to be down by 20 percent, we can expect competition for the remaining supply to be intense.)

   b. Once the crude oil has been allocated to refiners, decisions have to be made regarding what to produce. Refiners may choose to produce only one of the four products mentioned above, or they may decide to produce some of each. How does a firm in a competitive market answer the question of what to produce?

   c. Would different decisions on what to produce be made in September and October as winter is approaching than would be made in May and June when people are planning their summer vacations? Why? How does the market let firms know of differences in product demand at different times of year?

d. Finally, describe how the market determines who will get the products produced at the refinery. If goods are allocated by the market system, will shortages of any of the four products exist for an appreciable length of time? How do you know?

3. The competitive market mechanism is assumed to allocate resources *efficiently* by directing them to their highest valued uses. However, does this also mean that the results arising from the working of the market system are always *equitable*? That is, does the market system also ensure equal distribution of resources and/or products?

ANSWERS

Fill-in Questions

1. circular flow
2. resource (or factor); product
3. self-interest
4. real
5. money
6. barter; real flows
7. price system
8. resource (or factor)
9. dollar votes
10. invisible hand
11. competition
12. perfect competition
13. monopoly
14. competition
15. imperfect

Multiple Choice Questions

1. d
2. b
3. d
4. c
5. a
6. b
7. d
8. b
9. c
10. c
11. b
12. c
13. a
14. d
15. a

APPLICATIONS

1. a. Households supply resources to business firms.

b. Payment by firms for resources represents a cost of production for businesses and incomes to households.

c. Households spend money (incomes) in product markets for goods and services. This spending constitutes revenues for business firms.

d. The business sector supplies goods and services to households in return for household spending.

2. a. In the situation described, many firms would want to buy the available crude oil. Through competitive bidding for this resource, price would serve as a rationing device—those firms able to buy the highest price for the crude oil would obtain it.

b. The management would analyze the demand for each product in an effort to estimate sales revenue from particular products. Costs would also be analyzed in order to prepare profitability estimates for each product. Without more specific information, we cannot determine which product or mix of products would be most profitable to produce. We can only outline the process by which the refiners would arrive at the decision.

c. Changes in the demand for products would change revenue estimates and, therefore, the profit calculations. As winter approaches, we would expect the demand for heating fuel to increase. As more people bid for the supply of fuel oil, the price of fuel oil would increase. This higher price would signal the refiners to increase production of fuel oil and to cut back on less profitable items such as gasoline.

On the other hand, we would expect the demand for gasoline to be greatest during the summer months. Again, as the demand for gas increased, the price would rise. Refineries would respond to this price signal by increasing production of gasoline (where large profits would be earned) and curtailing production of the new less profitable heating fuel. In both cases, price signals the changes in consumer preferences and demand.

d. Price competition among consumers in product markets will determine who receives the goods that have been produced. In general, consumers and business firms with the greatest incomes will be able to buy more of the goods than those with smaller incomes. Shortages should not be a problem since, by assumption, prices may fluctuate freely. If demand should increase, markets will ration the goods among competing consumers by raising the price until it reaches an equilibrium where quantity demanded is again equal to quantity supplied. If demand decreases, the price will fall until equilibrium is reached.

3. The market mechanism would distribute resources equally *if* (and this is a big if) every individual had equal amounts of resources (dollar votes). Since income and wealth generally are not distributed equally, market alllocations tend to favor individuals who have more dollar votes. Many government activities are directed toward dealing with such inequities which have not been remedied by the market system.

Chapter 5

Households in the American Economy

LEARNING OBJECTIVES

The discussion of the circular flow model in Chapter 4 dealt with the interaction between households and businesses in the United States economy. In the present chapter, we take a closer look at the characteristics and actions of the household sector.

After reading Chapter 5, you should be able to:

1. distinguish the household as a social unit from the household as an economic unit;

2. explain the two basic roles played by households in the economy;

3. understand how the household can be viewed as a producer of satisfaction;

4. identify the major sources of household income and the factors causing differences in income levels among households;

5. explain how households, as a whole, use the income they receive;

6. identify the trends currently influencing the economic behavior of households.

CHAPTER OUTLINE

I. In economics, a household is not necessarily the same as a family group. Economists define a household as a person or group of people living under the same roof and functioning as an economic unit.

   A. In the circular flow of the American economy, households have two main functions.

      1. Households supply economic resources (land, labor, capital, and entrepreneurship) to businesses in exchange for income.

      2. Households act as consumers by spending their income on goods and services. This spending represents demand and thereby influences what and how much businesses will produce.

B. Households are also producers in the sense that they attempt to spend their income on that particular combination of goods and services which produces the greatest possible amount of satisfaction or utility for household members.

II. The sources of household revenue (income) are wages, rent, interest, proprietor's income, distributed corporate profits, and transfer payments from government. The total of these income payments is called personal income.

A. Wages and salaries, paid by producers to purchase labor, are the largest single source of household income.

1. The amount of such payments received by any given household (that is, the household's income level) depends on the quality and quantity of labor (or other resources) it supplies to businesses and the current market demand for the specific types of labor supplied.

2. Regional variations in income reflect regional differences in the availability of human resources and in the business demand for different types of labor.

B. Since the amount and quality of resources possessed and the prices for which they can be sold to businesses differ between households, income is unequally distributed throughout the economy. However, differences in dollar income between households do not necessarily reflect equivalent differences in living standards.

III. Households use their income to pay taxes to government, to save, and to purchase goods and services.

A. Disposable income is the amount of income available to households to spend or save after personal taxes (such as income, sales, or property taxes) have been paid.

B. Patterns of household saving and spending vary at different income levels. However, a household will spend its income with the goal of increasing the total satisfaction of its members.

IV. Analysis of 1970 Census data reveals a number of trends affecting the behavior and structure of American households.

A. The average number of household members is declining, as is the number of economically unproductive members. Consequently, household per capita income is increasing.

B. The median age of household members is decreasing. Since younger households tend to spend a greater fraction of their income than older households, the overall level of household spending is increasing.

C. Greater participation of women in the labor force has increased both household income and expenditures for goods and services produced outside of the home.

D. A rising level of educational achievement has had a positive impact on the level of household income.

E. The gradual shift of population from rural to urban areas has increased both household income and spending.

F. Median household income is rising.

V. Many decisions that affect the whole economy are made within the household.
    A. If households are unwilling to save, there will be less money available to
        businesses for expansion and capital improvement.
    B. Households' decisions about how much and what to consume are a major
        factor in determining what goods will be produced.
    C. The household sector's decision about how and at what price to employ
        their resources affects the economy's capacity to produce.

KEY TERMS

You should be familiar with the meaning of the terms listed below. For definition of
these terms, please refer to the glossary at the end of your textbook and to the appropriate section in this chapter.

household   dissave
saving   disposable personal income
personal income

CONCEPTS AND DEFINITIONS

Fill-in Questions

Complete each sentence by writing in the blank the most appropriate word or words
from the terms listed below or by circling the word in parentheses that is correct.

satisfaction   self-sufficient
wages   median household income
dissave   demand
quantity   taxes
disposable personal income   saving
salaries   personal income
household   quality

1. A household __dissave__ when its spending in a particular time
    period is greater than its income.

2. In economics any person or group of people living under the same roof and
    functioning as an economic unit is considered a __household__.

3. __Personal inc.__ is the total amount of income received by households
    in the form of wages, rent, interest, proprietor's income, distributed corporate
    profits, and government transfer payments.

4. Currently about 15 percent of total personal income is spent on the payment of
    __taxes__ to government.

5. _Disp. persn. inc._ is the amount of income a household has available for consumption and/or saving after all personal taxes have been paid.

6. A household is _self sufficient_ if it does not need to rely on economic exchange with other parties in order to satisfy its demand for goods and services.

7. The amount of income that is neither spent nor paid to the government in the form of taxes is called _saving_.

8. If half of all households in an economy earn less than $14,000 annually while the remaining half earns more than $14,000, then $14,000 is the _median household income_ for that economy.

9. The largest source of revenue for most American households is in the form of _wages_ and _salaries_.

10. The final "product" of a household is the _satisfaction_ of its members.

11. The amount of income a household receives depends primarily on the _quality_ and _quantity_ of the labor it has to sell and on the current _demand_ in the market for that labor.

Multiple Choice Questions

Circle the correct answer.

1. Economists view households as
   a. producers of marketable goods and services.
   b. having minimal influence on the production plans of businesses.
   c. being composed of family members only.
   d. sellers of input resources to businesses.

2. The largest single source of household income is
   a. wages.
   b. rent.
   c. interest.
   d. government transfer payments.

3. From the economist's perspective, the overall goal of the household is to
   a. maximize saving.
   b. maximize income.
   c. maximize utility.
   d. minimize taxes paid to government.

4. Differences in income levels among households across the United States

    a. accurately reflect differences in living standards.

    b. result only from differences in the productive abilities of the individuals comprising various households.

    c. tend to vary directly with the level of education achieved by household members.

    d. occur solely because some households supply greater quantities of labor to employers than other households.

5. The shift of population from rural to urban areas along with the ever-increasing number of working mothers has

    a. had no effect on the economic behavior of households.

    b. increased spending on goods and services.

    c. resulted in decreased household earnings.

    d. caused households in general to become more self-sufficient.

6. The amount of income available to the household depends on

    a. the quantity of labor it has to sell.

    b. the type of labor skills it has to sell.

    c. the demand for the particular type of labor it has to sell.

    d. all of the above.

7. If Mr. Jones' income is $40,000, while Mr. Smith's is just $20,000, Jones must

    a. have worked harder and longer than Smith.

    b. be better educated than Smith.

    c. be more highly skilled than Smith.

    d. possess resources having greater market value than Smith's.

8. Currently more than three-quarters of total personal income in the United States is

    a. paid to government in the form of taxes.

    b. spent on goods and services.

    c. saved.

    d. used to purchase food.

9. After paying all her taxes, Judy Higgins has $14,560 left over. This after-tax amount is Judy's

    a. disposable personal income.

    b. personal income.

    c. median income.

    d. saving income.

APPLICATION

1. Assume that an individual earns $23,000 per year as an electrician, $1200 in interest from savings accounts, and $3600 from the rental of a warehouse which he owns. His taxes amount to $6000 and he spends $21,000.

    a. His personal income is $ _____.
    b. His disposable income is $ _2760_____.
    c. His saving is $ _____.

ANSWERS

Fill-in Questions

1. dissaves
2. household
3. personal income
4. taxes
5. disposable personal income
6. self-sufficient
7. saving
8. median household income
9. wages; salaries
10. satisfaction
11. quality; quantity; demand

Multiple Choice Questions

1. d
2. a
3. c
4. c
5. b
6. d
7. d
8. b
9. a

APPLICATION

1. a. $27,800 The answer is arrived at as follows: $23,000 (wage) + $1,200 (interest) + $3,600 (rental income) = $27,800 (personal income, the total amount of income received from all sources).

    b. $21,800 The answer is arrived at as follows: $27,800 (personal income) — $6,000 (taxes) = $21,800 (disposable income, the amount available for spending or saving after taxes have been paid).

    c. $800   The answer is arrived at as follows: $21,800 (personal consumption) — $21,000 (personal consumption) = $800 (saving).

Chapter 6

Businesses in the American Economy

LEARNING OBJECTIVES

Economists divide the macroeconomy into three basic sectors: households, businesses, and government. In Chapter 5, the economic activities of households were discussed. Now, we are going to focus our attention on the behavior of businesses.

After reading Chapter 6, you should be able to:

1. describe the nature and understand the purpose of business enterprise in our economy;

2. discuss the principal forms of business organization and cite the advantages and disadvantages of each;

3. distinguish implicit costs from explicit costs;

4. identify the trends currently affecting the business sector that will probably influence the economy as a whole.

CHAPTER OUTLINE

I.   A business enterprise is an economic unit organized to produce goods and services by taking advantage of the efficiencies created by the specialization and division of labor. In the simple circular flow model, businesses buy input resources owned or controlled by households and pay wages and salaries to the households in return.

   A. While profit maximization has traditionally been viewed as the basic goal of private enterprise, some modern observers believe that businesses try to make only an acceptable level of profits.

   B. A plant is an individual producing unit of the land and capital (physical equipment) employed in the production process. A business firm is a business organization that produces goods and services in one or more plants. An industry is a group of firms that produce the same or similar commodities.

II.   In the United States today, three principal forms of business enterprise can be
      distinguished by the way they are organized and by the legal form they take:
      the individual proprietorship, the partnership, and the corporation.
      A. The individual proprietorship is the simplest form of business organiza-
         tion. One person, the proprietor, owns all of the productive property and
         bears sole legal responsibility for the success or failure of the firm.
         1. The lack of red tape in establishing a proprietorship, the prospect of suc-
            cess, and the desire to be one's own boss account for the popularity of
            this type of business organization.
         2. Limited financial and entrepreneurial resources make it difficult for the
            proprietor to compete effectively with other forms of business.
      B. Two or more people sharing direct ownership of, and responsibility for, a
         firm constitute a partnership.
         1. An advantage of a partnership is that the firm's financial and en-
            trepreneurial resources will probably be larger than those of an in-
            dividual proprietorship.
         2. The equal liability of all partners for business debts and the difficulty of
            reaching agreement on important decisions are disadvantages of this
            type of business organization.
      C. In the corporate form of business organization, the corporation is legally
         created as an entity separate from the persons who establish it. In the
         United States, the corporation has the major share of business activity.
         1. Some of the advantages associated with the corporation account for its
            popularity. Among them are:
            a. Liability of owners (shareholders) for debts incurred by the corpora-
               tion is limited to the amount invested by each in the company.
            b. Relatively easy access to substantial sums of money allows corpora-
               tions to produce large amounts of output and to take advantage of
               the cost economies available through large-scale production.
            c. The corporation is a more stable organization than other types of
               business enterprise, and this stability makes long-range planning
               easier.
            d. Since the maximum marginal rate of taxation on corporate profits is
               46 percent, incorporation serves as a tax advantage to some share-
               holders.
         2. One disadvantage of a corporation is that since corporate owners and
            managers are usually two different groups of people, there may be con-
            flicts of interest regarding appropriate operating policy for the firm.
III. The major source of income for all business firms is the revenue derived from the
      sale of output. A business's revenue is then spent in various ways.
      A. Business firms must pay sales, excise, payroll, and profits taxes. About
         one-sixth of total corporate revenue is used to pay taxes.
      B. Firms must also spend revenue to purchase the factors of production
         (labor, raw materials, machinery).
IV.   The firm has two types of costs: explicit costs (the costs, like those mentioned

above, that are recorded in the firm's account books) and implicit costs (the opportunity costs of being in business. These opportunity costs are not recorded in account books).

   A. Any revenue a firm receives that exceeds its explicit *and* implicit costs of production is called an economic profit.

V. Several trends within the business sector are likely to exert significant impact on the economy in general.

   A. Business firms are becoming larger, thus allowing a relatively few firms to dominate particular industries.

   B. Nonprofit organizations are growing in number and importance.

   C. Service industries are expanding rapidly in relation to other sectors of the economy.

   D. Firms are being held increasingly accountable for the safety of the items they produce.

KEY TERMS

You should be familiar with the meaning of the terms listed below. For definition of these terms, please refer to the glossary at the end of your textbook and to the appropriate section in this chapter.

profits	corporation
business firm	bond
plant	explicit costs
industry	implicit costs
individual proprietorship	economic profit
partnership	

CONCEPTS AND DEFINITIONS

Fill-in Questions

Complete each sentence by writing in the blank the most appropriate word or words from the terms listed below or by circling the word in parentheses that is correct.

business firm	purchase of input resources	individual proprietorship
revenue	industry	explicit costs
implicit costs	corporation	taxes
partnership	bonds	profits
economic profit	profit maximization	plant

1. The amount of money that the labor and capital resources owned and used by a company in its production process could have earned in some alternative employment is the firm's _____.

2. A(n) _____ is a group of firms offering the same or similar products in the marketplace.

3. Corporations often borrow money by selling _____ to the general public.

4. The term _____ has been defined differently by economists and accountants.

5. Actual monetary payments made by a firm for the purchase of input resources represent an (explicit/implict) cost of production.

6. Two or more people sharing direct ownership of and responsibility for a firm constitute a(n) _____.

7. An organization producing goods and services in one or more plants is called a(n) _____.

8. If Ms. Smith wishes to limit her maximum possible liability to the amount of money she invests in a firm, the form of business organization most appropriate for her investment is the _____.

9. Two major categories of business expenditures are _____ and _____.

10. A(n) _____ is an individual producing unit containing the land and capital resources utilized in the production process.

11. The type of business organization characterized by a single owner of all productive property, who assumes sole responsibility for the success or failure of the firm, is the _____.

12. A(n) _____ results when a firm's revenues exceed the sum of its explicit and implicit costs of production.

13. While _____ has traditionally been viewed as the basic goal of the business firm, some economists currently contend that firms attempt only to earn some target level of profits.

14. Most of a business firm's _____ comes from the sale of its output.

Matching Questions

From the list on the right, select the item that best matches each item on the left, and write its letter in the blank.

_____ 1. Seven out of every ten of these firms fail within five years of opening.

    a. partnership

_____ 2. The least common form of business organization.

    b. individual proprietorship

_____ 3. Type of business organization nor-   c. corporation
mally best able to take advantage
of the cost economies of large-
scale production.

Multiple Choice Questions

Circle the correct answer.

1. The form of business organization that accounts for about 60 percent of all
   output produced by private enterprise is the

   a. plant.

   b. corporation.

   c. individual proprietorship.

   d. partnership.

2. The popularity of the corporate form of business organization is partially accounted for by the fact that

   a. little red tape is encountered in establishing a corporation.

   b. most shareholders in publicly owned corporations play an important role in
   the policymaking process of the firm.

   c. great satisfaction is derived from being one's own boss.

   d. it provides some shareholders with a significant tax advantage.

3. Current trends within the business sector of the economy indicate that

   a. more than half of the labor force is employed in service industries.

   b. the average business firm is smaller today than it was 25 years ago.

   c. service industries, as a whole, realize greater total profits than manufacturing industries.

   d. the prevailing attitude toward consumers continues to be "let the buyer
   beware."

4. A firm realizes an economic profit when

   a. an explicit profit exists.

   b. explicit costs are greater than the implicit costs of production.

   c. its total revenue exceeds its implicit costs of production only.

   d. its revenue exceeds the total of its explicit and implicit costs of production.

5. Bell Telephone Company owns a building and machinery where Slimline
   telephones are made. This producing unit is called a(n)

   a. proprietorship.

   b. plant.

    c. industry.

    d. corporation.

6. The most common form of business organization is the

    a. individual proprietorship.

    b. firm.

    c. partnership.

    d. corporation.

7. An individual might decide on establishing a proprietorship, as opposed to one of the other types of business organization, because

    a. government statistics indicate that proprietorships are generally very profitable operations.

    b. of the relatively easy access to financial resources enjoyed by most proprietors.

    c. of the desire to make independent business decisions.

    d. the owner's liability is limited to the amount of money invested in the company.

8. The increasing importance of the corporate form of business organization over time has

    a. resulted in a greater degree of competition among firms in the economy.

    b. nearly eliminated the individual proprietorship as a form of business organization.

    c. reestablished profit maximization as the sole aim of business activity.

    d. largely separated the ownership and management functions.

9. If for several consecutive years a firm's total revenue is less than the sum of its explicit and implicit costs

    a. it should definitely go out of business.

    b. it has definitely been making an accounting loss.

    c. psychological factors may explain its willingness to continue production.

    d. it has been making an economic profit, but an accounting loss.

10. Ford, General Motors, and American Motors together constitute a(n)

    a. corporation.

    b. plant.

    c. business firm.

    d. industry.

APPLICATION

1. After serving 10 years as a bank vice-president earning $30,000 annually, John Dough decides to quit his job and open a pastry shop. In addition to his time, Mr. Dough invests $25,000, which had been earning 10 percent interest in a savings certificate, in the business. If total revenue in the first year of operation amounts to $50,000, while total explicit costs are $28,000, and Mr. Dough receives no salary during the course of the year,

   a. the total implicit costs of production are $ _____.

   b. economic profit is $ _____.

   c. Mr. Dough must be receiving "psychological" revenue equal to at least $ _____, if he decides to continue operating the pastry business. Why is this so?_____

   _____

   _____

ANSWERS

Fill-in Questions

1. implicit costs
2. industry
3. bonds
4. profits
5. explicit
6. partnership
7. business firm
8. corporation
9. taxes; purchase of input resources
10. plant
11. individual proprietorship
12. economic profit
13. profit maximization
14. revenue

Matching Questions

1. b
2. a
3. c

Multiple Choice Questions

1. b
2. d
3. a
4. d
5. b
6. a
7. c
8. d
9. c
10. d

APPLICATION

1. a. $32,500 $30,000 of foregone salary as a bank vice-president plus $2500 of foregone interest (10% on $25,000).

   b. $10,500 ($50,000 of total revenue minus explicit costs of $28,000 and implicit costs of $32,500).

   c. $10,500 (An economic loss of $10,500 indicates that Mr. Dough could increase his monetary income by $10,500 if he closed the pastry shop, returned to his banking position, and redeposited the $25,000 in a savings certificate. The fact that Mr. Dough remains in the pastry business means that he must be receiving nonmonetary or psychological income of at least $10,500 to compensate for his economic loss).

Chapter 7

Government in the American Economy

LEARNING OBJECTIVES

Having examined the economic rules of households and businesses in Chapters 5 and 6, we will discuss the remaining major sector of the domestic economy, the government. We will see that the shortcomings of the market economy and the price system described in Chapter 4 often create the need for government involvement in economic matters.

After reading this chapter, you should be able to:

1. explain why government intervention in a market economy is necessary;

2. understand the distinction between private and public goods;

3. assess the degree of efficiency with which the government, as opposed to private enterprise, provides goods and services to the public;

4. identify the major revenue sources and the major expenditure categories of federal, state, and local governments;

5. explain the basic principles that often serve as the basis for determining how the tax burden should be distributed among the members of society;

6. distinguish between progressive, proportional, and regressive taxes.

CHAPTER OUTLINE

I.   The government intervenes in economic matters to assure the smooth operation and correct the inherent inequities of the price system, to provide public goods and services, and to reduce the degree of macroeconomic instability.

A. While controversy exists regarding the proper extent of government intervention in the private sector, legislation has been enacted which attempts to: (1) protect the rights of buyers and sellers in the marketplace; and (2) maintain a high level of competition in the market.

B. The free play of market forces results in an unequal distribution of income among households throughout the economy. Since the degree of these income differences is considered too great, government attempts to redistribute income from the wealthy to the poor through taxation and other policies.

  C. The government provides many public goods and services to the society by acting either as a collective producer or as a collective purchasing agent.

    1. The market system has no efficient mechanism for responding to the demand for public goods such as highways and police protection because, unlike private goods, public goods are not subject to the exclusion principle (those who can pay the price get the benefits of the product, those who can't pay are excluded from the benefits). Because the exclusion principle cannot be applied to public goods, private producers are unable to produce them profitably.

  D. In an attempt to minimize undesirable fluctuations in economic activity, the federal government can alter its spending and taxation policies (fiscal policy). The Federal Reserve System, an independent agency of the federal government, can also try to reduce inflation and unemployment in the economy by manipulating the money supply (monetary policy).

II. Even though government provision of goods and services is often economically inefficient, we cannot conclude that society's welfare would necessarily be improved if the private sector provided all these products.

  A. Two possible ways to measure the government's efficiency are to analyze the product cost and compare it with a private firm doing similar work and to measure the government's ability to reach its stated production goals.

  B. Some reasons for government inefficiency include government rules, political considerations, and diseconomies of scale.

III. The primary source of federal, state, and local revenue is taxes.

  A. The largest single sources of federal, state, and local government revenue are personal income, sales, and property taxes, respectively.

  B. Revenue Sharing funds and other federal government grants are also significant revenue sources for state and local governments.

IV. Transfer payments and purchases of both input resources from households and finished products from private firms are the most important categories of government expenditure.

  A. Income security payments (such as Social Security payments) have replaced defense spending as the largest category of federal government spending. In 1978, these two items accounted for 56 percent of federal outlays.

  B. The largest local government expenditures are for education, police and fire protection, and welfare.

V. Two principles are often used by government in deciding how the tax burden should be distributed among the populace.

  A. The benefits-received principle states that people who gain most from the goods and services provided by the government should pay most in taxes.

  B. The ability-to-pay principle states that the amount of taxes an individual pays should be directly related to the individual's income.

VI. Taxes are classified as progressive, proportional, or regressive depending on whether *the amount of the tax payment as a percentage of income* rises, remains constant, or declines as one's income grows.
   A. With a progressive tax, the rate of taxation increases as the base amount taxed increases.
   B. With a proportional tax, the tax rate is the same regardless of the base amount taxed.
   C. With a regressive tax, rates decrease as the base amount taxed increases.

KEY TERMS

You should be familiar with the meaning of the terms listed below. For definition of these terms, please refer to the glossary at the end of your textbook and to the appropriate section in this chapter.

price fixing	benefits-received principle
private goods	ability-to-pay principle
exclusion principle	progressive tax
public or social goods	proportional tax
transfer payments	regressive tax

CONCEPTS AND DEFINITIONS

Fill-in Questions

Complete each sentence by writing in the blank the most appropriate word or words from the terms listed below or by circling the word in parentheses that is correct.

sales taxes	regressive
benefits-received	private
proportional tax	price fixing
income taxes	ability-to-pay
public	exclusion
transfer payments	private goods
property taxes	tax rate
progressive	

1. A(n) _____ requires that the amount of taxes paid as a percentage of income remains constant regardless of the taxpayer's level of income.

2. Governmental outlays for which the recipients provide no productive activity in return are called _____.

3. The primary source of revenue for most state governments is _____.

4. The _____ principle implies that a person who earns $30,000 annually should pay a larger tax bill than a person whose yearly income is $18,000.

5. Diamond rings are _____ goods.

6. A secret agreement among the nation's largest steel companies to increase prices by $3.00 per ton would constitute _____.

7. Purchasers of (public/private) goods are the sole consumers of the benefits which these items offer.

8. A tax is _____ when the percentage of one's income paid in the form of the tax is greater for people with low incomes than it is for those with high incomes.

9. The greatest share of revenue for the federal government in the United States comes from _____.

10. Defense missiles are _____ goods.

11. A $2.00 bridge toll for automobile passage is an example of a tax based on the _____ principle.

12. If you pay a security guard to keep watch over your home and this results in enhanced safety in the neighborhood as a whole, the _____ principle is not in operation.

13. Since private sector demand is nonexistent, _____ goods are not produced by businesses.

14. When the rate of taxation rises along with one's income, the tax is _____.

15. The primary source of revenue for local governments is _____.

Multiple Choice Questions

Circle the correct answer.

1. The largest single source of federal government revenue is

   a. the corporate income tax.

   b. the personal income tax.

   c. social insurance taxes and contributions.

   d. the sales tax.

2. Which of the following government activities is the *best* example of a public good or service?

   a. fire protection.

    b. welfare.

    c. elementary education.

    d. health care for the poor.

3. The exclusion principle does not apply to the consumption of

    a. Big Macs.

    b. automobile services.

    c. national defense services.

    d. health services.

4. The most expensive program in the federal government budget is

    a. income security.

    b. education.

    c. national defense.

    d. health.

5. If a tax is levied such that it results in rising tax bills as individual income increases, the tax is

    a. necessarily progressive.

    b. not proportional since each individual does not pay the same amount of taxes.

    c. based on the benefits-received principle.

    d. regressive if the tax bill represents a higher percentage of income for a poor person than a wealthy person.

6. If a tax is based on the ability-to-pay principle

    a. it cannot be regressive.

    b. each individual's tax bill directly reflects the benefits received from the provision of public goods and services.

    c. it could be proportional.

    d. it must be progressive.

7. An example of the government's redistribution policy is

    a. automobile pollution emission standards.

    b. legislation requiring nationwide unit pricing of food and health and beauty aids.

    c. national defense spending.

    d. free lunch programs for elementary school children from low income households.

8. Considering the traditional reasons for government intervention, the federal government might provide a particular good or service to the public

   a. if it can do so profitably.

   b. if an important private sector producer of this item declares bankruptcy.

   c. if private-sector demand for this product increases.

   d. if the benefits received from the consumption of the product cannot be confined to the purchaser.

9. One important reason for the inefficiency of federally provided goods and services is

   a. the long history of debilitating strikes by public employee unions.

   b. the diseconomy of large-scale production that affects some government programs.

   c. the inability to compete with private firms producing the same goods and services.

   d. the overall lack of formal education of government employees.

10. In recent years there has been a trend toward increased size of businesses. In 1967, the Federal Trade Commission reviewed 1350 mergers and acquisitions. The Justice Department filed suit against 10 of these firms. The main purpose of this action by the government is to

    a. prevent mergers.

    b. maintain a certain degree of competition.

    c. prevent companies from making large profits.

    d. redistribute corporate incomes.

APPLICATIONS

1. If Ms. Green pays $10,000 in taxes on an income of $50,000 and Ms. Rasmussen pays taxes of $5000 on an income of $25,000, this income tax is (progressive/proportional/regressive). (Circle the proper response.)

2. In the blank space, indicate whether the revenue necessary to finance each of the following government activities should be collected on the basis of the ability-to-pay or benefits-received principle.

   a. Installation of high-intensity street lights in a downtown business district. _____.

   b. A subsidized housing program for families earning less than $10,000 annually. _____.

   c. A Food Stamp program for the elderly. _____.

   d. Maintenance of a municipal parking lot. _____.

ANSWERS

Fill-in Questions

1. proportional tax
2. transfer payments
3. sales taxes
4. ability-to-pay
5. private
6. price fixing
7. private
8. regressive
9. income taxes
10. public
11. benefits-received
12. exclusion
13. public
14. progressive
15. property taxes

Multiple Choice Questions

1. b
2. a
3. c
4. a
5. d
6. c
7. d
8. d
9. b
10. b

APPLICATIONS

1. The tax is *proportional* because the *rate* of taxation, 20 percent is the same in both cases ($10,000 is 20 percent of $50,000 and $5,000 is 20 percent of $25,000).

2. a. benefits-received principle

   b. ability-to-pay principle

   c. ability-to-pay principle

   d. benefits-received principle

Chapter 8

Measuring National Income and Product

LEARNING OBJECTIVES

The basic economic concepts of production possibilities, supply and demand, and the circular flow of income which were introduced in earlier chapters are used in evaluating the overall performance of the economy. This study of the behavior of economic aggregates, such as gross national product and the rates of inflation and unemployment, is known as macroeconomics. Before considering macroeconomic *theory*, however, we must first understand how macroeconomic activity is *measured*.

After reading this chapter, you should be able to:

1. understand the purpose of the national income and product accounts;

2. define gross national product (GNP);

3. calculate GNP by using either the expenditures or income approach;

4. understand the limitations of GNP as a measure of both economic activity and economic welfare.

CHAPTER OUTLINE

I.   The system of national income and product accounts is used by economists to measure the economy's performance. These accounts tell us the value of the goods and services purchased by households from businesses in the product market, and the value of the goods and services that businesses buy from households in the resources market.
　　A. National accounts are an important aid in economic planning for government, businesses, and investors.

II. Gross national product (GNP), the total market value in monetary terms of all goods and services produced for final consumption in the economy during a given year, is the most basic measure of economic activity recorded in the national income accounts.

A. To arrive at an accurate measure of production, economists compensate for changes in the value of money. Therefore, nominal GNP (GNP measured in current dollars) is adjusted for the annual percentage change in overall prices by using a price index called the implicit price deflator. This adjusted figure is called real GNP (GNP measured in constant dollars).

B. To avoid double-counting, only the value of goods and services classified as final products (that is, products that will not be resold or processed further) is counted in GNP.

C. Because GNP measures the level of *productive* output, money transfers not involving current production (such as government transfer payments), the sale of second-hand goods, and security sales on the stock exchange are excluded from the measurement of GNP.

III. The two basic methods of calculating GNP are the expenditures approach and the income approach. The two different approaches are different sides of the same coin (GNP).

A. The expenditures approach measures the purchases of goods and services for final consumption by all buyers in the product market over the period of one year. The four major categories of national expenditures are personal consumption, investment, net exports, and purchases of goods and services by state, local, and federal governments.

1. Personal consumption includes all purchases of goods and services made by households. Personal consumption is often broken down into three categories: durable goods, nondurable goods, and services.

a. In the past 20 years, personal consumption has accounted for about two-thirds of national expenditures.

2. In national income accounting, investment is the amount of current output that adds to or replaces the national stock of real productive assets. This figure includes business investment in capital goods and inventories, and investments in residential housing.

3. Net exports is the value of goods and services exported from the economy minus the value of imported goods and services. (This figure can be a negative number.)

B. The income approach to measuring GNP adds together the amount of income generated annually in the process of producing goods and services for final consumption and the amount of two nonincome items (indirect business taxes and capital consumption allowance).

1. The types of income generated in the production process are wages and salaries, proprietor's income, rent, interest, and corporate profits. The sum of these income categories constitutes national income (NI), the amount paid out by businesses to purchase or to rent productive services.

2. Indirect business taxes are taxes (such as sales or business property taxes) that are often treated as part of manufacturing costs.

3. The capital consumption allowance (a system for charging for the depreciation of capital goods) is also added to a firm's costs of production.

IV. Gross national product is an imperfect measure of both economic activity and economic welfare.
   A. There are two basic problems with GNP as a measure of economic activity.
      1. Since only market transactions are considered in its calculation, GNP ignores productive nonmarket activity such as work done by women in the home.
      2. Because the valuation of services provided by the government does not include a normal profit return, GNP is less than it would be if these services were provided by private enterprise.
   B. Some of the problems of using GNP as a measure of economic welfare are:
      1. GNP overstates an economy's well-being because it does not take into account the negative side effects that result from the production of some goods and services.
      2. GNP understates an economy's well-being because it fails to account for economic goods (such as leisure) that are not produced and sold by businesses.
      3. GNP does not give any indication of how the current level of output is distributed among the members of society (that is, if it is equally or unequally distributed). Therefore, the issue of social welfare is not addressed.
V. Comparisons of the GNP of different countries cannot be interpreted too rigidly. Differences in population, structure of the economy, and national income accounting procedures make it difficult to make valid comparisons of GNP between countries.

KEY TERMS

You should be familiar with the meaning of the terms listed below. For definition of these terms, please refer to the glossary at the end of your textbook and to the appropriate section in this chapter.

national income and product accounts	net exports
gross national product (GNP)	national income
price index	wage and salary
value added	proprietor's income
durable goods	rent
nondurable goods	profits
services	interest
investment	indirect business taxes
inventories	net national product
gross investment	capital consumption allowance
net investment	per capita GNP

CONCEPTS AND DEFINITIONS

Fill-in Questions

Complete each sentence by writing in the blank the most appropriate word or words from the terms listed below or by circling the word in parentheses that is correct.

durable
gross investment
net exports
income
price index
expenditures
wage
depreciation
national income
net investment
personal consumption
interest
value added
services

rent
gross national product (GNP)
national income and product accounts
nondurable goods
proprietor's income
inventories
net national product
salary
services
capital consumption allowance
indirect business taxes
per capita GNP
profits

1. Autombiles, stereo systems, and TV sets are examples of (durable/nondurable) goods.

2. From a national income accounting perspective, _Investment_ is defined as the amount of current output that adds to or replaces the productive capacity of the economy.

3. The expenditure category dealing with the exchange of goods and services in international markets is known as _net exports_.

4. Real GNP is calculated by deflating nominal GNP by an appropriate _price index_.

5. Fringe benefits and tips are part of the _wage_ and _salary_ component of national income.

6. The _natl inc + product Accts_ provide a system for measuring the overall performance of the economy.

7. If depreciation of the economy's stock of productive assets is greater than gross investment, then _net investment_ is negative.

8. _interest_ includes all payments by businesses to the suppliers of borrowed money capital.

9. _GNP_ is the total market value of goods and services produced for final consumption in a given year.

10. _Nondurable_ goods are consumed or disposed of within the current time period.

11. If, in a given year, the sales of final goods and services exceed the production, then _inventories_ will probably be lower at the end of the year than they were at the beginning.

12. _Rent_ is the smallest element of national income.

13. The total of all business payments for land, labor, capital, and entrepreneurial ability in a given year is _natl. inc_.

14. The _Captl Cnsmpta allwnce_ provides a systematic method for the measurement of depreciation.

15. If country A has a GNP of $500 billion and a population of 50 million, while country B's GNP is $250 billion and 25 million people reside there, _per capita GNP_ is the same in both countries.

16. In order to avoid double-counting the _value-added_ approach may be used to determine the contribution of a particular good or service to GNP.

17. Corporate _profits_ that are distributed to shareholders are called dividends.

18. Firms attempt to pass _indirect bsnss tax_ (a nominee item) on to consumers in the form of higher prices.

19. Legal advice, dental care, and professional preparation of income tax returns are examples of _services_.

20. If the value of depreciation of real productive assets is subtracted from GNP, we have calculated _net natl product_.

21. The earnings of an owner-operated, unincorporated small business are classified as _proprtrs income_.

22. Of the four major components of national expenditures, the one that accounts for the largest share of expenditures is _persnl. cnsmptn_.

23. Net national product minus indirect business taxes equals _natl. inc._.

24. The capital consumption allowance is a system for calculating the _depreciatn_ of capital goods.

25. There are two basic approaches to calculating GNP. They are the _income_ approach and _expenditures_ approach.

26. The total value of real productive assets produced in one year is _gross investment_.

Matching Questions

From the list on the right, select the item that best matches each item on the left, and write its letter in the blank.

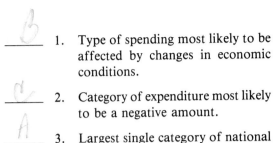

_____ 1. Type of spending most likely to be affected by changes in economic conditions.

_____ 2. Category of expenditure most likely to be a negative amount.

_____ 3. Largest single category of national expenditure.

_____ 4. Fastest growing component of national expenditure.

a. personal consumption

b. investment

c. net exports

d. government purchases of goods and services

Multiple Choice Questions

Circle the correct answer.

1. Gross national product in any given year is equal to the

    a. total value of goods and services produced for final consumption.

    b. total market value of goods and services purchased in the economy.

    c. total market value of goods and services produced for final consumption.

    d. total market value of goods and services produced in the economy.

2. Using the expenditures approach, an underestimate of GNP occurs if

    a. United States purchases of foreign-produced goods and services are ignored.

    b. government transfer payments are excluded from the analysis.

    c. purchases of used refrigerators are included in the analysis.

    d. the change in business inventories is ignored when total output exceeds the sales of goods and services for final consumption.

3. Which of the following is a measure of the value of a year's production after it has been adjusted for the consumption of capital goods during the year?

    a. net national product

    b. national income

    c. gross national product

    d. net personal income

4. Gross national product increases from one year to the next

    a. only if production, in real terms, increases.

    b. if prices rise an average of 5 percent, while real output remains constant.

    c. if business sales volume increases.

    d. only if the rate of increase in real output exceeds the rate of inflation.

5. Of the following candidates, the best measure of economic welfare is
   a. GNP adjusted for the rate of inflation.
   b. real GNP per capita.
   c. national income.
   d. nominal GNP.

6. Which of the following is equal to GNP minus the capital consumption allowance (depreciation)?
   a. net personal income
   b. national income
   c. disposable income
   d. net national product

7. In calculating GNP according to the expenditures approach, we ignore
   a. inventories if they are at exactly the same level at the end of the year as they were at the beginning of the year.
   b. the value of imports since this figure does not represent domestic production.
   c. the spending of transfer-payment recipients, because these payments do not represent productive activity.
   d. government spending on goods and services because GNP measures private-sector production only.

8. The nation's stock of productive assets grows if
   a. businesses spend to replace existing capital assets.
   b. gross investment equals depreciation.
   c. real GNP increases.
   d. net investment is positive.

9. The income approach to GNP measures
   a. the total costs of production for all producers of final products.
   b. all sources of household income.
   c. corporate dividends, but not profit that is retained by businesses.
   d. personal consumption, investment, net exports, and government purchases of goods and services directly.

10. The amount paid out by businesses in wages, salaries, interest, rents, and profits to purchase or to rent productive services is
    a. disposable income.
    b. net national product.
    c. national income.
    d. personal income.

11. All of these statements about GNP are correct *except*

    a. GNP is always expressed in monetary terms.
    b. GNP is a measure of the level of productive output.
    c. government transfer payments are included in GNP.
    d. GNP is arrived at by multiplying the quantity of units produced by the market price of each unit.

12. As an indicator of social welfare, per capita GNP

    a. tells us how output is actually distributed among the members of society.
    b. accounts for productive nonmarket transactions.
    c. is preferable to nominal GNP, but inferior to real GNP per capita.
    d. recognizes the impact of increased leisure time on the quality of life.

13. In order to avoid double-counting, all of the following are excluded from GNP except

    a. sales of securities on the stock exchange.
    b. sales of second-hand goods.
    c. gifts from one individual to another.
    d. government purchases.

14. Comparisons of nominal GNP between countries

    a. provide a good indication of relative living standards.
    b. provide a good indication of relative living standards if national income accounting procedures are the same in all nations.
    c. make highly industrial economies appear more successful than highly agricultural economies because nonmarket transactions are more prevalent in the former than in the latter.
    d. are more meaningful when differences in population and prices are also taken into account.

15. Which element of national income is the largest today?

    a. rental income
    b. proprietor's income
    c. wages and salaries
    d. corporate profits

APPLICATIONS

1. Indicate, by filling each blank space with either "yes" or "no," whether or not the following current year activities and transactions are included in the calculation of GNP.

  a. The purchase of a used pickup truck from your next-door neighbor for $1500. _____

  b. The purchase of 100 shares of stock in the Honeywell Corporation. _____

  c. The portion of a farmer's output that is consumed by his family. _____

  d. The value of the produce from your family's vegetable garden assuming the vegetables are not sold in the marketplace. _____

  e. The purchase of a previously owned home for $60,000. _____

  f. Having Joe's Auto Repair tune up your car for $39.99. _____

2. A baker purchases four eggs for 30¢, one cup of sugar for 25¢, two cups of flour for 15¢, a teaspoon of vanilla for 10¢, and one cup of butter for 50¢. After mixing the ingredients and baking, the result is a cake which sells for $2.00. What is the value added by the baker's mixing and baking of the cake? _____

3. Evaluate the following statement: "In 1971, nominal GNP was $1 trillion. By 1978, it reached $2 trillion. Therefore, our standard of living was twice as high in 1978 as it was in 1971."

4. Employing the accompanying data (in billions of dollars), calculate gross national product, net national product, national income and net investment using both the expenditures approach and the income approach. Show your calculations.

Corporate profits before taxes	$ 157.
Gross private domestic investment	316.
Wages and Salaries	1300.
Exports	200.
Indirect Business Taxes	190.
Personal Consumption expenditure	1350.
Interest	108.
Government purchases of goods and services	465.
Proprietors' Income	114.
Capital Consumption Allowance	230.
Imports	210.
Rental Income	22.

  a. Gross national product is $ _____.

  b. Net national product is $ _____.

  c. National income is $ _____.

  d. Net investment is $ _____.

ANSWERS

Fill-in Questions

1. durable
2. investment
3. net exports
4. price index
5. wage; salary
6. national income and product accounts
7. net investment
8. interest
9. gross national product (GNP)
10. nondurable
11. inventories
12. rent
13. national income
14. capital consumption allowance
15. per capita GNP
16. value-added
17. profits
18. indirect business taxes
19. services
20. net national product
21. proprietor's income
22. personal consumption
23. national income
24. depreciation
25. income; expenditures
26. gross investment

Matching Questions

1. b
2. c
3. a
4. d

Multiple Choice Questions

1. c
2. d
3. a
4. b
5. b
6. d
7. a
8. d
9. a
10. c
11. c
12. d
13. d
14. d
15. c

APPLICATIONS

1. a. no*

   b. no*

   c. yes

   d. no (assuming that the vegetables are not sold in the marketplace)

   e. no*

   f. yes

*The commissions on all of these sale transactions would, however, be included in GNP as part of the wages/salaries category.

2. 70¢

3. Since changes in population, prices, leisure time, etc., are ignored by the nominal GNP figures, we are unable to determine how the standard of living has changed during the seven-year interval.

4. a. $2121. Using the expenditures approach, GNP would equal the sum of the following elements of the national income and product accounts: gross private domestic investment, exports, personal consumption expenditures, government purchases of goods and services, and imports (remember to subtract the imports figure). Using the income approach, GNP would equal the sum of the following elements: corporate profits before taxes, wages and salaries, indirect business taxes, interest, proprietors' income, capital consumption allowance, and rental income.

   b. $1891 (NNP = GNP minus the capital consumption allowance)

   c. $1701 (NI = NNP minus indirect business taxes)

   d. $86 (net investment = gross investment minus the capital consumption allowance)

Chapter 9

Inflation, Unemployment, and Business Cycles

LEARNING OBJECTIVES

In the previous chapter, gross national product was defined and methods of calculating this measure of market economic activity were discussed. The purpose of this chapter is to introduce two or more important macroeconomic concepts—inflation and unemployment. We will discuss several types of inflation and unemployment and will investigate some of the causes of these problems. Finally, we will examine the interaction of inflation and unemployment during the various phases of the business cycle.

After reading this chapter, you should be able to:

1. define inflation and understand the causes of the various types of inflation;

2. recognize the impact of inflation on productive activity and the distribution of income;

3. know how the unemployment rate is measured and understand how this measure tends to both underestimate and overestimate the severity of the unemployment problem;

4. identify and understand the causes of the three basic categories of unemployment;

5. recognize the social and economic costs of unemployment;

6. understand the concept of a business cycle and be able to identify its phases;

7. be familiar with the various theories of the causes of business cycles.

CHAPTER OUTLINE

I.   The achievement of full employment and price stability is one of the main objectives of current macroeconomic policy because of their impact on economic activity and on our daily lives.

II. Inflation occurs when the general level of prices rises.
   A. Price indexes are used to measure the rate of inflation during any particular time period. In the United States, the Consumer Price Index (CPI), the Produce Price Indexes, and the implicit price deflator are the most commonly used measures of price changes.
      1. The CPI measures the price level of the goods and services purchased by an average American household, and although it has limitations, it is very influential both in shaping government economic policy and in adjusting incomes.
      2. The PPIs measure average changes in prices of goods at various stages of processing (finished goods, intermediate goods, and raw materials).
      3. The implicit price deflator of the GNP is the price index for gross national product, and because it covers so many goods and services, it can be used to measure broad price movements in the economy as a whole.
   B. While for theoretical purposes, inflation is usually classified as being of either the demand-pull or cost-push variety, it is difficult to categorize real-world episodes of inflation so neatly.
      1. Demand-pull inflation is caused by an increase in demand at a time when an economy cannot increase production or is unable to increase production fast enough to meet the increase in demand.
      2. Cost-push inflation is due to increased costs of production (increased profits and/or increased resource prices).
      3. Both demand-pull and cost-push inflation can be influenced by government spending and regulation and by consumer expectations of continued inflation.
   C. Inflation can occur at different rates. When the overall level of prices increases noticeably on a daily basis, hyperinflation exists. On the other hand, an annual rate of inflation of 5 percent or less is referred to as creeping inflation.
III. The costs of inflation are difficult to determine. However, when inflation is not fully anticipated, there are costs.
   A. Inflation can cause an arbitrary redistribution of income. Those who become relatively poorer because of inflation include people who lend money, people who save money, and those who live on fixed incomes.
   B. Inflation may also result in a decline in real output because it encourages many individuals to engage in speculative, as opposed to productive, activity as they attempt to protect themselves from rising prices.
IV. While unemployment can refer to any unused resource, most economists focus their attention on unemployed labor.
   A. The economic cost of unemployment on the production side of the national accounts is the value of output that could have been, but is not, produced; on the income side, the cost is the loss of wages and salaries (or rent and interest when land or capital resources are unemployed).
      1. This economic loss of output is represented by the GNP gap which is calculated by subtracting the actual GNP figure from the potential level

of GNP (that is, what GNP could have been if all resources had been fully employed).

B. There are also social costs of unemployment, including loss of skills and training, and increased domestic problems.

C. The unemployment rate is the fraction of unemployed persons in the civilian labor force (not including the Armed Forces).

   1. As a result of measurement difficulties, many people feel that the unemployment rate may underestimate the actual unemployment problem because it makes no allowance for the "hidden unemployed" or for those who are underemployed.

   2. There are also people who contend that the unemployment rate overestimates the unemployment problem because it does not distinguish between those who are actually unable to find work and those who have simply decided to leave the labor market for a period of time.

D. The three major types of unemployment are frictional, structural, and cyclical.

   1. Since frictional unemployment (caused by functional imperfections in the labor market) and structural unemployment (resulting from some structural change in the economy) are largely unavoidable, an unemployment rate of 4-5 percent is consistent with the notion of full employment.

   2. Cyclical unemployment results from a declining level of overall spending in the economy. The federal government undertakes fiscal and monetary policy in an attempt to eliminate this type of unemployment.

V. Business cycles are recurrent fluctuations in economic activity that vary in length and severity.

A. In its simplest form, the cycle can be divided into four phases: expansion (business activity increases), peak (capacity is fully used, full employment is achieved), recession (spending slows, investment declines), and trough (substantial unemployment, little investment).

   1. When studying fluctuations in business activity economists must take into account seasonal variations and the differences in sales of durable and nondurable goods.

B. Disagreement exists among economists regarding the causes of business cycles. Many theories have been proposed including some that relate business cycles to disturbances in the money supply or to technological change.

KEY TERMS

You should be familiar with the meaning of the terms listed below. For definition of these terms, please refer to the glossary at the end of your textbook and to the appropriate section in this chapter.

inflation	frictional unemployment
deflation	structural unemployment

Consumer Price Index
Producer Price Indexes
implicit price deflator
demand-pull inflation
cost-push inflation
hyperinflation
creeping inflation
unemployment rate

cyclical unemployment
GNP gap
business cycles
recovery
peak
recession
trough

CONCEPTS AND DEFINITIONS

Fill-in Questions

Complete each sentence by writing in the blank the most appropriate word or words from the terms listed below or by circling the word in parentheses that is correct.

implicit price deflator
frictional unemployment
deflation
recession
inflation
recovery
cyclical unemployment
Consumer Price Index
cost-push
unemployment

business cycles
peak
trough
demand-pull
labor
GNP gap
hyperinflation
Producer Price Indexes
structural

1. When ___deflation___ is unanticipated, the dollars repaid by debtors are worth *more* than the dollars that were originally borrowed.

2. The ___recovery___ phase of the business cycle is characterized by increasing levels of output, employment, and profits, but relatively constant prices.

3. Production is irretrievably lost to the economy when there is unemployed ___labor___.

4. If, in any given year, all of the major unions in the United States negotiate wage increases in excess of labor productivity gains, (cost-push/demand-pull) inflation will occur.

5. An economy that has the capacity to produce $2500 billion of output, but manages to produce just $2200 billion worth of goods and services for final consumption, suffers from a ___GNP gap___ of $300 billion.

6. Current changes in the ___PPI___ provide a good indication of how the Consumer Price Index will behave in the near future.

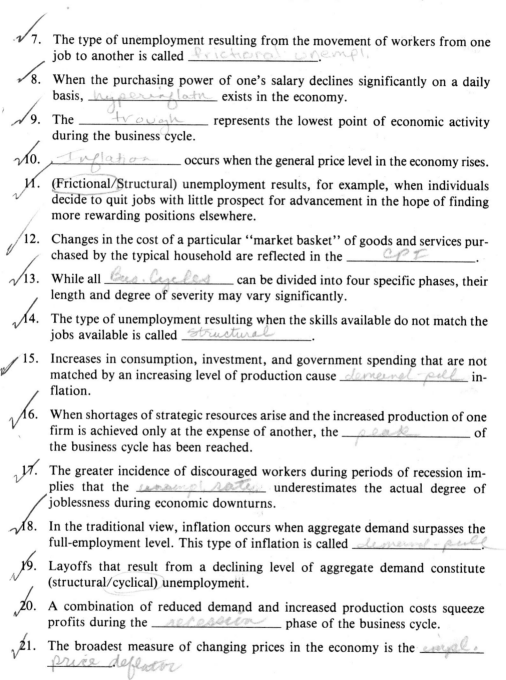

7. The type of unemployment resulting from the movement of workers from one job to another is called _frictional unempl._

8. When the purchasing power of one's salary declines significantly on a daily basis, _hyperinflatn_ exists in the economy.

9. The _trough_ represents the lowest point of economic activity during the business cycle.

10. _Inflation_ occurs when the general price level in the economy rises.

11. (Frictional/Structural) unemployment results, for example, when individuals decide to quit jobs with little prospect for advancement in the hope of finding more rewarding positions elsewhere.

12. Changes in the cost of a particular "market basket" of goods and services purchased by the typical household are reflected in the _CPI_.

13. While all _Bus. Cycles_ can be divided into four specific phases, their length and degree of severity may vary significantly.

14. The type of unemployment resulting when the skills available do not match the jobs available is called _structural_.

15. Increases in consumption, investment, and government spending that are not matched by an increasing level of production cause _demand-pull_ inflation.

16. When shortages of strategic resources arise and the increased production of one firm is achieved only at the expense of another, the _peak_ of the business cycle has been reached.

17. The greater incidence of discouraged workers during periods of recession implies that the _unempl. rate_ underestimates the actual degree of joblessness during economic downturns.

18. In the traditional view, inflation occurs when aggregate demand surpasses the full-employment level. This type of inflation is called _demand-pull_.

19. Layoffs that result from a declining level of aggregate demand constitute (structural/cyclical) unemployment.

20. A combination of reduced demand and increased production costs squeeze profits during the _recession_ phase of the business cycle.

21. The broadest measure of changing prices in the economy is the _implic. price deflator_

Matching Questions

From the list on the right, select the item that best matches each item on the left, and write its letter in the blank.

_a_   1.   Job loss resulting from decreased consumption spending by households.

                          a.   cyclical unemployment

_e_   2.   Job loss resulting from the decision to relocate from Chicago to Phoenix for climatic reasons.

                          b.   underemployed

_d_   3.   Those who stop looking for work upon experiencing difficulty and disappointment in searching for a job.

                          c.   frictional unemployment

                          d.   hidden unemployed

_b_   4.   Those whose talent greatly exceeds the skill requirements of their present job.

                          e.   structural unemployment

Multiple Choice Questions

Circle the correct answer.

1. In order for inflation to exist in the economy

   a. the prices of all goods and services must be rising.

   b. at least some prices must be rising, but no prices can be falling.

   c. the prices of most goods and services must be rising.

   d. the prices of all goods and services must be rising at the same rate.

2. If the Consumer Price Index in 1979 is 220.7 and the base year is 1967,

   a. a "market basket" of goods and services would cost $220.70 in 1979, if it cost $100 in the base year.

   b. the current annual rate of inflation is 120.7 percent.

   c. the price of every good and service in 1979 is 120.7 percent higher than it was in 1967.

   d. consumer prices in general are 220.7 percent higher in 1979 than they were 12 years earlier.

3. Suppose that you have plans to take a job for the summer. You are offered a job that you cannot begin until a week after school has ended. You decide to take the job since your pay will be quite high, but you are unemployed for one week. Your unemployment is

   a. structural unemployment.

   b. frictional unemployment.

   c. cyclical unemployment.

   d. none of these.

4. The Consumer Price Index

    a. assures accurate information on changes in the cost of living because the price of every consumer item produced in the United States is given consideration.

    b. guarantees that, regardless of the base year, the market basket of goods and services whose prices are monitored accurately reflects current-year purchases of households.

    c. attempts to give households in the economy an indication of how their cost of living is changing.

    d. accounts for changes in the quality of particular goods and services over time.

5. If higher prices could be attributed solely to attempts by producers to increase profit margins, this type of inflation could be characterized as

    a. demand-pull.

    b. cost-push.

    c. hyperinflation.

    d. creeping inflation.

6. Economists agree that creeping inflation

    a. does not really hurt anyone.

    b. stimulates economic activity if prices of economic resources rise faster than product prices.

    c. does not eliminate the incentive to save as long as the rate of interest paid on savings exceeds the rate of inflation.

    d. definitely causes consumers to develop a "buy now" attitude.

7. In discussing inflation in the post-Korean war period, John Kenneth Galbraith argued that industries dominated by big firms would tend to charge prices below maximum profit levels. Such firms, he suggested, are afraid that price increases will invite increased union demands that, once granted, are irreversible. They therefore wait until unions ask for higher wages and then raise prices shortly thereafter. These increased prices in turn encourage unions to increase their demands. The type of cyclical inflation described by Galbraith would be called

    a. hyperinflation.

    b. cost-push inflation.

    c. demand-pull inflation.

    d. excess demand.

8. If unanticipated deflation occurred in the economy

    a. everyone would be better off.

    b. those on fixed incomes would benefit.

   c. borrowers would be better off, because the dollars they would repay would be worth less than the dollars they originally borrowed.

   d. income would not be arbitrarily redistributed, as it is when inflation occurs.

9. According to current thinking, to achieve full employment

   a. cyclical unemployment must be eliminated.

   b. a zero rate of unemployment is necessary.

   c. the talents of each member of the labor force must be fully utilized.

   d. frictional unemployment must be eliminated.

10. The basic cause of business cycles is

   a. a source of disagreement among economists.

   b. underproduction and overconsumption following long periods of prosperity.

   c. the steady growth of the money supply over time.

   d. the lack of technological improvement in the United States economy over time.

11. As a result of a weakening interest in additional aircraft in this country both from private industry and the federal government, the aircraft industry has been suffering the pains of contraction. Thousands of workers at all levels have been laid off from such major companies as Boeing and Lockheed, particular in several West Coast cities. This type of unemployment is

   a. structural unemployment.

   b. frictional unemployment.

   c. cyclical unemployment.

   d. none of these.

12. During the course of the business cycle

   a. consumption spending is usually more volatile than investment spending.

   b. expenditures on consumer durables vary more than expenditures on consumer nondurables.

   c. all industries in the business sector are equally affected.

   d. the severity of the recessionary phase is matched by an equally intense recovery phase.

13. If you lose your job as a payroll clerk because the firm computerizes the payroll system, your job loss is an example of

   a. hidden unemployment.

   b. cyclical unemployment.

   c. frictional unemployment.

   d. structural unemployment.

14. The price controls of World War II were lifted in 1946. For a large number of people, there had been enforced saving during the war. Rationing and the sheer lack of consumer durables had kept spending down. Thousands of servicemen were also given various forms of bonuses upon leaving the service. As price controls were lifted, people scrambled for the goods that were available and prices rose by almost 25 percent in the second half of 1946.

The type of inflation experienced in 1946 was

a. cost-push inflation.

b. wage-push inflation.

c. demand-pull inflation.

d. profit-push inflation.

APPLICATIONS

1. Assume that an economy's potential GNP is $3000 billion, but that 5 million people are unemployed. Labor is the only unemployed resource and the average annual wage is $12,000.

   a. What is the actual level of GNP? $_____

   b. What is the size of the GNP gap? $_____

2. Assume that, in June, the civilian labor force is composed of 100 million individuals, and 94 million of these are employed.

   a. The unemployment rate in June is _____ percent.

   b. If, in July, 1 million individuals stop looking for work, while one million high school graduates begin searching for their first jobs, the unemployment rate in July is _____ percent.

3. If the Consumer Price Index, using 1967 as the base year, was 148 in 1975 and is 192 in 1979, prices have risen _____ percent since 1975.

ANSWERS

Fill-in Questions

1.	deflation	12.	Consumer Price Index
2.	recovery	13.	business cycles
3.	labor	14.	structural
4.	cost-push	15.	demand-pull
5.	GNP gap	16.	peak
6.	Producer Price Indexes	17.	unemployment rate

7. frictional
8. hyperinflation
9. trough
10. inflation
11. frictional

18. demand-pull
19. cyclical
20. recession
21. implicit price deflator

Matching Questions

1. a
2. c
3. d
4. b

Multiple Choice Questions

1.	c	8.	b
2.	a	9.	a
3.	a	10.	a
4.	c	11.	a
5.	b	12.	b
6.	c	13.	d
7.	b	14.	c

APPLICATIONS

1. a. $2940 billion [$300 billion potential GNP minus $60 billion (5 million times $2000) in wages = $2940]

    b. $60 billion ($60 billion is the difference between potential and actual GNP)

2. a. 6 percent (6 million people are unemployed; 6 million is 6 percent of 100 million)

    b. 6 percent (The 1 million people who stop looking for work drop out of the number of unemployed people because they are not looking for work. However, the addition of 1 million high school graduates to the number of unemployed people looking for work balances out the first loss of 1 million people. Therefore, the unemployment rate remains the same.)

3. 29.7 percent [44, the change in the CPI (192 − 148 = 44), is 29.7 percent of 148, the year to which we are comparing the 1979 CPI.]

Chapter 10

Total Spending: The Consumption and Investment Components

LEARNING OBJECTIVES

Unemployment and inflation were identified in the previous chapter as the two most serious problems facing macroeconomic policymakers. These problems exist largely because either too little or too much spending occurs in the economy. Since the level of aggregate spending is such an important determinant of macroeconomic performance, we separate total spending or aggregate demand into four basic components and study each individually. In this chapter, consumption and investment are examined. The determinants of these two types of spending are discussed, and the importance of each is assessed in terms of its impact on the macroeconomy.

After reading this chapter, you should be able to:

1. identify the determinants of consumption spending;

2. distinguish permanent income from current income and recognize how their respeetive impacts on the level of consumption spending differ;

3. understand the method by which firms decide whether or not to undertake certain investment projects;

4. identify the factors that affect business investment spending in the economy;

5. distinguish between the various types of investment spending.

CHAPTER OUTLINE

I.   Consumption is the largest single category of total spending or aggregate demand. It represents the amount of spending for goods and services undertaken by the household sector.

    A. The most important determinant of household spending is the size of its disposable income (DI). Part of a household's disposable income may also be used for saving (DI minus consumption). The amounts of income used for consumption spending and saving vary with the level of disposable income.

1. A consumption schedule shows the amount a household plans to spend at each possible level of disposable income at a specific point in time.
   a. The average propensity to consume (APC) is the percentage of a given total disposable income that is spent: $C/DI = APC$
   b. The marginal propensity to consume (MPC) indicates the fraction of new disposable income that is spent: $\dfrac{\text{change in } C}{\text{change in DI}} = MPC$
2. A saving schedule shows the amounts a household plans to save at each possible disposable income level at a specific point in time.
   a. The average propensity to save (APS) is the percentage of a given total income that is saved: $S/DI = APS$.
   b. The marginal propensity to save (MPS) is the fraction of new income that is saved: $\dfrac{\text{change in saving}}{\text{change in disposable income}} = MPS$
3. The consumption schedule shows two important facts: consumption varies directly with income level (as DI increases, C increases); and when DI changes, the change in consumption is less than the change in income.

B. Aggregate or total consumption is the sum of spending by all households in the economy. Aggregate disposable income is the most important determinant of aggregate consumption.
   1. Aggregate consumption is also influenced by the average age and size of households, stocks of liquid assets and consumer durable goods, level of private debt, consumer expectations, and cultural attitudes.

C. Some recent studies suggest that consumption spending responds more closely to changes in permanent income (a worker's average income level throughout his or her life) than to changes in current income.

II. The second major component of private spending is investment spending. Investment, which is the most volatile component of GNP, can be divided into three categories: business purchases of new plant and equipment, changes in business inventories, and residential construction. Business purchases of new plant and equipment are the largest category of investment spending.

A. In general, a prospective investment project will be undertaken if the estimated rate of return on the project exceeds the current market rate of interest.
   1. The relationship between the market rate of interest and investment is inverse (as the rate of interest declines, all other things equal, total investment spending will increase, and vice versa).

B. The major factors influencing business-investment decisions are innovation and technological advance, the current stock of fixed business capital, expectations regarding market behavior, and the current profitability of business.
   1. The volatility of business-investment spending is partially explained by the accelerator theory which states that changes in consumption spending will induce a change in investment spending that is proportionally even greater than the change in consumption.

C. Businesses also have funds invested in their inventories of goods and resources. In general, businesses tend to try to increase the size of their inventories when sales are rising or are expected to rise. If sales are constant or decreasing, businesses may try to cut back on their inventory investment.
  1. Because inventories are a more liquid kind of asset than most kinds of business saving, inventory investment is extremely volatile.
D. The level of residential construction activity is largely determined by population size, the level of personal income, credit availability, and migration trends.
  1. Many economists consider residential construction an important indicator of future economic trends. When construction increases, the outlook for economic expansion is good. Declines in residential construction are often seen as signs of a coming recession.
E. While investment spending is generally characterized as being subject to erratic change from one time period to the next, both fluctuating interest rates and the long-run nature of investment planning moderate the degree of variability in investment.

KEY TERMS

You should be familiar with the meaning of the terms listed below. For definition of these terms, please refer to the glossary at the end of your textbook and to the appropriate section in this chapter.

saving	marginal propensity to consume
consumption schedule	marginal propensity to save
saving schedule	liquid assets
average propensity to consume	permanent income
average propensity to save	accelerator theory

CONCEPTS AND DEFINITIONS

Fill-in Questions

Complete each sentence by writing in the blank the most appropriate word or words from the terms listed below or by circling the word in parentheses that is correct.

marginal propensity to consume	change in disposable income
change in consumption	average propensity to save
consumption schedule	saving schedule
saving	investment spending
liquid assets	average propensity to consume
profitability	accelerator theory
marginal propensity to save	permanent income

1. A _Consumption Schedule._ shows how household consumption varies as the level of disposable income changes.

2. A positive relationship exists between the stock of _liquid Assets_ and a household's level of consumption spending.

3. If a family spends $24,000 out of an annual disposable income of $30,000, its (average/marginal) propensity to save is .2 (6/30).

4. If individuals spend a higher-than-normal portion of income in years when their income is unusually low, and save a larger-than-normal portion of income in years when income is unusually large, consumption decisions are probably being made on the basis of _Permanent inc_ rather than current income.

5. The value of the _Marginal Propensity to Consume_ indicates the amount by which spending on goods and services changes in response to a change in disposable income.

6. When income changes, the change in consumption is (less than/greater than) the change in income.

7. If the Smith family's annual disposable income is, $20,000 and it spends $18,000, its _Average. Propens. Consume_ is .9.

8. A table illustrating the relationship between household saving and household disposable income is called a _Saving Schedule_.

9. The _Acceleration theory_ explains how, for example, a 10 percent increase in consumption spending might induce a 20 percent increase in investment spending.

10. Since any addition to income must be either spent or saved, the sum of the _Marginal Propensity to Consume_ and the _marginal prop to save_ must equal one.

11. _Saving_ is the portion of disposable income that is left over after current expenditures.

12. The _rate_ of consumption (increases/decreases) as the level of disposable income increases.

13. Stocks, bonds, and bank accounts are examples of _liquid Assets_.

14. If the market rate of interest declines from 10 percent to 6 percent, we would expect investment spending to (increase/decrease).

15. Long-range planning and fluctuating interest rates tend to stabilize _____ _Investment Spending_.

16. Consumption varies (directly/inversely) with income level.

17. The size of investment expenditures is determined by the investment's estimated _profitability_.

18. The average income that an earner expects over his or her working life is called _permanent. inc_

19. The marginal propensity to consume is expressed as $\dfrac{\text{change in } C}{\text{change in } DI}$.

Multiple Choice Questions

Circle the correct answer.

1. As the level of household disposable income increases

   a. the APC decreases.
   b. the MPC approaches one.
   c. saving increases and consumption decreases.
   d. the APS declines.

2. If a point on an aggregate consumption schedule lies below the 45-degree line,

   a. all disposable income is spent on goods and services.
   b. dissaving occurs in the economy.
   c. aggregate consumption is less than aggregate disposable income.
   d. the economy necessarily experiences unemployment.

3. The level of consumption in the economy increases

   a. as the stock of liquid assets declines.
   b. as the stock of consumer durable goods declines.
   c. as the average age of households increases.
   d. if consumers expect prices to fall in the future.

4. If a firm is considering the purchase of a new machine, it will invest

   a. if the estimated rate of return from the machine is greater than zero.
   b. only if the estimated rate of return on the machine exceeds the market rate of interest by at least the rate of inflation.
   c. if the estimated rate of return on the machine is greater than zero, and the firm has sufficient retained earnings to buy the machine.
   d. if the estimated rate of return on the machine exceeds the market rate of interest.

5. Historically, the most important cause of dramatic fluctuation in total investment spending has been

   a. annual changes in aggregate household consumption.
   b. the rise and fall of innovation investment.
   c. fluctuation in business' rate of profit from one year to the next.
   d. tax-law changes regarding acceptable methods of depreciating newly purchased capital goods.

6. Which of these equations is the average propensity to consume?

    a. $\dfrac{C + S}{DI}$

    b. $\dfrac{\text{change in } S}{\text{change in } DI}$

    c. $\dfrac{C}{DI}$

    d. $\dfrac{\text{change in } C}{\text{change in } DI}$

7. According to the accelerator theory, investment spending

    a. falls to zero if consumption spending fails to increase on an annual basis.

    b. declines if consumption spending remains constant after having increased in the previous time period.

    c. will increase as long as some capital goods wear out every year.

    d. will grow at an increasing rate for an indefinite period of time.

8. Fluctuations in investment spending are not always as great as that indicated by the accelerator theory because

    a. the level of residential construction is relatively constant over time.

    b. interest rates tend to be higher during periods of prosperity than during recessionary periods.

    c. of the short-term nature of investment planning.

    d. inventory investment is stable over time.

9. When a household considers its income to be temporarily low, it is likely to

    a. save an increasing percentage of its income.

    b. spend the same percentage of income it would if income were higher.

    c. spend a higher percentage of its income.

    d. save the same percentage of income it would if income were higher.

10. Assume that your family's disposable income is $10,000 and current consumption expenditures are $8500. In addition, your family's marginal propensity to consume is .8 regardless of the level of disposable income. Under these circumstances, it can be stated that

    a. the APS is .2.

    b. the APC will rise if disposable income increases.

    c. saving will increase by $150 if disposable income increases to $11,000.

    d. consumption expenditures will be reduced to $7700, if disposable income falls to $9000.

11. All of these are a major component of investment spending except

    a. education.

    b. residential construction.

    c. inventories.

    d. business purchase of plant and equipment.

12. The Estermyer Electric Co. is considering purchasing two trucks, priced at $8000 each, for its growing business. The estimated rate of return on these trucks is 9 percent. The firm will purchase the trucks

    a. as long as its retained earnings are at least $16,000.

    b. because the estimated rate of return is positive.

    c. if it can borrow funds at 8 percent in order to finance this project.

    d. even if it could earn 10 percent by depositing its retained earnings in a bank account instead of buying the trucks.

13. Suppose that you receive a relatively large and unexpected inheritance. What behavior would economists be likely to predict?

    a. You would be expected to go on a spending binge in which you would save practically nothing of your additional income.

    b. You would be expected to save a large proportion since you would not consider this to be a permanent increase in your annual income.

    c. You would be expected to dissave since you feel more secure.

    d. You would be expected to consume the same proportion of your inheritance that you consume of your regular income.

APPLICATIONS

1. The ABC Floor Waxing Co. is considering the purchase of a new machine, with a useful life of one year, at a cost of $2000. Furthermore, due to its technical superiority in comparison to machines currently in use, the new machine is expected to generate $2200 of net revenue for the company, *before* taking account of the cost of the machine.

    a. On the basis of the above information, the estimated rate of return on the machine is _____ percent.

    b. Even if ABC possesses sufficient retained earnings to purchase the machine outright, it should do so only if the market rate of interest is (greater than/less than) _____ percent.

2. Complete the following table depicting household consumption and saving at various levels of disposable income.

Disposable Income	Consumption	Saving
$10,000	$12,000	$ _____
20,000	18,000	_____
30,000	24,000	_____
40,000	_____	_____
50,000	_____	_____

a. The value of the MPS is _____.

b. Dissaving occurs when disposable income is $ _____.

c. The value of the APC is _____ when disposable income is $20,000 and _____ when disposable income is $40,000.

ANSWERS

Fill-in Questions

1. consumption schedule
2. liquid assets
3. average
4. permanent income
5. marginal propensity to consume
6. less than
7. average propensity to consume
8. saving schedule
9. accelerator theory
10. marginal propensity to consume; marginal propensity to save
11. saving
12. decreases
13. liquid assets
14. increase
15. investment spending
16. directly
17. profitability
18. permanent income
19. $\frac{\text{change in } C \text{ (consumption)}}{\text{change in DI (disposable income)}}$

Multiple Choice Questions

1.	a	8.	b
2.	c	9.	c
3.	b	10.	d
4.	d	11.	a
5.	b	12.	c
6.	c	13.	b
7.	b		

APPLICATIONS

1. a. 10 percent (Subtracting the cost of the machine from the net revenue gener-
    ated, we see that a $200 return was earned on a $2000 invest-
    ment. Dividing the dollar return by the cost of the machine, we
    arrive at a 10 percent estimated rate of return.)

    b. less than 10 percent (Since ABC posseses retained earnings sufficient to
    purchase the machine, the market rate of interest
    represents its opportunity cost; i.e., the rate of
    interest ABC could earn it if invested its retained
    earnings in their next best alternative, instead of in
    the machine. Therefore, if the market rate of interest
    exceeds 10 percent, ABC would invest its funds at this
    higher rate instead of settling for the 10 percent
    return from the machine.)

2.

Disposable Income	Consumption	Saving
$10,000	$12,000	$ – 2,000
20,000	18,000	+ 2,000
30,000	24,000	6,000
40,000	30,000	10,000
50,000	36,000	14,000

a. $.4 \left(\text{MPS} = \dfrac{\text{change in } S}{\text{change in DI}} = \dfrac{4,000}{10,000} = \dfrac{4}{10} = .4 \right)$

b. $10,000

c. The APC is .9 when disposable income is $20,000

$\left(\text{APC} = \dfrac{C}{\text{DI}} = \dfrac{18,000}{20,000} = \dfrac{9}{10} = .9 \right)$, and .75 when disposable income

is $40,000 $\left(\dfrac{C}{\text{DI}} = \dfrac{30,000}{40,000} = \dfrac{3}{4} = .75 \right)$

Chapter 11

The Equilibrium Level of Output and Income

LEARNING OBJECTIVES

Consumption and investment were introduced in the previous chapter as two important categories of spending in the macroeconomy. This chapter illustrates how consumption and investment combine to determine the level of output that will be produced in an economy. Discussion of the impact of government spending on the level of output is delayed until Chapter 12.

After reading this chapter, you should be able to:

1. demonstrate an understanding of the concept of macroeconomic equilibrium;

2. explain, through use of either the aggregate demand-aggregate supply or savings-equals-investment approach, how the equilibrium level of income or output for an economy is determined;

3. explain and demonstrate the paradox of thrift;

4. show why changes in consumption and investment spending cause greater than proportionate changes in output or income;

5. differentiate between the equilibrium level of income and the full-employment level of income.

CHAPTER OUTLINE

I. The level of output ultimately produced in response to a given level of consumption and investment spending in an economy is known as the equilibrium level of output or income.

   A. In this chapter the models used to explain how equilibrium is determined will be simplified by omitting the role of government spending and taxes. Thus, all national income will be classified as disposable income and will be equal to net national product (NNP) because there are no business taxes.

   B. We will also ignore the capital consumption allowance and use NNP instead of GNP in our discussion.

II. One approach to determining the equilibrium in the market for goods is the aggregate demand-aggregate supply approach. Using this approach, equilibrium will occur at that level of output that will generate sufficient income to produce the exact level of total spending needed to purchase all available goods and services (that is, the level of output at which quantity demanded equals quantity supplied).
  A. Aggregate demand measures the total amount of money (in current dollars) that all buyers are willing and able to spend on all goods and services at a given time.
    1. Aggregate demand (in this simplified model) equals investment spending for the year (I) plus consumption spending for the year (C).
  B. Aggregate supply is the total value (in current dollars) of all goods and services produced or available for purchase at a given time.
  C. Keynesian theory assumes that businesses will supply as many goods as spenders will buy, and that equilibrium will be reached when aggregate demand equals aggregate supply.
    1. A production level (aggregate supply) that is higher than total spending (aggregate demand) will not be maintained because suppliers would be left with goods on their hands.
    2. If aggregate supply is lower than aggregate demand, businesses will expand their production to meet the excess demand.
III. Another way to examine equilibrium is through the use of the savings-equals-investment approach. Using this approach, equilibrium will occur at the point at which saving (a temporary withdrawal from the circular flow) equals investment spending (an injection into the circular flow).
  A. If households want to save more than businesses want to invest, the imbalance will result in a decrease in total spending that will in turn lead businesses to cut back production to the point where saving again equals investment.
  B. If businesses want to invest more than households want to save, business firms will increase production until they reach the level of NNP that will call forth saving equal to the amount they want to invest.
IV. When all households decide to save more money, their saving plans begin a process of adjustment as the economy seeks a new equilibrium level of production. This adjustment eventually results in a reduction in the actual amount that households are able to save. This reduction in aggregate saving that follows a period of planned increases in saving is called the paradox of thrift.
V. If the level of either consumption or investment spending changes, the equilibrium level of output (NNP) will be altered by some multiple of the change in spending.
  A. The ratio that indicates the total change in income that will result from an initial change in consumption or investment spending is known as the multiplier.

1. The multiplier is the reciprocal of the marginal propensity to save (MPS). Thus, if we know the MPS or the marginal propensity to consume (MPC) we can calculate the multiplier:

$$\text{multiplier} = \frac{1}{\text{MPS}} = \frac{1}{(1 - \text{MPC})}$$

VI. There is no mechanism in the economy to ensure that equilibrium will be established at the full-employment level of income or output.
   A. If aggregate demand exceeds the full-employment level of NNP, an inflationary gap exists.
   B. If aggregate demand is less than the full-employment level of NNP, a deflationary gap exists.
   C. The problems of inflationary or deflationary gaps can be solved by efforts to alter the rates of spending or saving, for example, through government actions.

KEY TERMS

You should be familiar with the meaning of the terms listed below. For definition of these terms, please refer to the glossary at the end of your textbook and to the appropriate section in this chapter.

aggregate demand   multiplier
aggregate supply   deflationary gap
paradox of thrift   inflationary gap
multiplier effect

CONCEPTS AND DEFINITIONS

Fill-in Questions

Complete each sentence by writing in the blank the most appropriate word or words from the terms listed below or by circling the word in parentheses that is correct.

saving   multiplier
multiplier effect   paradox of thrift
aggregate demand   investment
aggregate supply   planned investment

1. If a(n) (inflationary/deflationary) gap exists in the economy, the equilibrium level of NNP exceeds the full-employment level of NNP.

2. The smaller the value of the marginal propensity to save, the larger the value of the _multiplier_.

3. The full-employment level of NNP is $750 billion. The equilibrium level of NNP is $650 billion. The (inflationary/deflationary) gap is equal to ___100 bill.___.

4. The total amount of money spent by all buyers on final goods and services in a given year is the level of ___Aggregate Demand___ in the economy.

5. Total investment exceeds ___planned. invstm.___ when *undesired* inventory accumulation occurs.

6. If ___aggreg. Supply___ exceeds ___Aggreg. Demand___ the equilibrium level of NNP is less than the currently produced level of output.

7. Significant unemployment of resources suggests that the economy is burdened by a(n) (inflationary/deflationary) gap.

8. If the multiplier is 5, then the MPS is ___1/5___ and the MPC is ___4/5___.

9. The two approaches to determining the equilibrium levels of output and income are the ___Aggreg.-Dem.___ approach and the ___Aggreg Supply___ equals ___Saving, Invest___ approach.

10. The equilibrium level of output (increases/decreases) if households decide to reduce the amount of saving out of any given level of disposable income.

11. If planned investment expenditures are greater than the amount of saving planned by households at the current level of output, ___Aggreg. Demand___ exceeds ___Aggreg. Supply___.

12. A decrease in consumption spending that elicits a much larger decrease in the equilibrium level of income provides evidence that the ___Multiplier Effect___ is at work in the economy.

13. If businesses want to invest $100 billion, but households want to save only $80 billion, the businesses will (increase/decrease) their levels of production.

14. The fact that an attempt by households in general to increase saving renders the economy unable to support this higher level of saving is explained by the ___Paradox of Thrift___

15. The ___Multiplier___ is a ratio that indicates the ultimate change in income that will result from an initial change in investment.

16. If aggregate demand is less than aggregate supply, the economy will (expand/contract) until equilibrium is reached.

17. A hypothetical economy has the following schedules (in billions of dollars).

Level of output and income	Intended investment	Saving
$ 25	$10	− $ 5
50	10	0
75	10	5
100	10	10

The equilibrium level of output and income is ___$100 bil___.

18. A hypothetical economy has the following schedules (in billions of dollars).

Level of output and income	Consumption	Investment
$ 25	$30	$15
50	50	15
75	60	15
100	80	15

The equilibrium level of output and income is _$75 bill_____.

Multiple Choice Questions

Circle the correct answer.

1. If the equilibrium level of output is $2 trillion and the full-employment level of output is $2.4 trillion,

   a. an inflationary gap exists.

   b. an increase in investment spending of $.4 trillion would allow the economy to reach the full-employment level.

   ⓒ aggregate demand is less than the full-employment level of output.

   d. a deflationary gap of $.4 trillion exists.

2. If the economy's current level of output is greater than the equilibrium level of output,

   a. inflation necessarily exists.

   b. unemployment necessarily exists.

   ⓒ planned saving exceeds planned investment.

   d. businesses experience an unexpected decrease in inventories.

3. In the economy shown below, the equilibrium level of output

   a. is X.

   ⓑ is Y.

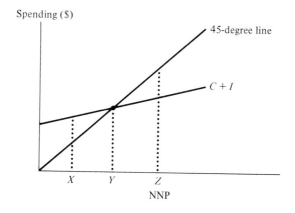

c. is Z.

d. cannot be determined due to insufficient information.

4. Using the graph from question 3, we can determine that

   a. businesses want to invest more than households want to save at the X level of output.

   b. Y is the full-employment level of output.

   c. an inflationary gap exists at the Z level of output.

   d. households and businesses wish to purchase more than is produced at the Z level of output.

5. The savings-investment graph below indicates that

   a. regardless of the level of NNP, a positive amount of saving occurs.

   b. households desire to save more than businesses want to invest at the B level of NNP.

   c. investment spending increases as the level of NNP grows.

   d. aggregate demand must equal aggregate supply at the C level of output.

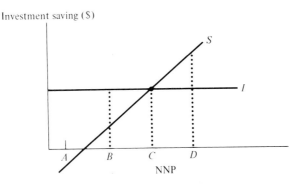

6. An increase in investment of $10,000 will result in

   a. exactly a $10,000 increase in the level of NNP.

   b. an increase in NNP that is some multiple of $10,000.

   c. an increase in NNP less than $10,000 because some of it will be saved.

   d. no change in the level of NNP.

7. What happens if the equilibrium NNP falls above full employment?

   a. Price levels fall.

   b. Income rises.

   c. Price levels rise.

   d. The equilibrium point changes.

8. If an increase in investment spending causes the aggregate demand curve to shift upward from $(C + I)$ to $(C + I_1)$, the equilibrium level of income will
   a. be unaffected because consumption will fall by the exact amount that investment increases.
   b. increase by the vertical distance AB.
   c. increase by the horizontal distance XY, which must exactly equal the vertical distance AB.
   d. increase by an amount greater than the vertical distance indicated by AB.

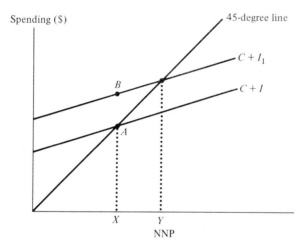

9. Viewing the accompanying graph, assume that the full-employment level of NNP is F and the current equilibrium output level is E. Under these circumstances,
   a. a deflationary gap equal to the vertical distance JK exists.
   b. an inflationary gap equal to the vertical distance JK exists.
   c. an inflationary gap equal to the horizontal distance FE exists.
   d. a deflationary gap equal to the horizontal distance FE exists.

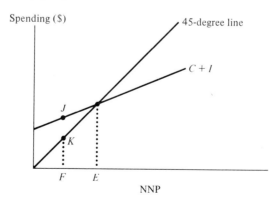

10. According to the paradox of thrift, if all households decide to increase saving

    a. businesses will decide to increase investment.
    b. the performance of the economy will improve, because thriftiness is a desirable trait for households to possess.
    c. their incomes will eventually be reduced to the point where they are unable to save more than they had in the past.
    d. the equilibrium level of income will increase.

11. If the marginal propensity to consume is .9, a $3 billion decrease in investment spending will ultimately cause

    a. the equilibrium level of income to decrease by $3 billion.
    b. the intended level of saving to decrease by $3 billion.
    c. the equilibrium level of income to decrease by $3.33 billion.
    d. aggregate demand to exceed aggregate supply at the original equilibrium level of income.

12. If the value of the marginal propensity to save increases,

    a. a $10 billion increase in consumption will cause a smaller increase in the equilibrium level of output than it did when the MPS was smaller.
    b. the value of the multiplier is unaffected, since it is equal to $1/(1 - MPC)$.
    c. the value of the multiplier increases.
    d. investment will increase because of the increased availability of funds for borrowing.

APPLICATIONS

1. a. what is the value of the multiplier if:

    (1) the MPC is .9? _____
    (2) the MPC is .8? _____

    b. Using economic (not mathematical) logic, explain why the value of the multiplier increases as the MPC increases.

    c. If investment spending increases by $25 billion, the level of income will ultimately increase by $_____ if the MPC is .9 and by $_____ if the MPC is .8.

2. Use the data below in answering the following questions.

    a. Calculate the level of aggregate demand corresponding to each level of output by filling in the blank spaces in the aggregate demand column.

    b. What is the equilibrium level of output? $_____ billion.

c. At the equilibrium level of output, saving is equal to $_____ billion.

d. If the economy temporarily produces $1200 billion of output, explain why you would expect output to expand in the ensuing production period.

e. If the economy temporarily produces $2000 billion of output, explain why you would expect output to contract in the next production period.

f. What is the value of the MPC in this example? _____

g. The value of the multiplier is _____.

h. If the economy is operating at the equilibrium level of output and consumption spending subsequently decreases by $10 billion, the new equilibrium level of income is $_____ billion.

Aggregate supply	Consumption	Investment	Aggregate demand
	(all figures are in billion of $)		
$1000	$1200	$40	$_____
1200	1320	40	$_____
1400	1440	40	$_____
1600	1560	40	$_____
1800	1680	40	$_____
2000	1800	40	$_____
2200	1920	40	$_____

3. Assume that the economy is at equilibrium. For each of the cases below, indicate whether there will be a rise (+) or fall (−) in national output and income assuming that all other things are equal.

a. Households decide that they wish to spend a higher proportion of their incomes because there are several new products they wish to buy.

b. Households decide to save a larger proportion of their incomes because they think prices will fall in the future.

c. Businesses find that by using new computerized techniques they can keep smaller inventories and wish to do so.

d. Businessmen expect prices for their goods to rise in the future so they wish to build up their inventories.

4. Fill in the following table which shows the impact of a $2 million increase in investment spending on income, consumption, and saving when the marginal propensity to save is .1 and the marginal propensity to consume is .9.

	Change in income	Change in consumption	Change in saving
Round 1: Increase in investment	$2,000,000	$_____	$_____
Round 2	$1,800,000	$_____	$_____
Round 3	$_____	$_____	$_____
All other rounds	$_____	$_____	$_____

ANSWERS

Fill-in Questions

1. inflationary
2. multiplier
3. deflationary; $100 billion
4. aggregate demand
5. planned investment
6. aggregate supply; aggregate demand
7. deflationary
8. 1/5; 4/5
9. aggregate demand-aggregate supply; saving; investment
10. increases
11. aggregate demand; aggregate supply
12. multiplier effect
13. increase
14. paradox of thrift
15. multiplier
16. contract
17. $100 billion
18. $75 billion

Multiple Choice Questions

1.	c	7.	c
2.	c	8.	d
3.	b	9.	b
4.	a	10.	c
5.	d	11.	b
6.	b	12.	a

APPLICATIONS

1. a. (1) $10 \left(\text{if the MPC} = .9 \text{, then the MPS} = .1 \text{ and the multiplier} = \frac{1}{1/10} \text{ or } 10 \right)$

    (2) 5

    b. As the value of the MPC increases, people spend a greater fraction of any increase in disposable income than they did in the past. This generates a greater increase in demand during each round of the multiplier process. Consequently, producers respond by increasing output and income accordingly. The magnitude of the change in income, therefore, varies directly with the size of the MPC.

    c. $250 billion; $125 billion (The multiplier = 10, 10 × $25 billion = $250 billion; the multiplier = 5, 5 × $25 billion − $125 billion.)

2. a. The aggregate demand $(C + I)$ figures are as follows: $1240, $1360, $1480, $1600, $1720, $1840, $1960.

    b. $1600 (aggregate supply = aggregate demand)

    c. $40 (at equilibrium, saving must equal investment)

    d. Because when aggregate supply is $1200, aggregate demand is $1360. Consequently, producers find their inventories shrinking unexpectedly and respond to this situation by increasing production.

e. Because when aggregate supply is $2000, aggregate demand is just $1840. Consequently, inventories of unsold goods pile up and output is reduced in the next production period.

f. $.6 \left(\text{aggregate supply} = \text{income. Thus, the MPC} = \dfrac{\text{change in consumption}}{\text{change in income}} = \dfrac{120}{200} = \dfrac{6}{10} \text{ or } .6 \right)$

g. $2.5 \left(\text{multiplier} = \dfrac{1}{\text{MPS}} = \dfrac{1}{(1 - \text{MPC})} = \dfrac{1}{(1 - .6)} = \dfrac{1}{.4} = 2.5 \right)$

h. $1575 [the multiplier is 2.5. Therefore a $10 billion decrease in consumption spending will give rise to a $25 billion decrease in income (2.5 × $10 billion). $1600 billion (equilibrium) minus $25 billion = $1575 billion.]

3. a. +

   b. −

   c. −

   d. +

4.

	Change in income	Change in consumption	Change in saving
Round 1: Increase in investment	$ 2,000,000	$ 1,800,000	$ 200,000
Round 2	$ 1,800,000	$ 1,620,000	$ 180,000
Round 3	$ 1,620,000	$ 1,458,000	$ 162,000
All other rounds	$14,580,000	$13,122,000	$1,458,000
Total	$20,000,000	$18,000,000	$2,000,000

Round 1: The change in consumption (C) is $1,800,000 (change in income × MPC = $2,000,000 × .9 = $1,800,000).

The change in saving (S) is $200,000 (change in income minus change in C = $2,000,000 − $1,800,000 = $200,000)

Round 2: Change in C is $1,620,000 ($1,800,000 × .9)

Change in S is $180,000 ($1,800,000 − $1,620,000)

Round 3: Change in income is $1,620,000. This figure is arrived at as follows: The Round 2 change in C ($1,620,000) gives rise to a $1,620,000 increase in demand. Producers will want to meet this additional demand with $1,620,000 of output. The production of this output will in turn give rise to $1,620,000 additional income. Thus, the Round 2 change in consumption becomes the change in income in Round 3.

Change in C is $1,458,000 (.9 × $1,620,000)

Change in S is $162,000 ($1,620,000 − $1,458,000)

All other rounds (and Total): In order to figure the change in income in all other rounds, we must first figure the total change in income arising from the increased investment of $2,000,000. Given the MPS of .1, we know the multiplier is 10. Thus, we know the total change arising from the initial increase in investment will be $20,000,000. In order to find the change in income for all other rounds, we then subtract the sum of the changes in income of Rounds 1, 2, and 3 ($5,420,000) from the total change in income ($20,000,000). The change in income for all other rounds is $14,580,000.

The change in C for all other rounds is $13,122,000 ($14,580,000 × .9).

The change in S for all other rounds is $1,458,000 ($14,580,000 − $13,122,000).

The total change in C is $18,000,000 ($20,000,000 × .9).

The total change in S is $2,000,000 ($20,000,000 − $18,000,000). Note that the total change in S is equal to the initial increase in investment in Round 1.)

Chapter 12

Fiscal Policy: Government Spending and Taxation

LEARNING OBJECTIVES

In Chapter 11 we examined the process by which the equilibrium level of output is determined in an economy with only the household and business sectors. In this chapter we extend our analysis in order to determine the impact of the government sector on economic activity. Government strategies for stabilizing the economy through the use of fiscal policy are given special attention.

After reading this chapter you should:

1. be familiar with the discretionary and nondiscretionary fiscal policy tools that may be used by government;

2. be aware of the role politics plays in the discretionary fiscal policy process;

3. understand how government spending and taxation affect the equilibrium level of income;

4. recognize the impact of discretionary fiscal policy on government budgets and the public debt.

CHAPTER OUTLINE

I. Fiscal policy is the action taken by government to alter the level of its expenditures and taxes in order to bring about desired changes in economic activity. In the United States, the federal government uses fiscal policy in an attempt to minimize inflation and unemployment, and to promote economic growth.

   A. Nondiscretionary fiscal policy consists of built-in stabilizers that automatically cushion any fluctuations in economic activity. It is designed to reduce the impact that changes in net national product (NNP) have on on the level of disposable income.

      1. The progressive tax structure is one type of nondiscretionary fiscal tool.

        a. If NNP decreases, national income (NI) will decrease. Because of the progressive tax structure, the percentage decrease in taxes collected will be greater than the percentage decline in NI. Therefore, spending which is a function of disposable (after-tax) income will not decrease in proportion to the decrease in NI since taxes have also decreased.

b. If NNP increases, NI will increase, but so will the amount of taxes collected. The increase in DI is therefore smaller than the increase in NI, and the taxes act as a brake on expansionary economic activity.

c. Government is often reluctant to decrease spending when tax revenues decrease. If a budget deficit arises, the government can finance it by selling bonds or by increasing the money supply. If tax revenues increase, the government may use the budget surplus to increase its spending or to redeem bonds, or it may hold the surplus revenues in Treasury deposits.

(1) If the economy is operating at a high rate of employment and the government holds the extra revenues out of the circular flow, spending will decrease and NNP will decrease. The contractionary effect of increased tax revenues produced by increases in NNP is called fiscal drag.

2. Transfer payments and other types of subsidies paid by the federal government also dampen the effects of changes in NNP.

a. If NNP drops, businesses will cut back production, unemployment will increase, and NI will decrease. But because of increases in government transfer payments, such as unemployment compensation, workers will still have money to spend, and spending will not decline in proportion to the decline in NI.

b. If NNP rises, NI will also rise. However, transfer payments will decrease and tax revenues will increase, thus guarding against excessive spending when NNP increases.

B. Discretionary fiscal policy is the purposeful alteration of the rates of taxation or government spending in order to help establish equilibrium NNP at a full-employment, noninflationary level.

1. The government may try to stabilize the economy by changing its level of spending on goods and services.

a. If the economy is faced with a deflationary gap, government can increase its spending on goods and services. This increase will lead to an increase in aggregate demand which will in turn, cause the equilibrium level of NNP to rise.

b. If the economy is faced with an inflationary gap, government can decrease its spending to decrease aggregate demand. This decrease in aggregate demand will cause NNP to fall to a noninflationary level.

2. The government may also increase the effectiveness of the built-in stabilizers by purposefully altering its expenditures on transfer payments or by altering the rates of taxation.

a. When NNP rises, the government may act to decrease its transfer payments and increase tax rates.

           b. When NNP falls, government may increase its transfer payments and enact a tax cut.

        3. Since discretionary fiscal policy is subject to the political process, policy decisions may sometimes reflect what is best for politicians and their constituencies rather than what is best for the entire country.

        4. A lengthy time lag between the time that an economic problem arises and the time that discretionary policies begin to alleviate the problem may also reduce the effectiveness of discretionary fiscal policy.

II.   The addition of government spending and taxation to the consumption, saving, and investment activity of households and businesses alters the equilibrium level of output (NNP).

   A. Government spending represents an addition both to aggregate demand and to investment (an injection into the circular flow). As such, it results in a higher equilibrium level of NNP.

      1. Aggregate demand = consumption spending + business investment + government spending $(C + I + G)$.

      2. Increases or decreases in government spending are subject to the multiplier effect.

   B. Personal income taxation reduces disposable income and, therefore, consumption spending. Like saving, it represents a leakage from the circular flow and, in itself, causes the equilibrium level of NNP to decline.

      1. Using the saving-equals-investment approach, the equilibrium equation now reads: saving + taxes = business investment + government spending.

      2. Increases or decreases in the amount of taxes collected are subject to the multiplier effect.

   C. Since the expansionary impact of a given amount of government spending on aggregate demand outweighs the contractionary impact of an equal dollar amount of taxation, equal amounts of government spending and taxation will increase the equilibrium level of NNP.

III. In the process of altering government spending and rates of taxation in an attempt to stabilize the economy, the government budget is rarely balanced.

   A. The government often finances budget deficits by borrowing money from households and businesses through the sale of bonds. The total dollar value of government bonds outstanding constitutes the public debt.

      1. Although some controversy exists over its impact on the economy, most economists agree that the public debt is not sufficiently large (relative to GNP), to pose a threat to the stability of the economy.

KEY TERMS

You should be familiar with the meaning of the terms listed below. For definition of these terms, please refer to the glossary at the end of your textbook and to the appropriate section in this chapter.

fiscal policy
nondiscretionary fiscal policy
  (automatic stabilizers)
fiscal drag

discretionary fiscal policy
budget deficit
budget surplus
public debt

CONCEPTS AND DEFINITIONS

Fill-in Questions

Complete each sentence by writing in the blank the most appropriate word or words from the terms listed below or by circling the word in parentheses that is correct.

discretionary
nondiscretionary
$C + I + G$
multiplier effect
fiscal policy
fiscal drag
budget surplus
budget deficit

money
public debt
transfer-payments system
impact lag
decision lag
time lag
bonds
progressive tax structure

1. With the introduction of government, the aggregate expenditures for the economy are _~~fiscal drag~~_ . _C + I + G_

2. _Nondiscretionary_ fiscal policy operates automatically.

3. The deflationary effect of a progressive tax on a growing economy is called _fiscal drag_ .

4. _Discretionary_ fiscal policy requires deliberate government action.

5. When the amounts of government spending and revenues collected are the same, NNP will (decrease/(increase)) in the long run.

6. Annual government expenditures in excess of revenues result in a _Budget deficit._ .

7. Contractionary _discretionary_ fiscal policy may be difficult to implement because it is unpopular among politicians.

8. The progressive tax structure is one type of _nondiscretionary_ fiscal policy.

9. _Nondiscretionary_ fiscal policy reduces, but does not eliminate, the effects of economic fluctuations on the level of disposable income.

10. The term _fiscal policy_ encompasses all attempts by government to improve macroeconomic conditions by altering its levels of taxation and spending.

11. If NNP is decreasing, government should ((increase)/decrease) its spending and (increase/(decrease)) the rate of taxation.

12. To the extent that government bondholders are United States citizens, we owe the _Public debt_ to ourselves.

13. Under noninflationary circumstances, _fiscal drag_ occurs when the additional tax revenue generated by higher levels of economic activity are held idle by government.

14. Time lags and politics limit the effectiveness of _discretionary_ fiscal policy.

15. When NNP is rising transfer payments (increase/~~decrease~~) and taxes (~~in-crease~~/decrease).

16. Changes in government spending and taxation are subject to the _multiplier effect_

17. If the federal government wishes to reduce inflationary pressures in the economy, it may deposit a _Budget Surplus_ with the United States Treasury instead of, for example, retiring a portion of the national debt.

18. Two types of nondiscretionary stabilizers are the _Progressive tax_ and the _Transfer Payment System_ _structure_

19. The extent of Congressional debate regarding any proposed change in either government spending or rates of taxation largely determines the length of the _decision lag_.

20. Fiscal drag is a limitation of _Nondiscretionary_ fiscal policy.

21. That period of time between the recognition of, for example, significant unemployment and the time that Congressionally-approved increased government spending begins to reduce unemployment in the economy constitutes the _time lag_ of discretionary fiscal policy.

22. The government can finance a budget deficit by increasing the supply of _money_ or by selling _bonds_.

23. The _impact lag_ associated with an increase in public works spending is usually significantly longer than that associated with a decrease in the rate of personal income taxation.

24. Government spending is one form of _discretionary_ fiscal policy.

Multiple Choice Questions

Circle the correct answer.

1. During a period of rising economic activity, the automatic stabilizer likely to have the greatest effect on disposable income is

   a. progressive personal income taxation.

   b. proportional personal income taxation.

   c. regressive personal income taxation.

   d. an increase in the rate of personal income taxation.

2. At equilibrium, which of the following is true?

   a. $S + G = I + T$

   b. $S + T = I + G$

   c. $S + I = T + S$

   d. $S - T = I - G$

3. An appropriate response to the existence of fiscal drag would be

   a. a decrease in government spending, since this would reduce the burden of government on the private sector of the economy.

   b. a decrease in the rate of personal income taxation.

   c. a decrease in Social Security payments.

   d. a decrease in veterans' benefits.

4. If the government balances its budget, the overall effect on income is

   a. deflationary.

   b. neutral.

   c. expansionary.

   d. either expansionary or deflationary.

5. Assuming that the MPC is the same for all income groups, the effect of a $40 million increase in public works spending on the equilibrium level of income will be the same as a

   a. $40 million increase in investment spending.

   b. $40 million decrease in taxation.

   c. $40 million increase in taxation.

   d. $40 million increase in government transfer payments.

6. Which of the following discretionary fiscal policy proposals is least politically feasible?

   a. an increase in defense spending.

   b. an increase in the corporate income tax.

   c. an increase in Social Security payments.

   d. an increase in the personal income tax.

7. The most serious problem with discretionary policy as a stabilizing tool is

   a. reaching political agreement.

   b. timing.

   c. the creation of a public debt.

   d. none of these.

8. Assume that equilibrium in an economy composed of only household and business sectors is established at the $1000 billion level of output. The MPC is .9. If a government sector is then introduced with government spending of $50 billion and taxation of $50 billion,

   a. the equilibrium level of income remains at $1000 billion.

   b. the increased government spending will be inflationary.

   c. aggregate demand is unaffected as government spending rises by $50 billion, causing consumption to decline by $50 billion.

   d. the equilibrium level of income rises to $1050 billion.

9. In the early 1960s President Kennedy requested a tax cut from Congress. Walter Heller, the Chairman of the Council of Economic Advisers, argued that the growth of the economy was being slowed by "excessive" taxation. The tax cut was meant to

   a. reduce fiscal drag.

   b. eliminate a surplus.

   c. combat inflation.

   d. restrict the Vietnam war.

10. If the president is given the power, during times of emergency, to change government spending or taxes without Congressional approval

   a. the impact lag associated with discretionary fiscal policy is significantly reduced.

   b. the recognition lag associated with discretionary fiscal policy is significantly reduced.

   c. the decision lag associated with discretionary fiscal policy is significantly reduced.

   d. the impact lag is reduced, but the recognition lag is longer.

11. A surtax with corresponding increases in government expenditures is actually

   a. deflationary.

   b. undetermined.

   c. neutral.

   d. expansionary.

12. Suppose you are a member of Congress and must vote on a new budget. A report from the president's economic advisors estimates that the economy is operating $20 billion below the full-employment level of income and output. They also estimate that MPC = .75. You know that you could eliminate the gap by voting for additional direct expenditures of $5 billion, but you know that your constituents would never stand for an increase in the national debt.

   What else could you do to eliminate the gap?

    a. Increase transfer payments by $20 billion and increase taxes by $20 billion.

    b. Increase both taxes and expenditures for goods and services by $5 billion.

    c. Increase both taxes and expenditures for goods and services by $20 billion.

    d. Nothing that would not lead to an increase in the national debt.

13. When the government sector is included with the household and business sectors of the economy, equilibrium occurs at that level of output where

    a. consumption plus investment equals aggregate supply.

    b. planned investment plus government spending equals planned saving plus taxes.

    c. planned saving equals planned investment.

    d. government spending equals taxes.

14. If government spending is increased by $10 billion and taxation is increased by $8 billion and the MPC is .8,

    a. aggregate demand is unaffected as the increases in both government spending and taxation completely neutralize one another.

    b. the net effect on aggregate demand is an increase of $3.6 billion.

    c. the net effect on aggregate demand is an increase of $10 billion.

    d. a budget surplus of $2 billion exists.

15. If an economy has a stable price level, the government can deal with a problem of excessive unemployment by

    a. increasing taxes while holding spending constant.

    b. taxing in excess of spending.

    c. spending in excess of taxation.

    d. reducing its role in the economy.

16. If the government increases taxation by $25 billion and the MPC is .8,

    a. the aggregate demand curve will shift upward by $25 billion.

    b. the aggregate demand curve will remain in its initial position since taxation does not affect consumption, investment, or government spending.

    c. the aggregate demand curve shifts downward by $25 billion.

    d. the aggregate demand curve shifts downward, but this shift is less than $25 billion.

APPLICATIONS

1. Identify the following examples of fiscal policy as either discretionary (D) or nondiscretionary (ND).

a. A Congressional decision to extend the maximum collection period for unemployment compensation from 13 to 65 weeks. _____

b. Increasing the personal exemption on the federal personal income tax from $750 to $1500 per person. _____

c. A decrease in personal income taxes paid by the general public as the level of NNP falls. _____

d. A decrease in the amount of unemployment compensation paid by government as the economy expands. _____

e. A change in the definition of "unemployed" which allows previously uncovered groups to qualify for unemployment compensation. _____

2. Assuming an MPC of .9, explain how the equilibrium level of NNP is affected by increases of $10 billion in both government spending and taxation.

3. a. Fill in the blank spaces in the table below, assuming that the MPC is .9.

   b. The equilibrium level of output is $_____ billion.

   c. The level of saving at the equilibrium level of income is $_____ billion.

   d. If the full-employment level of income or output is $100 billion less than the equilibrium level of output, the economy is experiencing (inflation/unemployment). (circle one)

   e. Using the information in Part d, government spending would have to (increase/decrease) by $_____ in order to establish equilibrium at the full-employment level of output.

Aggregate supply	Taxes	Disposable income	Consumption	Investment	Government spending	Aggregate demand
		(All figures are in billions of dollars.)				
$1525	$25	$_____	$1455	$60	$40	$_____
1625	25	$_____	$_____	60	40	$_____
1725	25	$_____	$_____	60	40	$_____
1825	25	$_____	$_____	60	40	$_____
1925	25	$_____	$_____	60	40	$_____
2025	25	$_____	$_____	60	40	$_____
2125	25	$_____	$_____	60	40	$_____

ANSWERS

Fill-in Questions

1. consumption spending + business investment + government spending $(C + I + G)$
2. nondiscretionary
13. fiscal drag
14. discretionary
15. decrease; increase
16. multiplier effect

3. fiscal drag
4. discretionary
5. increase
6. budget deficit
7. discretionary
8. nondiscretionary
9. nondiscretionary
10. fiscal policy
11. increase; decrease
12. public debt

17. budget surplus
18. progressive tax structure; transfer-payments system
19. decision lag
20. nondiscretionary
21. time lag
22. money; bonds
23. impact lag
24. discretionary

Multiple Choice Questions

1.	a	9.	a
2.	b	10.	c
3.	b	11.	d
4.	c	12.	c
5.	a	13.	b
6.	d	14.	b
7.	b	15.	c
8.	d	16.	d

APPLICATIONS

1. a. D
   b. D
   c. ND
   d. ND
   e. D

2. With an MPC of .9, the multiplier is 10. Therefore, the $10 billion increase in government spending will increase the equilibrium level of NNP by $100 billion.

   While the increase in government spending directly increases aggregate demand by $10 billion, the increase in taxation does not affect total spending or aggregate demand directly. The increase in taxation first causes disposable income to decline by $10 billion. With an MPC of .9, the $10 billion decrease in disposable income results in a $9 billion decrease in consumption. This decrease in spending is also subject to the multiplier of 10. Thus, the equilibrium level of NNP declines by $90 billion as a result of the $10 billion increase in taxation.

   Since the increased government spending raises NNP by $100 billion and the increased taxation reduces NNP by $90 billion, the overall impact of both actions is to increase the equilibrium level of NNP by $10 billion.

3. a.

Aggregate supply	Taxes	Disposable income	Consump-tion	Invest-ment	Government spending	Aggregate demand
		(all figures in billions of dollars)				
$1525	$25	$1500	$1455	$60	$40	$1555
1625	25	1600	1545	60	40	1645
1725	25	1700	1635	60	40	1735
1825	25	1800	1725	60	40	1825
1925	25	1900	1815	60	40	1915
2025	25	2000	1905	60	40	2005
2125	25	2100	1995	60	40	2095

Disposable income = aggregate supply − taxes

Consumption is figured as follows: Disposable income increases by $100 billion each time. Given the MPC of .9, we know that consumption will increase by $90 billion each time DI increases. Thus, $1455 (the original consumption figure) + $90 billion (the increase in consumption) = $1545 (the new consumption figure); $1545 billion + $90 billion = $1635, and so on.

Aggregate demand = Consumption + investment + government spending

b. $1825 billion (the point at which aggregate supply = aggregate demand)

c. $75 billion ($I + G$ must equal $S + T$ at the equilibrium level)

d. inflation

e. $ − 10 billion

Chapter 13

The Importance of Money in an Economy

LEARNING OBJECTIVES

The use of money as a medium of exchange in our economy facilitates the purchase and sale of goods and services. In addition to this most obvious role, however, money acts as a standard of value and represents one way in which wealth may be held. In this chapter, we initially discuss these functions of money and then, using a macroeconomic perspective, we consider how fluctuations in the amount of money existing in the economy at any time may influence prices, employment, and production levels.

After reading this chapter you should:

1. have a better understanding of how money functions in an economy;

2. know how the money supply is usually defined and why other potential definitions of the money supply receive less attention;

3. be familiar with the basic factors affecting the demand for money;

4. understand the various theories regarding the role of money in determining the levels of prices, output, and employment in the economy.

CHAPTER OUTLINE

I.   Any item that is considered money serves as a medium of exchange, a standard of value, and a store of wealth.
   A. The use of money as a medium of exchange facilitates and speeds up economic transactions.

II. In the United States, currency (coins and paper money) and demand deposits (checking accounts) are the two major kinds of money. Together they constitute M_1 the most basic definition of the money supply.
   A. Since the face value of coins is greater than the value of the metal from which they are made, our coinage is a token money.

    B. Since paper money has no inherent value and is not backed by a precious metal such as gold or silver, the general public relies on the government to undertake the actions necessary to maintain the market value of paper money.

        1. A "fiat" money system is one in which paper money need not be backed by any set amount of precious metal.

    C. Demand deposits account for approximately 75 percent of our money supply.

    D. Near monies (such as time deposits and Treasury securities), like money, can be converted easily into currency or demand deposits, but unlike money, they are not widely accepted as a medium of exchange.

        1. Some economists argue that the basic definition of the money supply should be expanded to include funds deposited in savings and time accounts (M_2).

III. According to Keynes, people keep money on hand in order to undertake transactions (transactions demand), to allow them to meet unexpected contingencies (precautionary demand), and to speculate about the future course of prices (speculative demand).

    A. The amount of money that people keep on hand to undertake transactions and meet unexpected contingencies depends largely on their income. The amount of money held for speculative purposes is determined primarily by the market rate of interest.

        1. A liquidity preference curve (a demand curve for money) shows the amount of liquid assets people desire to keep on hand at various interest rates, assuming that all other factors that may affect money demand remain constant.

            a. The quantity of money held varies inversely with changes in the interest rates. When interest rates are high, less money is held; when interest rates are low, more money is held.

            b. Changes in the level of income and in psychological expectations can cause a shift in the liquidity preference curve.

IV. The Quantity Theory of Money (Money Supply × Velocity = Price × Quantity) deals with the relationship of price level and the money supply and is used to make predictions about the macroeconomic impact of changes in the money supply.

    A. Velocity (the number of times each dollar is spent or turned over within a stated period of time) can be measured by dividing the dollar value of GNP by the money supply (M) $\cdot$ $V = \dfrac{\text{GNP}}{M}$ or $MV = \text{GNP}$.

        1. Since GNP equals the quantity of all final goods and services times their prices ($Q \times P$), the quantity theory is generally expressed as $MV = PQ$.

    B. $MV = PQ$ shows us that changes in the supply of money (assuming velocity is constant) can affect the price level (P) and/or production level (Q).

        1. Classical economists assumed that V and Q were relatively constant. Therefore, they believed that changes in the money supply would result in proportionate changes in prices—if M increased, P would also increase and vice versa.

2. In the Keynesian view, increases in M are often counteracted by decreases in V, with no change in P and Q. Thus, to affect P and Q, some other agent (such as the government) must ensure that increases in M would be spent (that is, that V would remain the same or increase), thus stimulating the economy.

3. Chicago School economists believe that, since fluctuations in velocity are minor, changes in the money supply are largely reflected in changing price and/or production levels, depending upon the current state of the economy.

V.   The interaction between the demand and supply curves for money determines the interest rate (the price of money).

A. When the interest rates are high, business investment spending declines. If interest rates are low, business investment rises. This relationship between the level of the interest rate and the level of investment is called the marginal efficiency of investment (MEI).

B. Since we know that the interest rate varies with the money supply, we can draw the following relationships to show the effects of the money supply on the level of net national product (NNP):

If M increases $\longrightarrow$ the interest rate increases $\longrightarrow$ investment decreases $\longrightarrow$ NNP decreases.

If M decreases $\longrightarrow$ the interest rate increases $\longrightarrow$ investment decreases $\longrightarrow$ NNP decreases.

1. The extent to which a change in M will affect NNP depends on the shape of the liquidity preference and MEI curves.

KEY TERMS

You should be familiar with the meaning of the terms listed below. For definition of these terms, please refer to the glossary at the end of your textbook and to the appropriate section in this chapter.

monetary theory	M_2
M_1	transactions demand
currency	precautionary demand
commodity value	speculative demand
token money	liquidity preference curve
"fiat" money system	quantity theory of money
demand deposits	velocity
near-monies	marginal efficiency of investment (MEI)

CONCEPTS AND DEFINITIONS

Fill-in Questions

Complete each sentence by writing in the blank the most appropriate word or words from the terms listed below or by circling the word in parentheses that is correct.

liquidity preference curve	precautionary demand
velocity	medium of exchange
quantity theory of money	interest rates
marginal efficiency of investment	"fiat" money system
level of income	quantity
M_1	near monies
M_2	store of wealth
commodity value	market rate of interest
speculative demand	speculative demand
price	demand deposits
transactions demand	monetary theory
standard of value	token money

1. The sum of all paper money, coins, and checking accounts in the economy at any point in time constitutes ___M_1___.

2. If the money supply increases, but both price and production levels remain constant, ___velocity___ must fall.

3. The ___precautionary demand___ for money exists because some people set aside a portion of their funds for a "rainy day."

4. According to the Keynesian view of the ___Quantity theory of $___, changes in the money supply do not always affect the level of aggregate demand in the economy.

5. Studying ___Monetary theory___ helps us understand the macroeconomic implications of changing the money supply.

6. The ___liquidity preference curve___ illustrates how the amount of money held by the public responds to changes in the opportunity cost of holding money.

7. The monetary value of a coin is equal to its ___Commodity value___ if the coin's purchasing power is determined by the value of the materials used to manufacture the coin.

8. The type of money used in the great majority of all transactions is ___DD___.

9. If the ___marginal efficiency of investment___ curve becomes flatter, an increase in the interest rate from, for example, 12 percent to 13 percent will cause investment to decline by a greater amount than it would have if the curve were steeper.

10. When incomes rise in the economy and people desire to purchase more goods and services, their ___transactions demand___ for money increases.

11. A "___fiat money system___" exists in your society if, as dictator, you declare that fig leaves, and only fig leaves, may be used to pay all private and public debts.

12. M_1 plus the amount of deposited funds in savings and time accounts equals ___M_2___.

13. While they may be easily converted into currency or demand deposits, funds in savings and time accounts are examples of _near-monies_ because they cannot be directly used to purchase goods and services.

14. Since the commodity value of the metals in the Susan B. Anthony $1 coin is about 26¢, this coin is an example of _token $_.

15. If people expect prices to fall in the near future, their _speculative demand_ for money will increase in the current time period.

16. The two major determinants of the demand for money are _interest rate_ and _level of inc_.

17. By far the largest component of the money supply consists of _DD_.

18. The three major functions of money are _medium of exchnge_, _standard of value_, and _store of wealth_.

19. Money supply × velocity = _Price_ × _Quantity_.

20. The amount of money held for speculative purposes is determined primarily by the _market rate of interest_

21. All other things being equal, if the interest rates increase, the amount of money held in demand deposits will (increase/decrease).

22. Changes in the level of income can cause the _liquidy preference_ curve to shift.

23. _Velocity_ measures the number of times a dollar is spent in a given time.

24. When interest rates are high, business investment (increases/decreases).

25. The relationship between interest rates and quantity of money held is (direct/inverse) and the relationship between interest rates and business investment is (direct/inverse).

26. If the money supply increases, NNP can be expected to (increase/decrease).

27. The extent to which NNP changes with changes in the money supply depends on the shape of the _liquidy preference_ and the _MEI_ curves.

Multiple Choice Questions

Circle the correct answer.

1. Money serves as a medium of exchange in the sense that

    a. exchange cannot take place without the use of money.

    b. it is generally acceptable as a means of payment for goods and services.

   c. it is one way in which wealth may be held.

   d. the United States Treasury will exchange one dollar's worth of gold for every dollar bill presented for conversion by a United States citizen.

2. In the United States economy, most monetary transactions are undertaken with

   a. coins.

   b. checks.

   c. paper money.

   d. credit cards.

3. If the metallic value of a coin exceeds its face value

   a. the coin is token money.

   b. the Treasury will issue more coins in an attempt to reduce the metallic value.

   c. the coin will likely cease to operate as a medium of exchange.

   d. the coin will no longer be considered legal tender for the payment of all public and private debts.

4. Americans have confidence that the federal government will not create excessive amounts of paper money

   a. only to the extent that they believe government officials will exercise good judgment in monetary matters.

   b. because paper dollars in circulation are backed by a stock of gold in Fort Knox.

   c. since legislation exists that limits the issue of paper money.

   d. because they have the right to exchange their paper money for precious metals at the United States Treasury.

5. Funds deposited in savings accounts are not included in the M_1 definition of the money supply because they

   a. do not serve as a store of wealth.

   b. are not generally accepted as a medium of exchange.

   c. cannot easily be converted into currency.

   d. could not adequately serve as a standard of value.

6. If the level of income in the economy increases, the liquidity preference curve

   a. shifts to the left because the opportunity cost of holding money increases.

   b. shifts to the right as people desire to hold more money in order to undertake a greater level of transactions.

   c. shifts to the left, indicating that people prefer less liquidity and more goods and services.

   d. is unaffected, since this curve shows the relationship between the interest rate and the quantity of money demanded rather than the relationship between income and quantity of money demanded.

7. If the level of GNP is $1.5 trillion and the money supply is $300 billion

    a. each dollar is spent an average of 5 times in the purchase of final goods and services.

    b. an increase in the money supply will be inflationary.

    c. the velocity is .2.

    d. an increase in the money supply will reduce the unemployment rate.

8. According to the Classical view of the Quantity Theory of Money, an increase in the money supply will

    a. raise prices, while both velocity and the level of output decrease.

    b. result in an increased level of production.

    c. increase the level of aggregate demand.

    d. be completely offset by a decrease in velocity.

9. The Keynesian and Chicago School interpretations of the Quantity Theory differ in that

    a. Keynesians assume that velocity is essentially constant, while the Chicago economists believe that velocity varies significantly in the short run.

    b. Chicagoans assume that the economy always operates at full employment, while Keynesians hold that significant unemployment may exist at any point in time.

    c. Keynesians believe that prices are unlikely to increase, while Chicagoans feel that prices will definitely increase, in response to an increase in the money supply.

    d. Keynesians believe that velocity is much less predictable than Chicagoans believe it to be.

10. If the money supply is increased during a recessionary period,

    a. prices will increase proportionately.

    b. NNP will increase more if the MEI curve is steep rather than flat, all other things constant.

    c. NNP will increase more if the liquidity preference curve is steep rather than flat, all other things constant.

    d. velocity increases and NNP rises more than proportionately.

11. If an economy is experiencing a recession, the most likely Keynesian policy recommendation for remedying this situation is

    a. decreasing the money supply.

    b. increasing the money supply.

    c. decreasing government spending.

    d. increasing government spending.

12. Which statement is correct of the Chicago School or the "new" new economics?

    a. It assigns a primary role to the velocity of money.

    b. It emphasizes the use of government spending in changing prices and output.

    c. It is associated with John Maynard Keynes.

    d. It assigns a primary role to the money supply.

13. If M = money supply, V = velocity, P = prices, and Q = quantity of output, the quantity theory of money is usually expressed as

    a. $MP = VQ$.

    b. $MV = PQ$.

    c. $\dfrac{M}{V} = \dfrac{P}{Q}$

    d. none of these.

14. In response to events during the 1930s, Keynes reasoned that

    a. an increase in the money supply had been counterbalanced by a decrease in velocity.

    b. an increase in the money supply would assure an increase in the level of output and employment.

    c. an increase in the money supply inevitably caused an increase in prices.

    d. none of these.

15. Why are time deposits and near money not usually considered to be part of the money supply?

    a. They require 30 to 60 days notice for withdrawal.

    b. They do not represent values of goods and services.

    c. They earn interest.

    d. They cannot be exchanged directly for goods and services.

16. Liquidity preference refers to

    a. the willingness of households to save.

    b. the preferred interest rate on savings.

    c. the relationship between the willingness to hold money and the interest rate.

    d. none of these.

17. The money supply (M_1) consists of

    a. demand deposits and currency.

    b. currency.

    c. credit cards and currency.

    d. currency and savings accounts.

18. Coins are said to have a commodity value when

    a. the value of metal used is significantly below the exchange value.
    b. the value of metal or material used is equal to the exchange value.
    c. they can be exchanged for commodities.
    d. none of these.

19. Token money is any form of exchange in which the value of

    a. the metal (or commodity) is the same as the exchange value.
    b. the metal is greater than the exchange value.
    c. its exchange is very low.
    d. the metal (or other material used) is significantly lower than the exchange value.

APPLICATIONS

1. Assume that the following macroeconomic data is at your disposal. M = money supply; P = average price per unit; and Q = quantity of units of output.

    $M = \$400$ billion

    $P = \$2$

    $Q = 800$ billion

    $V = \dfrac{GNP}{M}$

    $GNP = P \times Q$

    a. The level of GNP in this economy is $\$ \underline{\ \ 1600\ \ }$.
    b. The value of velocity is $\underline{\ \ 4\ \ }$.
    c. As a Classical economist, if the money supply increases to $450 billion, what would happen to the values of V, P, Q, and GNP? Explain.

2. During the 1930s, interest rates were quite low. Those people who had income or savings kept them in the form of demand deposits and currency regardless of the amounts involved. Which of the liquidity preference curves below represents this situation best?

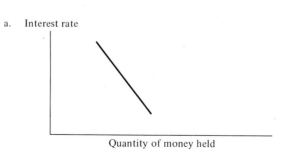

a. Interest rate

Quantity of money held

b.   Interest rate

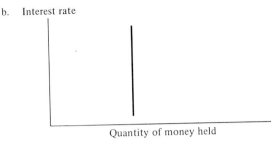

Quantity of money held

c.   Interest rate

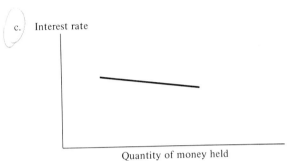

Quantity of money held

d.   Interest rate

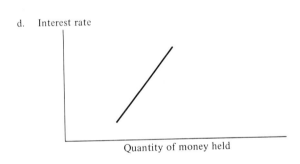

Quantity of money held

3. For each description below indicate whether the type of demand for money is transactions (T), precautionary (P), or speculative (S).

a. You have decided to keep $200 on hand for fear you might have to travel home in an emergency. P

b. You want to get stereo components but you think you might do better if you wait for the newest Japanese models. S

c. You have decided to keep $300 in your checking account to pay for rent, food, entertainment, clothes, and books. T

d. You have noticed that tuition has been rising. You decide to keep additional funds in your checking account in case unexpected expenditures arise. P

ANSWERS

Fill-in Questions

1. M_1

2. velocity

3. precautionary demand

4. Quantity Theory of Money

5. monetary theory

6. liquidity preference curve

7. commodity value

8. demand deposits

9. marginal efficiency of investment

10. transactions demand

11. "fiat" money system

12. M_2

13. near monies

14. token money

15. speculative demand

16. level of income; interest rates

17. demand deposits

18. medium of exchange; standard of value; store of wealth

19. price; quantity

20. market rate of interest

21. decrease

22. liquidity preference

23. velocity

24. decreases

25. inverse; inverse

26. increase

27. liquidity preference; marginal efficiency of investment

Multiple Choice Questions

1.	b	6.	b	11.	d	16.	c
2.	b	7.	a	12.	d	17.	d A ← e think
3.	c	8.	c	13.	b	18.	b
4.	a	9.	d	14.	a	19.	d
5.	b	10.	c	15.	d		

APPLICATIONS

1. a. $1600 billion (GNP $= P \times Q$)

    b. 4 $\left(V = \dfrac{\text{GNP}}{M} \right)$

    c. When the money supply increases, people have more money than is needed for transactions purposes. Since velocity is assumed to be constant, people spend this additional money, thereby increasing aggregate demand. According to the Classicals, however, the economy is already producing as much as it possibly can, so the increased demand simply serves to drive up prices. Overall, then, both V and Q remain constant at 4 and 800 billion, respectively, while P rises to $2.25. (Note that prices increased by 12-1/2 percent in response to a 12-1/2 percent increase in the money supply.) GNP rises from $1600 to $1800, but the entire increase is accounted for by higher prices because the number of units of output produced is constant.

2. c

3. a. P

    b. S

    c. T

    d. P

Chapter 14

Commercial Banks and the Creation of Money

LEARNING OBJECTIVES

As noted in Chapter 13, demand deposits account for about 75 percent of the basic money supply M_1. Since these deposits rest in commercial banks, the commercial banking system is an important part of the process by which the economy's money supply is altered. The purpose of this chapter is to investigate the mechanics of how the level of demand deposits, and therefore the money supply in the banking system expands or contracts.

After reading this chapter, you should be able to:

1. explain the purpose of reserve requirements;

2. determine the level of a bank's required reserves after examining the bank's balance sheet;

3. explain how a check, written against one bank and deposited in another, clears through the banking system;

4. explain how money is created in the bank lending process;

5. calculate the amount of lending that can be prudently undertaken by a bank, given the current condition of its balance sheet and its reserve requirement;

6. identify the factors that tend to limit the amount by which the money supply expands as a result of a given increase in bank reserves.

CHAPTER OUTLINE

I. The United States banking system is composed of a central bank, known as the Federal Reserve System (the Fed) and approximately 14,700 commercial banks.

    A. A bank's balance sheet summarizes its financial position at a given time and provides an easy way to show what happens at a bank when a financial transaction occurs.

1. Assets are things of value that the bank owns (such as cash, loans, bonds).
2. Liabilities are things of value that the bank owes to creditors (such as demand deposits).
3. Net worth is the value of the capital stock owned by the bank's stockholders.

II.   The primary function of the Federal Reserve System is to control the size of the money supply.

A. Banks are required by the Fed to hold a specified percentage of their deposit liabilities either in the form of bank vault cash or on deposit with the Fed. This percentage is called the reserve ratio or reserve requirement.
1. Through reserve requirements, the Fed controls the amount of money commercial banks can lend. This control over credit enables the Fed to counteract overexpansion or overcontraction in the economy.
2. The amount by which a bank's actual reserves exceeds its required reserves constitutes excess reserves.

B. In order to earn income, a bank either lends its excess reserves to borrowers or uses its excess reserves to purchase interest-bearing government securities.
1. In making a loan, the bank usually creates a checking account in the amount of the loan for the borrower. Since demand deposits are a major component of the basic money supply, the demand deposits created when banks make loans increase the money supply.
a. Any bank can create money in an amount equal to its excess reserves. The banking system as a whole, however, can expand loans, and thus increase the money supply, by some multiple of the amount of excess reserves. This multiple is equal to the reciprocal of the reserve ratio.
(1) The maximum possible expansion of the money supply is not usually achieved, however, because banks may be reluctant to lend excess reserves, the public may be reluctant to borrow them, or customers may reduce bank reserves by making cash withdrawals (currency leakage).
2. When a bank uses its excess reserves to purchase government securities, the money supply is not immediately affected. However, as long as these funds remain in the banking system, the ultimate increase in the money supply is the same as if the bank had lent its excess reserves.
3. When loans are repaid by borrowers or banks sell government securities to the public, the money supply declines.

KEY TERMS

You should be familiar with the meaning of the terms listed below. For definition of these terms, please refer to the glossary at the end of your textbook and to the appropriate section in this chapter.

commercial bank   net worth
central bank   reserve ratio
balance sheet   reserve requirement
assets   excess reserves
liability

CONCEPTS AND DEFINITIONS

Fill-in Questions

Complete each sentence by writing in the blank the most appropriate word or words from the terms listed below or by circling the word in parentheses that is correct.

assets	commercial bank
net worth	reserve requirement
liability	reserve ratio
central bank	excess reserves
The Federal Reserve System	balance sheet

1. The central bank in the United States is the _Fedrl. Resrve Systm_

2. If a bank is required to hold reserves of $8 million against $100 million of deposits, the ___R. R.___ is 8 percent.

3. The primary purpose of the _Centrl. bank_ is to control the size of the money supply.

4. Loans and government securities are two important ___assets___ of commercial banks.

5. The proportion of demand deposits that the banks must hold on deposit with the Fed is the ___R. R.___.

6. A bank's financial condition may be determined by examining its _balance sheet._

7. If the ___R.R.___ is increased, the amount of bank lending which can be supported by a given level of reserves is reduced.

8. While demand deposits represent an asset for the depositor, they are a ___liabilities___ for the bank.

9. The reserves held by a bank in addition to those required legally are called _excess reserves_

10. Like most private firms, the basic objective of a _commercial bank_ is to maximize profits.

11. A bank may eventually find itself with insufficient reserves to cover its deposits if it lends more than its _excess reserves_

12. A bank's _net worth_ is equal to its assets minus its liabilities.

13. (Liabilities/Assets) are owed by a bank; (liabilities/assets) are owned by the bank.

Multiple Choice Questions

Circle the correct answer.

1. Analysis of the United States banking system reveals that

    a. all commercial banks are members of the Federal Reserve System.

    b. all commercial banks are chartered by the federal government.

    c. most banks are not members of the Federal Reserve System.

    d. about three-quarters of all bank deposits are held by banks that are not members of the Federal Reserve System.

2. If Ms. Travis deposits a $100 check, written against the First National Bank, into her checking account at the Second Bank of Hesperia

    a. the Second Bank's demand deposits increase by $100, and its reserves decrease by $100 after the check clears through the banking system.

    b. both the demand deposits and reserves of the First Bank decrease by $100 after check clearance.

    c. the Second Bank's demand deposits increase by $100, and the First Bank's demand deposits decrease by $100, but reserves at both banks are unaffected.

    d. the amount of demand deposits in the banking system as a whole increases.

3. The Federal Reserve System imposes reserve requirements against bank deposits

    a. in all commercial banks.

    b. in order to ensure that banks have sufficient funds on hand to meet customers' demands for cash.

    c. in order to limit the amount of lending undertaken by commercial banks in the Federal Reserve System.

    d. in order to protect the funds of depositors.

4. If the reserve ratio is 15 percent, and the Bank of Banning has $3 million of demand deposits, $100,000 cash in its vault, and $500,000 on deposit with the Federal Reserve System,

    a. it has actual reserves of $600,000.

    b. its actual reserves are $350,000 less than its required reserves.

    c. it has excess reserves of $50,000.

    d. it would be imprudent for the bank to increase its lending.

5. When a bank transfers funds from its vault to its reserve account with the Federal Reserve System, the bank's

   a. assets rise and its liabilities decline.

   b. liabilities rise and its assets decline.

   c. overall level of liabilities is unchanged, but the composition of its liabilities is altered.

   d. overall level of assets is unchanged, but the composition of its assets is altered.

6. If a bank has $10,000 of excess reserves and the reserve ratio is 10 percent

   a. the bank may choose to place these funds on deposit with the Federal Reserve System and earn the passbook rate of interest.

   b. it can prudently lend $10,000 to borrowers.

   c. it must use these funds either to make loans or purchase government securities.

   d. it can prudently lend $100,000 to borrowers.

7. If you borrow $50,000 from a bank

   a. the money supply is unaffected if you take the loan in the form of cash.

   b. the liabilities of the bank are unaffected, if a demand deposit in the amount of the loan is created for you.

   c. the money supply increases only if the bank creates a demand deposit for you in the amount of the loan.

   d. the loan is a liability for you, and an asset for the bank.

8. If the reserve ratio is 15 percent, and a bank lends $100,000 to the Porter Construction Co., the money supply will ultimately increase by

   a. less than $667,000 if some funds leak out of the banking system during the loan expansion process.

   b. less than $667,000 million if some banks decide to buy government securities with excess reserves instead of making loans.

   c. $667,000 million.

   d. more than $667,000 million if banks lend funds only to low-risk borrowers.

9. When a borrower repays a loan by writing a check to the bank

   a. the amount of reserves in the banking system declines.

   b. the money supply declines by the amount of the check.

   c. the amount of bank loans outstanding is reduced, but the money supply is unaffected.

   d. the money supply eventually declines by some multiple of the amount of the check.

10. The sale of government securities by a bank to the general public

    a. leaves the amount of reserves in the banking system unaffected.

    b. is necessary if a bank has excess reserves.

    c. increases the amount of demand deposits in the banking system.

    d. necessarily indicates that the bank wants to make more loans.

11. With a reserve ratio of 20 percent, an increase in demand deposits of $150,000 at the Benjamin Franklin Bank will increase

    a. required reserves by $150,000 and actual reserves by $150,000.

    b. required reserves by $30,000 and actual reserves by $30,000.

    c. required reserves by $30,000 while actual reserves remain constant.

    d. required reserves by $30,000 and actual reserves by $150,000.

12. Which of these is a major function of the central bank in the United States?

    a. controlling the flow of money

    b. controlling credit

    c. setting reserve requirements

    d. all of the above are functions

13. Which of these is an asset of a commercial bank?

    a. demand deposits

    b. capital stock

    c. a loan owed by the bank

    d. reserves in an account with the Fed

14. Which of these is a liability of a commercial bank?

    a. United States government securities

    b. demand deposits

    c. property

    d. reserves in an account with the Fed

15. When a new commercial bank is established,

    a. owners invest money by establishing checking accounts.

    b. all of the invested funds are used to purchase property.

    c. some of the invested funds are used as cash reserves.

    d. none of these.

16. When one customer writes a check to another customer of the same bank

    a. the check does not go through the Federal Reserve System.

    b. the check must clear through the Federal Reserve System.

c. the bank subtracts the appropriate amount from both accounts.

d. the bank adds the appropriate amount to both accounts.

17. How is a check written on Bank *A* cleared after it is deposited in Bank *B*?

   a. The check goes to the Federal Reserve board.

   b. The Fed credits the account of Bank *B* and debits the account of Bank *A*.

   c. The check is sent directly from Bank *B* to Bank *A*.

   d. None of these.

18. In 1933, President Roosevelt declared a "banking holiday." All banks were closed and preparations were made for government audits. Those banks found to be sound were reopened with government approval. This action reassured customers about those banks allowed to reopen. You would suspect that an effect of this reassurance was to

   a. prevent the money supply from contracting further.

   b. expand the money supply.

   c. reduce the money supply.

   d. prevent the money supply from expanding.

19. Government policy from 1929 to 1939 comes under heavy criticism. Some critics argue that the money supply should have been expanded rapidly. Others argue that the creation of excess reserves would have had little effect anyway. All of the following statements explain why there would be little effect *except*

   a. it is unlikely that the money supply would expand by some multiple of the excess reserves.

   b. individuals and businesses were not eager to borrow money.

   c. bankers were generally unwilling to make loans.

   d. prices would simply rise in proportion to the increase in the money supply.

APPLICATIONS

1. The San Bernardino City Bank's balance sheet recently looked like this:

Assets		Liabilities & net worth	
Cash	$ 30,000	Capital stock	$1,000,000
Reserves with Fed (RWF)	90,000	Demand deposits	800,000
Loans	680,000		
Government securities	1,000,000		

Assume that the reserve ratio on demand deposits is 10 percent.

a. The San Bernardino City Bank has excess reserves of $ 40,000 _____

b. The City Bank uses all its excess reserves to purchase securities issued by the Cucamonga Water District. The Water District, in turn, deposits these funds in its checking account with the Bank of the West. Assuming check clearance has occurred, record both transactions on the respective balance sheets below. Use arrows (↑ , ↓) to indicate whether a particular account is increasing or decreasing, and show the *exact* amount by which each account is affected. (NOTE: In the following balance sheets, show only the items that are affected by the transactions. It is not necessary to repeat the *entire* balance sheet.)

San Bernardino City Bank		Bank of the West	
Assets	Liabilities & net worth	Assets	Liabilities & net worth

c. Assuming that the Bank of the West was just meeting its reserve requirement prior to the Cucamonga Water District's deposit, how much in excess reserves does it now possess? $_____

d. The Bank of the West uses its excess reserves to grant Lee Higgins a mortgage loan for the purchase of a home. Lee writes a check in the amount of the loan to the previous homeowner. The check is subsequently deposited in a checking account at the Pacific National Bank. Show how the balance sheets at both banks are affected once the check is cleared through the banking system. (NOTE: Show all of the transactions mentioned in Part d, not just the transaction dealing with check clearance.)

Bank of the West		Pacific National	
Assets	Liabilities & net worth	Assets	Liabilities & net worth

e. Using the M_1 definition of money, what is the net change in the money supply as a result of the transactions involved in Parts b and d? _____

f. The maximum amount that the money supply could possibly be expanded as a result of the excess reserves originally held by the San Bernardino City Bank is $_____.

ANSWERS

Fill-in Questions

1. Federal Reserve System (the Fed)
2. reserve ratio or reserve requirement
3. central bank
4. assets
5. reserve requirement or reserve ratio
6. balance sheet
7. reserve requirement or reserve ratio
8. liability
9. excess reserves
10. commercial bank
11. excess reserves
12. net worth
13. liabilities; assets

Multiple Choice Question

1. c	8. a	14. b
2. b	9. b	15. c
3. c	10. a	16. a
4. a	11. d	17. b
5. d	12. d	18. a
6. b	13. d	19. d
7. d		

APPLICATIONS

1. a. $40,000 [Required reserves on $800,000 of demand deposits are $80,000. Actual reserves (cash plus reserves at the Fed) are $120,000. Excess reserves, therefore, are $40,000.]

    b.

San Bernadino City Bank	
Assets	**Liabilities & net worth**
RWF ↓ $40,000	
Securities ↑ $40,000	

The purchase of securities by San Bernardino City increases its security holdings by $40,000. Its reserves with the Fed (RWF) account are reduced by $40,000 when the check it issued to the Cucamonga Water District is deposited in the Bank of the West and eventually clears through the banking system.

| **Bank of the West** | |
Assets	Liabilities & net worth
RWF ↑ $40,000	Demand Deposits ↑ $40,000

When the Cucamonga Water District deposits its check at the Bank of the West, the Bank's demand deposits increase by $40,000 and its RWF increases by the same amount after the check clears.

c. $36,000   [The $40,000 increase in demand deposits raises required reserves by $4,000 (10 percent). Actual reserves have increased by $40,000, however, so the Bank of the West has $36,000 of excess reserves.]

d.

| **Bank of the West** | |
Assets	Liabilities & net worth
Loans ↑ $36,000	Demand deposits ↑ $36,000
RWF ↓ $36,000	Demand deposits ↓ $36,000

| **Pacific National** | |
Assets	Liabilities & net worth
RWF ↑ $36,000	Demand deposits ↑ $36,000

The loan transaction increases both the Bank of the West's loans and its demand deposits by $36,000. When the previous homeowner deposits your check in his checking account at Pacific National, this bank's RWF and demand deposits increase by $36,000. As this check clears through the banking system, RWF and demand deposits at the Bank of the West are reduced by $36,000.

e. $76,000 ($40,000 increase in demand deposits in Part b, plus $36,000 increase in demand deposits in part d. Note that in Part d there is no net change in demand deposits at the Bank of the West because the two transactions offset each other.)

f. $400,000   (Since the reserve ratio is 10 percent, the reciprocal of the reserve ratio is 10. With $40,000 of excess reserves, therefore, the maximum possible expansion of the money supply is $40,000 times 10 or $400,000. The transactions in Parts b and d show only a portion of this money-supply expansion process.)

Chapter 15

The Federal Reserve System and Monetary Policy

LEARNING OBJECTIVES

One of the main purposes of the previous chapter was to demonstrate how a change in bank reserves ultimately results in a change in the economy's money supply. Since changes in the money supply usually alter the level of GNP, it is evident that the Federal Reserve can influence GNP by increasing or decreasing the amount of reserves available to the banking system. In this chapter we examine the methods used by the Fed to manipulate bank reserves in order to change the money supply and thereby influence macroeconomic activity.

After reading this chapter you should be able to:

1. discuss the basic organization of the Federal Reserve System, its relationship to other branches of the federal government, and the services it provides to member banks;

2. cite the objectives of monetary policy and demonstrate an appreciation for the difficulty of achieving these objectives;

3. explain the methods used by the Fed in attempting to attain its macroeconomic goals.

CHAPTER OUTLINE

I. The Federal Reserve System was established in 1913 in order to ensure a flexible money supply, achieve a uniform currency, and supervise bank activities.

    A. There are 12 regional Federal Reserve banks across the United States and a Board of Governors in Washington, D.C.

    B. Only about 40 percent of all commercial banks are members of the Federal Reserve System, but about 75 percent of all demand deposits reside in these banks.

    C. Like other banks, the Fed has a balance sheet. Included in its assets are gold certificates, Special Drawing Rights, United States securities, and loans to commercial banks. Included in its liabilities are Federal Reserve notes (paper dollars), member bank reserves, Treasury deposits, and capital accounts.

 D. The Fed was established as an independent central banking system to act in the public interest. Therefore, the Federal Reserve Act contains safeguards to insulate the Fed against political pressure from governmental agencies and from private groups.

II. In addition to making and implementing monetary policy decisions, the Fed also performs some routine administrative and supervisory functions that improve the operational efficiency of the banking system.

 A. The Fed provides check-clearing services to member banks.

 B. When a bank needs additional currency in order to meet the demands of its customers, the Fed ships the requested amount of currency to the bank and subtracts a corresponding sum from the bank's reserve account.

 C. The United States Treasury, in essence, has its checking account with the Fed, so the Fed extends a range of services to the Treasury just as a commercial bank provides various services to its depositors.

 D. The Fed periodically examines the books of member banks to ensure that they follow accepted practices.

III. The basic objectives of monetary policy are to secure and maintain a high level of employment and reasonably stable prices.

 A. If significant unemployment exists in the economy, an increase in the money supply will likely increase aggregate demand, which in turn will cause both production and employment to rise.

 B. Decreasing the money supply may reduce inflationary pressure by reducing aggregate demand.

 C. Unfortunately, price stability and a high level of employment are often mutually inconsistent. For example, the Fed may decide to decrease the money supply to restrain inflation, but this decrease can simultaneously result in an increase in unemployment.

 D. The effectiveness of monetary policy is reduced if unexpected changes in velocity occur or if investment does not respond predictably to interest-rate changes.

IV. Open-market operations and changes in reserve requirements and the discount rate are the basic tools employed by the Fed in implementing monetary policy.

 A. Open-market operations involve the sale or purchase of United States government securities in the open market.

  1. Decisions regarding open-market operations are made by the Open-Market Committee, which is composed of the Board of Governors and five Federal Reserve bank presidents.

   a. To increase the money supply, the Fed buys securities from commercial banks or from the general public. These purchases inject funds into the banking system, thus creating excess reserves and permitting banks to increase lending.

      b. To decrease the money supply, the Fed sells securities to commercial banks or to the general public. Such sales reduce the amount of reserves in the banking system, and thus reduce bank lending.

  B. The Fed may also adjust reserve requirements in order to implement monetary policy.

     1. A reduction in the reserve ratio creates excess reserves for all banks and as a result creates the possibility for the money supply to be increased by some multiple of the amount of excess reserves.

     2. An increase in the reserve ratio curtails bank lending.

     3. Note that a cut in the reserve requirement simply gives member banks the *opportunity* to expand loans if they want to. An increase in the reserve requirement, on the other hand, *forces* commercial banks to decrease their lending activity.

  C. The discount rate is the interest rate at which commercial banks borrow from the Fed. Borrowing increases the reserves of commercial banks and, consequently, their capacity to lend. Thus, the Fed can also implement monetary policy by changing the discount rate.

     1. An increased discount rate discourages bank borrowing, which decreases reserves of commercial banks, thus decreasing their lending capacity and the money supply.

     2. A reduction in the discount rate would allow commercial banks to increase their reserves. This would make it possible for banks to increase their loans thus increasing the money supply.

V. In addition to altering the money supply, the Fed also employs a variety of selective credit controls in an attempt to influence activity in particular sectors of the economy. Among these are controls on stock market credit, installment credit, and the interest rates on deposits.

KEY TERMS

You should be familiar with the meaning of the terms listed below. For definition of these terms, please refer to the glossary at the end of your textbook and to the appropriate section in this chapter.

Federal Reserve banks	capital accounts
gold certificates	open-market operations
Special Drawing Rights	discount rate
Federal Reserve notes	prime rate
Treasury deposits	margin requirements

CONCEPTS AND DEFINITIONS

Fill-in Questions

Complete each sentence by writing in the blank the most appropriate word or words from the terms listed below or by circling the word in parentheses that is correct.

Treasury deposits	Special Drawing Rights
discount rate	prime rate
Federal Reserve banks	open-market operations
margin requirements	Board of Governors
Federal Reserve notes	capital accounts
clearing	gold certificates

1. The ____*FDR*____ are technically owned by the member commercial banks in each of 12 districts.

2. The policy of the Fed is established by the *Board of govs.*

3. If IBM applied to the Bank of America for a loan to develop a new line of computers, it would probably be charged the ___*Prime rate*___.

4. *Fed. Reserve notes* are paper currency and appear as liabilities on the Fed's balance sheet.

5. The Fed uses the reserve accounts of member banks to balance accounts when checks drawn on one bank are deposited in another. This operation by the Fed is called a(n) ___*clearing*___ operation.

6. The intent of raising the ___*discount rate*___ is to discourage bank borrowing from the Fed.

7. *Specl. drawing rights* are sometimes called "paper gold" and can be used by governments to finance balance-of-payments deficits.

8. Accumulated Fed profits that have not been returned to the Treasury plus the money paid by member commercial banks to purchase stock in their regional Federal Reserve banks constitute the *capital accounts* on the Fed's balance sheet.

9. When the Fed delivers currency to a member bank, the Fed (debits/credits) the member bank's account for the amount of cash delivered.

10. The basic source of ___*Treasury deposits*___ in Federal Reserve banks is federal government tax receipts.

11. If the Fed is alarmed at the degree of speculation occurring in financial markets, it may impose higher *margin requirments* on the purchase of stock.

12. If the Open-Market Committee decides to buy a large quantity of bonds, bond prices will (increase/decrease) and interest rates will (increase/decrease).

13. When a member bank delivers cash to the Fed, the Fed (debits/credits) the member bank's account by the amount delivered.

14. _Gold certificates_ provide the Fed with a claim against gold held by the Treasury.

15. The Fed changes the amount of excess reserves in the banking system most effectively by undertaking _open-market operations_

16. The Fed can create excess reserves by (increasing/decreasing) the reserve requirement.

17. The interest that the Fed charges for loans to member banks is called the _discount rate_ .

18. For each item below, indicate whether it is an asset (A) or a liability (L) of the Federal Reserve banks.

    a. _A_____ United States government securities
    b. _L_____ Federal Reserve notes
    c. _L_____ member bank reserves
    d. _A_____ certificates for the Fed's gold desposits at Fort Knox
    e. _A_____ discounts
    f. _L_____ capital accounts

Multiple Choice Questions

Circle the correct answer.

1. The Federal Reserve System is independent of political pressure in the sense that

   a. only the president can reappoint an individual to a second 14-year term as a member of the Board of Governors.
   b. member commercial banks do not own the district Federal Reserve banks, and thus have little say in monetary policy matters.
   c. Congress has no direct supervisory authority over the Fed.
   d. the president makes only two Board of Governors appointments annually.

2. If significant unemployment exists in the economy, the Fed will

   a. attempt to decrease the money supply.
   b. not increase the money supply as this will definitely result in higher prices.
   c. undertake whatever policy is recommended by the president.
   d. attempt to stimulate aggregate demand by increasing the money supply.

3. Monetary authorities can selectively increase the funds available for home mortgages by

   a. increasing interest rates.
   b. allowing savings and loan institutions to pay higher returns on time deposits than banks.

c. allowing banks to pay higher returns on time deposits than savings and loan associations.

d. reducing interest rates.

4. If the Fed decreases the money supply

a. it is attempting to increase production and employment.

b. its actions will be neutralized if velocity unexpectedly decreases.

c. both interest rates and investment will increase.

d. it is probably attempting to reduce inflationary pressures in the economy.

5. The Fed purchases securities in the open market if

a. it desires to increase the amount of reserves in the banking system.

b. it believes it will be able to make a profit by selling the securities at a higher price sometime in the future.

c. security prices are low relative to stock prices.

d. it wishes to curtail bank lending.

6. If the Fed buys $10 million of government securities from commercial banks

a. the Fed's security holdings increase by $10 million and its reserves decline by $10 million.

b. actual reserves at commercial banks increase by $10 million.

c. demand deposits at commercial banks immediately increase by $10 million.

d. the money supply immediately increases by $10 million.

7. When the Fed sells government securities (bonds) in the open market

a. the price of bonds increases.

b. investment spending on plant and equipment increases.

c. the interest rate on government bonds increases.

d. the Treasury is able to borrow at a lower rate of interest.

8. When the Fed sells securities to the public rather than to a commercial bank

a. bank reserves and demand deposits are reduced by the amount of the transaction.

b. banks are unaffected by the securities transactions.

c. bank reserves and security holdings increase by the amount of the transaction.

d. the amount of funds available for bank lending increases.

9. Monetary policy actions may be ineffective in expanding economic activity because

a. the Fed is sometimes unable to locate sellers when it wishes to buy securities in the open market.

    b. the Fed is reluctant to buy securities if it feels that security prices will decline in the future.

    c. Fed purchases of securities oftentimes fail to increase bank reserves.

    d. banks are sometimes reluctant to make loans even if Fed actions have supplied them with excess reserves.

10. Reducing the reserve ratio

    a. is the most commonly used tool of expansionary monetary policy.

    b. reduces banks' required reserves, but does not affect actual reserves.

    c. increases the amount of reserves in the banking system.

    d. is an appropriate antiinflationary policy action.

11. Considering the effectiveness of the various monetary policy tools at the Fed's disposal, the most likely way for the Fed to deal with inflation would be to

    a. sell securities in the open market.

    b. increase the reserve ratio on bank deposits.

    c. use moral suasion to persuade banks to curtail lending.

    d. raise the discount rate.

12. An increase in the discount rate

    a. significantly reduces bank reserves.

    b. always causes the prime rate to increase.

    c. usually indicates that the Fed will attempt to contract economic activity in the future.

    d. usually results in a stock market rally.

13. If, in addition to undertaking open-market operations, the Fed wishes to employ one of its selective credit controls to help stimulate the economy, it may

    a. increase the margin requirement on the purchase of stock.

    b. reduce down-payment requirements on installment purchases.

    c. reduce repayment periods on consumer loans.

    d. request that banks refrain from making "speculative" loans.

14. Which of the following is *not* a function of the district Federal Reserve banks?

    a. supervision of member commercial banks.

    b. provision of a check-clearing service to member commercial banks free of charge.

    c. holding the reserve deposits of member banks.

    d. making loans to households and businesses.

15. The consolidated balance sheet of the 12 district Federal Reserve banks reveals

    a. that one of the Fed's largest assets is the amount of cash which it holds.

    b. the amount of credit the Fed extends to commercial banks.

    c. that the Federal Reserve notes in circulation are assets of the Fed.

    d. that the Fed's gold holdings are equal to 25 percent of the Federal Reserve notes in circulation.

16. The effect of a reserve requirement of 100 percent would be to

    a. increase the commercial banking system's power to expand the money supply.

    b. increase the commercial banking system's power to contract the money supply.

    c. eliminate the banking system's ability to expand or contract the money supply.

    d. eliminate any possible profit by commercial banks.

APPLICATIONS

1. Considering the basic tools at the Fed's disposal, give three specific policy recommendations that could be made in an attempt to reduce unemployment.

2. a. Show the balance-sheet transactions for both the Fed and the Lawrence National Bank when the Fed buys $1 million of securities from Lawrence National. Use arrows (↑ , ↓) to indicate whether a particular account is increasing or decreasing, and show the exact amount by which each account is affected.

Fed		Lawrence National	
Assets	Liabilities & net worth	Assets	Liabilities & net worth

    b. Assuming that Lawrence National was just meeting its reserve requirement prior to its sales of securities to the Fed and that the reserve ratio is 20 percent, what is the maximum amount that the money supply in the economy as a whole can possibly increase as a result of the Fed's purchase of securities? $_____

    c. If, instead of Lawrence National, *you* had sold $1 million of securities to the Fed, show how both the Fed's and Lawrence National's balance sheets would be affected, assuming you deposited the $1 million check from the Fed in your checking account at Lawrence National.

	Fed		Lawrence National	
Assets	Liabilities & net worth	Assets	Liabilities & net worth	

d. Making the same assumptions made in Part b, what is the maximum amount that the money supply in the economy as a whole can possibly increase as a result of the Fed's purchase of securities and your deposit of the Fed's check in your checking account at Lawrence National? $_____

ANSWERS

Fill-in Questions

1. Federal Reserve banks
2. Board of Governors
3. prime rate
4. Federal Reserve notes
5. clearing
6. discount rate
7. Special Drawing Rights
8. capital accounts
9. debits
10. Treasury deposits
11. margin requirements
12. increase; decrease
13. credits
14. gold certificates
15. open-market operations
16. decreasing
17. discount rate
18. a. A
    b. L
    c. L
    d. A
    e. A
    f. L

Multiple Choice Questions

1.	c	9.	d
2.	d	10.	b
3.	b	11.	a
4.	d	12.	c
5.	a	13.	b
6.	b	14.	d
7.	c	15.	b
8.	a	16.	c

APPLICATIONS

1. The Fed might buy securities in the open market, reduce the reserve ratio, or decrease the discount rate.

2. a.

Fed		Lawrence National	
Assets	**Liabilities & net worth**	**Assets**	**Liabilities & net worth**
Bonds ↑ $1 million	Reserves ↑ $1 million	Bonds ↓ $1 million Reserves ↑ $1 mill.	

   b. $5 million. (Lawrence National now has excess reserves of $1 million. The reciprocal of the reserve ratio is 5. Therefore, the $1 million of excess reserves times 5 equals $5 million.)

   c.

Fed		Lawrence National	
Assets	**Liabilities & net worth**	**Assets**	**Liabilities & net worth**
Bonds ↑ $1 million	Reserves ↑ $1 million	Reserves ↑ $1 million	Demand deposits ↑ $1 million (your checking account deposit)

   d. $5 million. (The money supply increases by $1 million when you deposit the check from the Fed in your checking account at Lawrence National. Since the bank's reserves also increase by $1 million in this transaction, the bank has excess reserves of $800,000—the remaining $200,000 of reserves must be held against the newly created $1 million of demand deposits. Consequently, with the reserve ratio of 20 percent, the money supply can expand by an additional $4 million ($800,000 × 5). The maximum possible expansion of the money supply, then, is $1 million plus $4 million equals $5 million.

   Comparing Parts b and d of this question, note that the maximum possible expansion of the money supply is $5 million, regardless of whether the Fed buys securities from a commercial bank or from the general public.

Chapter   16

Business Cycles, Fiscal and Monetary Policies: An Overview

LEARNING OBJECTIVES

The basic principles of macroeconomics were introduced in Chapters 8-15. Various economic aggregates and their measurement were discussed, and theories regarding their behavior were presented. Since the macroeconomy does not tend naturally toward full employment or price stability, the government's fiscal and monetary policy-making role was also examined.

Equipped with this background, we now review the experience of the American macroeconomy over the past five decades.

After reading this chapter, you should:

1. be familiar with the various phases of the business cycle;

2. be aware of the way in which particular economic variables tend to behave during the various phases of the business cycle;

3. be able to comment on the effectiveness of monetary and fiscal policy in dealing with inflation and unemployment during the past 50 years.

CHAPTER OUTLINE

I. Business cycles are characterized by four phases of economic activity—recovery, peak, recession, and trough.
   A. The government usually increases spending and/or cuts taxes, while the Fed increases the money supply in an attempt to stimulate aggregate demand during the recovery phase.
   B. As the economy nears full employment, further increases in demand tend to cause per-unit production costs to rise. Consequently, inflation becomes a problem at the peak of the cycle. At this point monetary policy usually becomes tighter in an attempt to alleviate inflationary pressures.
   C. As consumers begin to satisfy their demand for durable goods during the peak phase, spending for these items slows down. Spending may also be curtailed as consumer resistance to higher prices appears.

1. Investment begins to drop in response to these developments, and the overall reduction in aggregate demand leads to undesired inventory accumulation and to the lower levels of production and employment associated with recession.

D. The trough of the business cycle is characterized by relatively low levels of consumption and investment spending, substantial unused productive capacity, and a pessimistic business community.

II. An examination of the monetary and fiscal policies undertaken during the past 50 years indicates how the Federal Reserve System and the federal government have dealt with the fluctuations in economic activity associated with the business cycle.

A. During the 1930s the United States suffered through the longest and deepest depression in its history.

1. While monetary policy was generally expansionary during this time period, discount rate and reserve requirement increases were untimely and may have prolonged and worsened the economic downturn.

2. Although federal government expenditures rose significantly during the decade, they were partially offset by higher levels of taxation at both the state and the federal level. Consequently, fiscal policy was much less expansionary than is commonly believed.

B. Government spending and aggregate demand skyrocketed during World War II, and the unemployment rate was minimal. Monetary policy was also expansionary in order to accommodate war-related economic activity. The imposition of wage and price controls may have helped restrain inflation during this period.

C. Reduced government spending in the early postwar years was largely offset by increased consumer and producer durable goods purchases. As a result, production continued at high levels. With the removal of the wage and price controls, however, prices rose sharply.

1. Through 1948, although federal fiscal policy was contractionary, state and local government spending mushroomed, and inflation persisted.

2. Instead of concentrating on reducing the rate of inflation, the Fed aimed their activities at minimizing interest rates. Monetary policy was expansionary and, under the existing economic circumstances, inflationary.

D. Despite the Korean war and mild recessions in 1953-1954 and 1957-1958, the decade of the 1950s was generally prosperous.

1. There was little active countercyclical fiscal policy during the decade because the Eisenhower administration supported a "balanced-budget" philosophy.

2. Monetary policy was basically tight during the entire decade with the Fed pursuing an antiinflationary policy.

E. The American economy grew rapidly during the sixties. Resources were fully employed between 1965 and 1969, but excess demand generated serious inflationary pressures.

1. The Kennedy administration, believing that fiscal drag allowed high unemployment rates to persist, initiated several expansionary fiscal measures. The most significant actions undertaken were the personal and corporate income-tax-rate reductions in 1964. Aggregate demand further expanded as a result of the defense spending associated with the escalation of the Vietnam war, and with the economy already operating at full capacity, prices rose significantly.

2. Monetary policy was expansionary throughout much of the 1960s. When inflation accelerated in the latter part of the decade, the Fed chose to attack the problem by raising interest rates, while the money supply continued to grow rapidly. In hindsight, it appears that a reduced rate of monetary expansion would have been more appropriate.

F. The seventies was a period of simultaneous inflation and unemployment.

1. Although a number of fiscal and monetary policies were undertaken to deal with inflation and unemployment (such as wage and price controls, tax reductions, and changes in the discount rate), the effectiveness of traditional monetary and fiscal policy measures has been questioned.

CONCEPTS AND DEFINITIONS

Fill-in Questions

Complete each sentence by writing in the blank the most appropriate word or words from the terms listed below or by circling the word in parentheses that is correct.

recovery
peak
recession
trough
expansionary fiscal policy
deficit financing

new economics
fiscal drag
easy money policy
unemployment
inflation
expansionary

1. Increases in government spending and tax-rate reductions are examples of _expansionary_ fiscal policy.

2. _fiscal drag_ refers to the contractionary impact of higher government tax receipts that result from a growing economy.

3. Resource shortages, increased per-unit production costs, and rising prices prevail at the _peak_ of the business cycle.

4. Proponents of _new economics_ rejected the notion that fiscal prudence required annually balanced budgets.

5. _Recession_ looms on the horizon when consumers and producers consider their stocks of durable goods to be adequate and when households, in general, save a greater portion of their incomes.

6. A(n) _Expansionary fiscal policy_ is most appropriate when significant unemployment, but minimal inflation, exists in the economy.

7. During the early stages of an economic _recovery_, increases in aggregate demand stimulate production, but exert little influence on the price level.

8. _Deficit financing_ is necessary when government expenditures exceed tax receipts.

9. Widespread unemployment, business pessimism, and price reductions in competitive industries characterize the _____ of the business cycle.

10. Indicate the stage of the business cycle described by the characteristics below.

   a. _Peak_ The economy approaches full employment. Businesses are unable to meet increased demand so prices rise.

   b. _Recession_ Consumers have large stocks of durables on hand and are in no hurry to buy more. New investment drops. Banks tend to contract the money supply.

   c. _Recovery_ Confidence and consumer credit grow. Rapid increase in new investment.

   d. _Trough_ Businesses permit idle capacity to wear out without replacement. Interest rates are low, but there are few borrowers.

11. The main economic problem in the 1970s was simultaneous _____ _inflation_ and _unempl._.

12. The fiscal measures as a result of World War II were aggressively _expansionary_ _____.

13. During the war, the Fed kept interest rates (high/low) to keep down the costs of the national debt.

14. The basic problem in the early postwar years (1945 to 1949) was _____ _inflation_.

Multiple Choice Questions

Circle the correct answer.

1. By purchasing significant amounts of government securities in the open market in the early post-World War II years, the Fed

   a. increased the interest rate on government securities.

   b. contributed to inflationary pressures existing in the economy at that time.

   c. reduced the price of government securities.

   d. increased the Treasury's cost of borrowing.

2. A tight money policy is appropriate

   a. during peak periods when the economy has been operating at full capacity, and resource shortages have developed.

   b. during the trough phase of the business cycle.

   c. when significant excess capacity exists in the economy.

   d. when producers can increase output without experiencing increased costs per unit of output.

3. During the recovery phase of the business cycle

   a. an increase in the money supply is necessary to facilitate the expansion of economic activity.

   b. GNP increases, while prices decline.

   c. the Fed sells securities in the open-market in order to reduce the amount of reserves available to the banking system.

   d. government spending is reduced, since private sector spending increases.

4. During the 1930s, federal government fiscal policy was

   a. highly expansionary, as President Roosevelt injected huge amounts of money into the economy through government spending on public-works projects.

   b. not as effective as it could have been as a result of the government's reluctance to completely abandon its "balanced-budget" philosophy.

   c. contractionary, because large budget surpluses were realized throughout the decade.

   d. complemented by expansionary policies at the state and local government levels.

5. The economic downturn of the 1930s was probably aggravated by

   a. the deficit financing of public-works projects.

   b. discount-rate reductions early in the decade.

   c. the government's decision to fight inflation rather than unemployment.

   d. the Fed's decision to increase reserve requirements in 1937.

6. The "new economics" of the Kennedy-Johnson era was "new" in the sense that it recognized for the first time that

   a. without government intervention the economy would not tend toward full employment.

   b. wage and price controls are the only effective methods of dealing with inflation.

   c. budget deficits in most years would be necessary for the maintenance of economic growth.

   d. the budget need not be annually balanced, but must be balanced over the long run.

7. In the early 1960s the economy experienced fiscal drag in that

  a. budgetary deficits threatened the solvency of the federal government.

  b. sluggish investment spending slowed economic expansion.

  c. higher corporate and personal income-tax rates dragged the economy into recession.

  d. as tax receipts rose with the level of economic activity, the expansionary impact of fiscal policy was reduced.

APPLICATIONS

1. Explain how the Fed's attempt to provide low-cost debt financing arrangements for the Treasury in the early post-World War II years affected the Fed's ability to achieve price stability.

ANSWERS

Fill-in Questions

1. expansionary
2. fiscal drag
3. peak
4. new economics
5. recession
6. easy money policy or expansionary fiscal policy
7. recovery
8. deficit financing
9. trough
10. a. peak
    b. recession
    c. recovery
    d. trough
11. inflation; unemployment
12. expansionary
13. low
14. inflation

Multiple Choice Questions

1. b
2. a
3. a
4. b
5. d
6. c
7. d

APPLICATIONS

1. In order to keep interest rates low, the Fed bought significant amounts of securities in the open market. This increased the demand for securities, raised

their price, and reduced interest rates. The Treasury then borrowed at these lower rates.

From an economic-stabilization perspective, the Fed's security purchases greatly increased the amount of reserves available to the banking system. The money supply rose accordingly and added to the inflationary pressures already existing in the economy. Thus, monetary policy was expansionary in order to facilitate Treasury borrowing, when it should have been contractionary in order to stabilize prices.

Chapter 17

Stabilization: Problems and Policies

LEARNING OBJECTIVES

While monetary and fiscal policy actions have generally been beneficial, the macroeconomic experience of the United States indicates how difficult it is to achieve economic stability. In the present chapter, we discuss why the attainment of simultaneous full employment and price stability has proven to be such an elusive goal and discuss some of the problems encountered by policymakers in pursuing this goal.

After reading this chapter, you should:

1. be familiar with the Phillips curve and the trade-off between the rates of inflation and unemployment it proposes;

2. be able to explain the Classical, Keynesian, and Monetarist viewpoints regarding economic stabilization;

3. recognize how political realities affect the ability of policymakers to implement stabilization measures;

4. be familiar with the concept of stagflation and some of the nontraditional policies that have been proposed to deal with this problem.

CHAPTER OUTLINE

I. The two most basic goals of economic stabilization policy are full employment and price stability.

    A. The Phillips curve illustrates a proposed inverse relationship between the rates of unemployment and inflation—that is, in order to have lower rates of inflation, an economy must accept higher rates of unemployment, and vice versa.

        1. According to some economists, the unemployment-inflation trade-off worsened during the 1970s. Others claim that there is no long-run relationship between inflation and unemployment.

B. The Classical, Keynesian, and Monetarist views regarding how to achieve and maintain a stable economy differ.
   1. Classical economists believed that the economy would naturally operate at full capacity. In this self-regulating economy, government intervention was largely unnecessary.
   2. Keynes argued that there are no natural forces working within the economy that assure the achievement of full employment. Discretionary monetary and fiscal policy must be undertaken by the government in order to attain this goal.
   3. Monetarists, like the Keynesians, hold that there is no natural mechanism operating within the economy to assure full employment. Unlike the Keynesians, however, monetarists place little faith in the ability of fiscal policy to stabilize the economy. Instead, they recommend altering the money supply as the most appropriate method of effecting desired changes in economic activity.
C. Several factors limit the ability of monetary and fiscal policies to deal effectively with inflation and unemployment.
   1. The time lags associated with both monetary and fiscal policy are sometimes so long that specific policy actions prove inappropriate because of unexpected changes that often occur in the economy.
   2. Public opinion sometimes restricts the number of options available to policymakers, and it can also affect the choice of whether fiscal or monetary policies are employed.
   3. The public's expectations regarding the future course of monetary and fiscal policy may result in policy actions widening, rather than reducing, fluctuations in economic activity.
   4. Implementing contractionary fiscal policy through a reduction in government spending may be politically difficult because vested-interest groups resist proposed cutbacks.
   5. Conflicts between multiple goals also limit policymakers. The desire to avoid balance-of-payments problems, to achieve economic growth, and to pursue noneconomic goals, such as a clean environment or a strong national defense, may limit both the number of tools at the policymaker's disposal and the types of policies that can be undertaken.

II. Stagflation, a combination of unsatisfactory economic growth and persistent inflation, has been the outstanding economic problem of the 1970s.
   A. Once individuals and firms notice that the rate of inflation is continually high, they respond to it in ways that perpetuate the inflation even during recessions.
   B. In addition to traditional monetary and fiscal policy tools, wage and price controls have been employed in the fight against inflation. Their effectiveness, however, is questionable, and many economists claim that controls attack only the symptoms, and not the underlying causes, of inflation.
      1. Some alternatives to the traditional policies used to regulate inflation include changes in government taxes, regulations, and subsidies and indexing

(allowing tax brackets to change proportionately to the price level). Training programs, public-service employment, improved labor-market information, and the provision of incentives for employers to reduce discriminatory hiring practices are long-term policies aimed at reducing hardcore unemployment in the economy.

III. Although stabilization policies have not eliminated macroeconomic problems, they have enabled us to avoid the type of disaster that characterized the economy in the Great Depression of the 1930s.

KEY TERMS

You should be familiar with the meaning of the terms listed below. For definition of these terms, please refer to the glossary at the end of your textbook and to the appropriate section in this chapter.

Phillips curve
Say's law
stagflation

CONCEPTS AND DEFINITIONS

Fill-in Questions

Complete each sentence by writing in the blank the most appropriate word or words from the terms listed below or by circling the word in parentheses that is correct.

Classical economists	Humphrey-Hawkins Act
Keynesian	cost-push inflation
Monetarists	Say's law
New Economic Policy	stagflation
jawboning	Phillips curve
indexing	

1. The _New Economic Policy_ of the Nixon administration attempted to alleviate inflation through the imposition of wage and price controls and reduce unemployment by implementing expansionary monetary and fiscal policies.

2. Government efforts to persuade firms to limit price increases and unions to limit wage demands are examples of _jawboning_ .

3. _Monetarists_ claim that fiscal policy measures, unaccompanied by changes in the money supply, have no long-term effect on the level of economic activity.

4. A basic implication of _Say's Law_ is that whatever is produced in a given time period will be purchased.

5. Sluggish economic growth and a persistently high rate of inflation constitute _Stagnation._.

6. Since the unemployment rate associated with any given rate of inflation was greater in the 1970s than in the 1960s, some economists contend that the _Phillips Curve_ has shifted to the right.

7. Considering full employment a natural state of affairs, _Classical economists_ believed that government intervention in the economy was largely unnecessary.

8. Without _indexing_, an individual pays a higher rate of personal income taxation as his/her money income increases, despite the fact that real income may be unchanged.

9. The _Humphrey-Hawkins Act_ sets goals of 3-4 percent unemployment and 3 percent inflation for 1983, but provides no specific economic plan for achieving these goals.

10. Boosting government spending, lowering taxes, and increasing the money supply are the _Keynesian_ remedies for unemployment.

11. The concept of _cost-push inflation_ attributes most of the rise of the price level to unions and monopolistic businesses.

12. A technique that serves to prevent transfers of wealth when prices change unexpectedly is _indexing_.

13. The Phillips curve states that there is a(n) (direct/inverse) relationship between inflation and unemployment.

14. The _Phillips curve_ proposes a trade-off between the rate of unemployment and the rate of inflation.

Multiple Choice Questions

Circle the correct answer.

1. The contention by some economists that the Phillips curve shifted outward during the 1970s implies that

    a. an inflation-unemployment trade-off no longer exists.

    b. full employment can be attained at a lower rate of inflation than was previously possible.

    c. less monopoly power is being exercised by business and labor unions.

    d. the inflation-unemployment trade-off has deteriorated.

2. Classical economists believed that the economy would usually operate at full employment because

    a. interest-rate fluctuations would equate desired saving and desired investment thereby ensuring that aggregate demand would equal aggregate supply at the full-employment level of output.

b. households spend all of the income they receive so aggregate demand equals aggregate supply.

c. the "invisible hand" would move the economy to an equilibrium position.

d. according to the Employment Act of 1946, the federal government assumed responsibility for maintaining full employment.

3. According to the Keynesian perspective

a. the money supply must grow at a fixed annual rate in order to stabilize the economy.

b. government action is usually necessary to stabilize the economy.

c. expansionary fiscal policy, in itself, is an ineffective method of reducing unemployment.

d. changes in the money supply have no lasting impact on the economy.

4. In assessing the relative advantages and disadvantages of discretionary monetary and fiscal policy, it is clear that

a. the recognition lag is much longer for monetary policy than it is for fiscal policy.

b. the decision lag is shorter for monetary policy than it is for fiscal policy.

c. the operational lag for both monetary and fiscal policy is almost nonexistent.

d. most Keynesians view monetary policy as superior to fiscal policy in terms of effectiveness.

5. Contractionary fiscal policy is sometimes difficult to implement because

a. the housing industry lobbies strongly against the Fed's attempts to decrease the money supply.

b. the public is currently opposed to increases in government spending.

c. previous budgetary commitments limit the areas in which government spending cuts can be effected.

d. taxes cannot be reduced without a concurrent reduction in the provision of government services.

6. Policymakers may be reluctant to undertake contractionary fiscal policy measures when

a. significant inflation exists in the economy.

b. the rate of economic growth is considered excessive.

c. the general public believes that government is becoming "too big."

d. the president plans to seek reelection in the near future.

7. An economy would likely be suffering from stagflation if the rate of economic growth (adjusted for inflation) is

a. 6 percent, and the rate of inflation is 10 percent.

b. 1/2 percent, and the rate of unemployment is 8 percent.

c. 1/2 percent, and the rate of inflation is 9 percent.

d. 4 percent, and the rate of inflation is 3 percent.

8. When inflationary expectations develop in the economy

   a. unions often demand that cost-of-living escalator clauses be built into employee contracts.

   b. people's actions are unaffected by changes in the cost of living.

   c. people tend to postpone purchases in the hope that prices will decline in the near future.

   d. businesses tend to reduce prices as a show of good faith to their customers.

9. Passage of the Humphrey-Hawkins Act

   a. provides policymakers with a new set of tools with which to battle inflation and unemployment.

   b. insures that stagflation will be eliminated by 1983.

   c. does not necessarily mean that policymakers are better equipped to deal with inflation and unemployment.

   d. requires the federal government to balance its budget annually.

10. Public-service job programs

   a. represent an attempt to reduce hardcore unemployment in the economy.

   b. have greatly reduced the unemployment rate among women.

   c. have caused shortages of skilled labor in the private sector, as workers find public-sector jobs more attractive.

   d. serve only to increase the rate of inflation in the economy.

APPLICATION

1. Consider the hypothetical situation in which there has been a sudden and simultaneous 20 percent drop in both wages and prices. John Doe has just lost a job paying $5 an hour. He discovers that he can get another job— several, in fact—that pay $4 an hour. Thinking he is having particularly bad luck, he keeps looking. Although he would actually be as well off at $4 as he had been at $5 because of the drop in prices, he does not recognize the fact. What effect does such inadequacy of information have on the economy?

_____

_____

ANSWERS

Fill-in Questions

1. New Economic Policy
2. jawboning
3. Monetarists
4. Say's law
5. stagflation
6. Phillips curve
7. Classical economists

8. indexing
9. Humphrey-Hawkins Act
10. Keynesian
11. cost-push inflation
12. indexing
13. inverse
14. Phillips curve

Multiple-Choice Questions

1. d
2. a
3. b
4. b
5. c

6. d
7. c
8. a
9. c
10. a

APPLICATION

1. The unemployment rate will rise as workers remain unemployed for longer periods of time.

Chapter 18

Economic Growth Theory and the United States' Record

LEARNING OBJECTIVES

In addition to full employment and price stability, which were discussed in Chapters 16 and 17, a basic national goal is economic growth—that is, the production of an ever-increasing amount of goods and services. In this chapter, the factors affecting economic growth are identified and the relative importance of each in the growth of the United States economy is evaluated. Furthermore, a discussion of the costs and benefits associated with economic growth is presented.

After reading this chapter, you should be able to:

1. distinguish between changes in real gross national product and changes in economic welfare;

2. isolate the factors that have significantly contributed to the growth of the United States;

3. appreciate how a nation's cultural heritage may affect its economic performance;

4. identify the distinguishing features of the traditional theories of economic growth;

5. identify the costs and benefits which accompany economic growth.

CHAPTER OUTLINE

I. Economic growth is defined as an increase in real gross national product—that is, gross national product adjusted for price changes.

    A. Most economies do not grow at a steady rate. Instead, real GNP tends to grow in a cyclical fashion.

        1. An economy's health cannot be measured by its volume of production alone; its rate of growth is also important.

        2. Other factors to consider when discussing an economy's health as measured by real GNP include cultural activity, leisure time, and valuable services not included in GNP.

    B. Economic growth does not necessarily imply an improved standard of living.
      1. One indicator of standard of living is real GNP per capita which is calculated by dividing a nation's real GNP by the size of its poulation. Should real GNP grow faster than population grows, real GNP per capita rises. Under these conditions, the economy grows *and* the standard of living improves.
        a. Even real GNP per capita is an imperfect measure of standard of living, because many factors affecting our economic well-being (such as leisure) cannot be measured in monetary terms.

II.   Several factors determine an economy's rate of growth.
    A. The supply of human resources (labor), natural resources (land), capital, entrepreneurship, and the level to technology greatly influences an economy's ability to expand.
      1. An increase in the supply of any of these resources or an improvement in technology increases the productive capacity of the economy, thereby causing its production-possibilities curve (PPC) to shift outward (to the right).
    B. Economic growth is also influenced by changes in the level of demand which originate from the household, business, and government sectors of an economy.
      1. Growth does not occur unless there is sufficient spending to warrant the production of a greater amount of output than was produced in the previous time period.
        a. Expanding markets through population growth at home and through increased international trade stimulate investment which in turn leads to increases in production, employment, and income.
    C. Noneconomic factors such as religion, social custom, and political institutions may also either promote or retard economic growth.

III. The growth experienced by the United States economy is often traced to technological improvements and an abundance of resources (both natural and human).
    A. Utilization of a vast amount of natural resources during the nineteenth century westward expansion supported rapid economic growth.
    B. Population growth ultimately enlarged the labor force and increased the productive capacity of the economy.
      1. A higher level of educational attainment among Americans has resulted in a better skilled labor force which has also significantly contributed to economic expansion.
    C. Technological improvements, which permit more efficient use of resources, have been a major cause of growth in the American economy.

IV. Historically, theories of economic growth have attached varying importance to particular economic resources, technology, and the behavior of specific economic variables.
    A. Classical economists (such as Adam Smith, David Ricardo, and Thomas Malthus) generally ignored the possibility of technological advance. As a

result, they believed that growth would be restricted by either limited natural resources or unchecked population expansion.

B. Neoclassical economists incorporated technological advancement into their view of the economic-growth process. In addition, they concluded that interaction between the rates of saving, interest, and profit would assure a generally steady rate of economic growth.

C. Keynes emphasized the importance of total spending (demand), and specifically the contribution of government to total spending, in the economic-growth process.

   1. Post-Keynesians, on the other hand, concentrate on the role played by investment in economic expansion.

   a. Harrod and Domar introduced the concept of a capital/output ratio which holds that an increase in output and, therefore, changes in income are a function of capital accumulation or the investment rate.

V. Economic growth inflicts some costs upon society, in addition to generating benefits.

A. Inflation and pollution are often the by-products of economic growth.

   1. Since economic growth is a response to increased aggregate demand, inflationary pressures tend to mount when the economy approaches full employment.

   2. Increased production during periods of economic growth is often accompanied by pollution and environmental deterioration.

B. Besides providing additional employment opportunities, economic growth helps reduce absolute levels of poverty and alleviates a variety of domestic social and financial problems.

VI. Some policies that might accomplish overall growth for the United States include upgrading the quality of the labor force through training and education, encouraging increased capital formation, and increasing expenditures on technological research and development.

KEY TERMS

You should be familiar with the meaning of the terms listed below. For definition of these terms, please refer to the glossary at the end of your textbook and to the appropriate section in this chapter.

economic growth
capital/output ratio

CONCEPTS AND DEFINITIONS

Fill-in Questions

Complete each sentence by writing in the blank the most appropriate word or words from the terms listed below or by circling the word in parentheses that is correct.

capital/output ratio	entrepreneurial function
per capita GNP	technological advancement
natural resources	economies of scale
human resources	economic growth
stock of capital goods	real GNP

1. In modern economies, growth is considered to be a real increase in _____ _____.

2. Economic growth in nineteenth-century America was greatly helped by the availiability of a seemingly unlimited supply of _____.

3. If the price level remains constant, an increase in GNP indicates that _____ has occurred.

4. _____ allows a given amount of economic resources to produce a greater amount of output than in previous time periods.

5. Economic growth can be represented as a shift in the production-possibilities curve to the (right/left).

6. The _____ is directly affected by the amount of investment undertaken by businesses.

7. If, in a given year, prices increase by 10 percent, real output remains constant, and the population expands by 5 percent, _____ rises.

8. The attainment of higher levels of education over time has improved the quality of _____ in the United States economy.

9. A reduction in the _____ means that a greater increase in output is associated with each additional dollar of capital investment.

10. According to Schumpeter, a central feature in the decay of capitalistic economic systems would be the eventual obsolescence of the _____.

11. Growth may result from an increase in the supply of factors of production. An increase in population is likely to result in an increase in GNP but may cause a fall in _____.

12. _____ can generate increases in the supply of final products by providing production methods that are more efficient.

13. Firms may also become more productive as they increase in size. These increases in supply result from _____.

14. For each of the conditions below, indicate whether it will encourage or discourage growth.

    a. _____ The economy operates at a level below full employment.

    b. _____ A larger percentage of the population enters the labor force.

c. _____ American scientists, engineers, and educators migrate to Canada and Australia.

d. _____ There is an increase in the number of people completing work-training programs.

e. _____ Interest rates are kept at a very high level.

f. _____ Businesses pay a special tax every time they expand their plants.

Matching Questions

Select the name on the right which is most closely identified with each statement on the left, and write the corresponding letter in the blank space.

_____ 1. Economic growth is limited by diminishing returns.   a. Adam Smith

_____ 2. Economic growth slows as short-   b. John Maynard Keynes
ages of natural resources arise.

_____ 3. Uncontrolled population expan-
sion restricts economic growth.   c. David Ricardo

_____ 4. Government spending may be
necessary to promote economic   d. Thomas Malthus
growth.

Multiple Choice Questions

Circle the correct answer.

1. The importance of technological improvement to economic growth was initially recognized by

    a. David Ricardo.

    b. Thomas Malthus.

    c. the Neoclassical economists.

    d. Adam Smith.

2. Economic well-being is

    a. determined solely by the rate of economic growth.

    b. accurately measured by changes in GNP.

    c. accurately measured by changes in real GNP.

    d. sometimes affected by factors that cannot easily be measured in monetary terms.

3. If money GNP declines, but real GNP rises

    a. economic growth occurs.

b. the standard of living necessarily improves.

c. prices have risen, but real output has risen even faster.

d. the economy experiences recession.

4. When the production-possibilities curve shifts outward,

   a. economic growth necessarily occurs.

   b. economic growth necessarily occurs if the economy operates at a point on this new curve.

   c. resources that were previously unemployed are now utilized.

   d. aggregate demand increases.

5. Economic growth is

   a. dependent on sufficient demand to purchase the increasing amount of goods and services produced.

   b. characterized by a constant rate of increase in output for prolonged periods of time.

   c. sometimes limited by social and religious beliefs, such as adherence to the Puritan Ethic in eighteenth and nineteenth-century America.

   d. inevitable, since population growth guarantees a constantly increasing labor force and, therefore, an increase in the productive capacity of the economy.

6. David Ricardo used the concept of diminishing returns to explain why

   a. producers reduce output when product prices fall.

   b. economic-growth strategies that are successful in industrialized nations may fail in nonindustrialized nations.

   c. using a continually growing labor force in combination with a constant amount of land ultimately results in smaller and smaller increases in output.

   d. economic growth usually follows a cyclical pattern.

7. More so than his predecessors, Keynes stressed the importance of

   a. natural resources in the economic-growth process.

   b. aggregate demand in the economic-growth process.

   c. human resources in the economic-growth process.

   d. technological advances in the economic-growth process.

8. The increasing level of output that characterizes periods of economic expansion is

   a. always accompanied by higher prices.

   b. usually accompanied by a worsening unemployment problem.

   c. usually accompanied by increased environmental pollution.

   d. usually accompanied by an increase in the incidence of poverty.

9. The government may promote economic growth in the short run by

   a. decreasing government spending, in order to allow for more private-sector spending.
   b. relentlessly pursuing the goal of price stability.
   c. increasing taxes on individuals instead of businesses.
   d. undertaking policies that reduce interest rates.

10. An increase in GNP necessarily indicates that

    a. the standard of living has improved.
    b. the monetary value of currently produced output is greater than it was in the previous time period.
    c. economic growth has occurred.
    d. the level of real output currently produced in the economy is greater than it was in the previous time period.

11. Which of these could contribute to the increased productivity of the American work force?

    a. longer periods of education
    b. increased energy available for work resulting from a reduction in the work week
    c. a law making retirement mandatory at age 65
    d. all of these

12. According to Classical economists, we could account for economic growth by

    a. identifying increases in demand.
    b. changes in tastes.
    c. identifying those factors that contributed to an increase in supply.
    d. none of these.

13. Which of the following is most likely to have said that the population would grow at a geometric rate if unchecked while food production could grow at only an arithmetic rate?

    a. Thomas Malthus
    b. David Ricardo
    c. John Stewart Mill
    d. John Maynard Keynes

14. In the early part of American history, it was considered virtuous to save money and improper to spend it on frivolous items. This type of belief is likely to lead to

    a. population growth.
    b. accumulation of capital.

c. rapid advances in technology.

d. none of these.

APPLICATION

1. Evaluate the following statement: "An outward shift of the production-possibilities curve indicates that economic growth has occurred."

ANSWERS

Fill-in Questions

1. real GNP
2. natural resources
3. economic growth
4. technological advancement
5. right
6. stock of capital goods
7. per-capita GNP
8. human resources
9. capital/output ratio
10. entrepreneurial function

11. per-capita GNP
12. technological advancement
13. economies of scale
14. a. discourage
    b. encourage
    c. discourage
    d. encourage
    e. discourage
    f. discourage

Matching Questions

1. c
2. a
3. d
4. b

Multiple Choice Questions

1. c	6. c	11. d
2. d	7. b	12. c
3. a	8. c	13. a
4. b	9. d	14. b
5. a	10. b	

APPLICATION

1. An outward shift indicates that the economy is *capable* of producing more output than it did previously, but the shift does not necessarily mean that the

economy *is* producing more. If at least a portion of the increased productive capacity is utilized, production increases and economic growth results. If the additional capacity is unused, however, production does not rise and there is no economic expansion.

Chapter 19

Economic Growth in Less Developed Countries

LEARNING OBJECTIVES

After examining the growth of the highly industrialized United States economy in Chapter 18, we now turn our attention to the economic performance of less developed countries (LDCs) in Africa, Asia, and Latin America. The characteristics shared by LDCs that make economic growth so difficult are identified, and strategies for development are investigated. An increasingly popular strategy, the formation of commodity cartels among LDCs, receives special attention.

After reading this chapter, you should:

1. be familiar with the general characteristics of LDCs;

2. understand why LDCs have experienced such great difficulty in achieving and sustaining economic growth;

3. know the various development plans available to LDCs and be able to assess the feasibility of such plans;

4. be able to evaluate the impact that the formation of international cartels has had on the development prospects of LDCs.

CHAPTER OUTLINE

I. Although the term "less developed country" cannot be precisely defined, most LDCs have some common features.

    A. Low real per-capita GNP, small-scale agriculture, rapid population growth, an inadequately educated labor force, extremely unequal distribution of income, rudimentary industry, and reliance on one or two primary commodites for export characterize most LDCs.

        1. While most LDCs exhibit a number of these features, it is difficult to generalize about LDCs. Consequently, there is no single strategy for development that is universally acceptable.

II. Attempts to implement development plans are often frustrated by limited economic resources, the inability or unwillingness to adopt advanced technology, traditional cultural and social attitudes, and economic imperialism.

A. Despite the fact that most LDCs are populous, the *quality* of human resources is often low. Illiteracy, few opportunities for on-the-job training in management-level positions, and serious health problems frequently limit the productivity of the labor force.

B. Since most households are too poor to save, the amount of funds available for capital formation is small. In addition, profitable investment opportunities are few. Therefore, little investment occurs, and the stock of physical capital is not large enough to support significant economic development.

C. Because employing the latest technological advancements usually requires large-scale production and a skilled work force, LDCs use technologically inefficient production processes. As a result, they are unable to compete effectively with more developed countries in the production of manufactured goods.

D. Insufficient private physical capital is accompanied by an inadequate stock of public capital that would facilitate modern production (infrastructure). Rudimentary transportation networks and communications systems are often incapable of supporting large-scale industrial activity in the private sector.

E. Basic social and cultural values are sometimes in conflict with the efficient operation of an advanced economy.

F. Some individuals claim that LDCs are manipulated by economic imperialists, countries that seek to influence the political atmosphere or, that want to secure an uninterrupted flow of a strategic resource from the LDC. Such actions may inhibit or distort development by subordinating the LDCs interests to those of the imperialist nation.

   1. LDCs may nationalize industries in response to apparent imperialist actions. In doing so, the government assumes ownership of a firm that was formerly privately owned.

III. Various economic-development schemes have been attempted, but each has been confronted with problems.

A. The human-capital approach stresses improvement of human capital through better education and improved health.

   1. Providing free education through a public school system is a long-run plan to improve the quality of human resources, but it is expensive. Governments have also established programs to teach already employed workers basic reading and writing skills.

   2. Free vaccinations and inoculations, public health clinics, and improved nutrition also enhance the quality of the labor force in the long run.

B. The capital accumulation approach to economic development may appear attractive at first, but many LDCs do not possess a labor force sufficiently skilled to use new capital efficiently. Furthermore, obtaining funds for the purpose of building up capital stock has proven a difficult task, even through taxation.

C. Highly developed countries and many private, national, and international organizations have provided foreign aid to LDCs in the form of loans, grants, capital goods, technical assistance, food, and so on.
   1. While humanitarianism is a factor, foreign aid is often the result of the desire of Western and non-Western nations both to secure economic and political influence in and to create military alliances with LDCs. Therefore, the needs of the LDCs often play second fiddle to the donors' intentions.
   2. Due to limited success in spurring economic growth, to LDC criticism, and to the need to attend to pressing domestic problems, donor countries have curtailed foreign-aid programs in recent years.
      a. Some LDCs now feel that reliance on foreign aid represents a dependency relationship that is both undesirable in itself and a reminder of earlier colonial status.
D. Most LDCs employ some type of centralized economic planning in an attempt to better coordinate development efforts.
IV. In recent years international cartels, groups of countries producing the same product, have been formed. Their purpose is to limit the supply of a particular product and thereby raise the market price above the competitive price.
A. LDCs whose major source of foreign exchange and government revenue is derived from the sale of primary commodities such as copper or oil, may find it advantageous to belong to a cartel since a cartel may minimize commodity price fluctuations and thus stabilize export earnings.
B. Since all LDCs do not possess the same resource base, the overall impact of cartels is not necessarily beneficial. For example, while skyrocketing oil prices have aided the development efforts of OPEC nations, it has been difficult for non-member LDCs to pay for the imported oil that is vital to their economic existence.

KEY TERMS

You should be familiar with the meaning of the terms listed below. For definition of these terms, please refer to the glossary at the end of your textbook and to the appropriate section in this chapter.

economic development	nationalization
infrastructure	cartel
economic imperialism	

CONCEPTS AND DEFINITIONS

Fill-in Questions

Complete each sentence by writing in the blank the most appropriate word or words from the terms listed below or by circling the word in parentheses that is correct.

education
economic development
human capital
Third World
dependency relationship
physical capital
centralized planning

infrastructure
health
nationalization
economic imperialism
cartel
save

1. Foreign-aid programs are often criticized because they foster (a)n _____ between the donor and recipient countries.

2. Public-sector investment programs are necessary in most LDCs in order to develop a(n) _____ adequate to support economic development.

3. The less developed countries of Africa, Asia, and Latin America constitute the _____.

4. A(n) _____ is a monopoly in the sense that, acting as a single producer, it can manipulate market price by restricting supply.

5. In order to maintain the desired balance between growth in the public and private sectors of economies, many LDCs have adopted some form of _____ _____.

6. Free educational and health services provided by LDC governments represent an effort to improve the quality of _____.

7. Efforts by a United States firm, operating a plant in Brazil, to influence the outcome of a Brazilian election might be considered an example of _____ _____.

8. _____ in many LDCs is thwarted by a rate of population growth that exceeds the rate of increase in real GNP.

9. Since most households in LDCs are unable to save, the amount of funds available to enlarge the stock of _____ is small.

10. The _____ of a firm's assets is sometimes the response of a host government to the suspected imperialistic policies of a multinational corporation.

11. The stock of physical capital in LDCs is usually (small/large) This condition results from the inability of most of the households to _____.

12. The stock of public capital goods, such as power and highway systems, is called a(n) _____.

13. For most developing countries, the scarcest resource is _____.

14. The chief means of developing human capital is through _____ _____. Human capital can also be increased by improving _____ _____.

Multiple Choice Questions

Circle the correct answer.

1. A characteristic shared by most LDCs is
   a. a highly mechanized agricultural industry.
   b. a highly skilled labor force.
   c. the need to import most manufactured goods.
   d. the need to import labor to offset the impact of a dwindling labor force.

2. The inability of LDCs to accumulate physical capital is partially accounted for by the
   a. tendency of households to save rather than invest.
   b. reluctance of businesses to invest due to the instability of government.
   c. tendency of government to invest excessively in human capital.
   d. lack of demand for consumer goods caused by a slow rate of population growth.

3. Economic development in many LDCs is hindered by a
   a. high rate of population growth that significantly restricts growth in real GNP per capita.
   b. real GNP growth rate that is significantly less than those rates achieved by developed nations.
   c. labor force that is usually highly educated, but possess little technical skill.
   d. high rate of unemployment caused by the use of capital-intensive production processes.

4. United States foreign aid to LDCs
   a. has dwindled since the 1950s and now accounts for about 10 percent of GNP.
   b. has largely solved the problems faced by LDCs.
   c. is undertaken for strictly humanitarian purposes.
   d. is considered excessive by some individuals because of the limited past success of such programs.

5. The recent trend toward the establishment of international commodity cartels has
   a. generally improved the development prospects of all LDCs.
   b. reduced fluctuations in both export earnings and the cost of imports for LDCs as a whole.
   c. tended to increase the rate of inflation in most nations.
   d. improved the development prospects of participating LDCs, without adversely affecting the economies of nonparticipating LDCs.

6. If a business is nationalized
   a. the government assumes control of the firm's assets.
   b. its previous owners are guaranteed compensation by the government.
   c. its employees are cited for their patriotism and civic pride.
   d. its previous owners must not have been native citizens.

7. Government programs aimed at improving the health of the populace
   a. represent an attempt to improve the stock of physical capital.
   b. are aimed at upgrading the quality of human capital.
   c. only hinder development efforts because they tend to accelerate population growth.
   d. may enhance social well-being, but have no impact on economic development.

8. The claim that most LDCs lack an adequate infrastructure refers to the limitations on economic development imposed by
   a. a poorly skilled labor force.
   b. an insufficient stock of public goods.
   c. a small stock of private physical capital.
   d. the inability of LDCs to employ the latest technological advances in producing manufactured goods.

9. In order to encourage LDC investment
   a. dividend income from foreign firms may be taxed at a lower rate than dividends received from domestic companies.
   b. participation of foreign-owned firms in the economic-development process may be restricted.
   c. individuals may be permitted to offer their labor in producing capital goods in lieu of paying taxes.
   d. many governments have imposed regulations that have been extremely effective in limiting the amount of money that native citizens take out of the country.

10. Foreign aid is
    a. a source of much-needed investment funds for LDCs.
    b. necessarily imperialistic and therefore cannot be beneficial to an LDC's development efforts.
    c. usually in the form of grants that can be used for any purpose deemed appropriate by the recipient nation.
    d. no longer sought by LDCs, because these nations now recognize that reliance on aid establishes an undesirable dependency relationship with the donor country.

11. Many LDCs are requiring foreign firms to employ or train a certain percentage of local citizens for jobs within the company. This effort is an attempt to

    a. decrease the amount of income going to the local citizenry.
    b. increase the stock of human capital.
    c. discourage investment by foreign companies.
    d. prevent profits from leaving the country.

12. Foreign companies in LDCs hire local labor for which they pay wages, and income is generated throughout the economy. The income generated is likely to be low, however, if

    a. the industry is labor-intensive.
    b. the industry is capital-intensive.
    c. the company also purchases other inputs locally.
    d. none of these.

APPLICATION

1. Select the development strategy on the right that is most closely associated with each specific program mentioned on the left, and write the corresponding number in the blank space.

    _____ a. Formation of the World Coffee Producers Group.

    _____ b. Government payment of educational expenses for students to study abroad on the condition that they return to work in the country upon completing their education.

    _____ c. Tax credits for business spending on plant and equipment.

    _____ d. Development of inexpensive soil nutrients for an LDC by a United Nations agricultural research team.

    1. developing human capital
    2. accumulating capital goods
    3. foreign aid
    4. cartel participation

ANSWERS

Fill-in Questions

1. dependency relationship
2. infrastructure
8. economic development
9. physical capital

3. Third World
4. cartel
5. centralized planning
6. human capital
7. economic imperialism

10. nationalization
11. small; save
12. infrastructure
13. physical capital
14. education; health

Multiple Choice Questions

1. c
2. b
3. a
4. d
5. c
6. a

7. b
8. b
9. c
10. a
11. b
12. b

APPLICATION

1. a. 4
   b. 1
   c. 2
   d. 3

Chapter 20

Elasticity of Demand and Supply

LEARNING OBJECTIVES

As noted in Chapter 3, changes in the price of a commodity will influence the amount demanded by consumers as well as the quantity made available by business firms. The nature of these relationships is spelled out in the laws of demand and supply. In this chapter, we extend and refine the analysis of demand and supply by looking at the extent to which quantity demanded or supplied responds to a price change. With a knowledge of elasticity, we can better analyze market data and the possible effects of alternative governmental policies.

After reading this chapter, you should be able to:

1. define elasticity of demand and elasticity of supply;

2. compute various elasticities and interpret the results;

3. identify the determinants of demand and supply elasticity, and specify which determinants have signficance in the short run and which are of greater importance in the long run;

4. analyze the impact of governmental programs to control prices that are above or below the market equilibrium;

5. utilize elasticity data to analyze the impacts of governmental programs of taxation.

CHAPTER OUTLINE

I. Elasticity refers to the responsiveness of the demand for a commodity to changes in price.
    A. Elasticity is measured by the ratio of the percentage change in quantity demanded to the percentage change in price. Both the numerator and the denominator of this ratio are expressed as percentages.

$$\frac{E}{D} = \frac{\% \triangle Q}{\% \triangle P} = \frac{\triangle Q}{Q} \div \frac{\triangle P}{P}$$

    1. The demand for a commodity is elastic if this ratio (called the elasticity coefficient) is greater than 1; that is, if the percentage change in quantity demanded is greater than the percentage change in price.

    2. The demand for a commodity is inelastic if the percentage change in quantity demanded is smaller than the percentage change in price so that the elasticity coefficient is less than 1.

    3. The demand for a commodity is of unit elasticity if the percentage change in quantity is equal to the percentage change in price so that the elasticity coefficient equals 1.

B. For most commodities, demand is elastic over certain price ranges and inelastic over others. On a straight demand curve, the upper half of the curve is the elastic range; the lower half of the curve is the inelastic range.

    1. If a demand curve is horizontal, demand is perfectly elastic. For a demand curve of this type, consumption is infinite until a certain price is reached above which none of the good will be demanded.

    2. If a demand curve is vertical, demand is infinitely inelastic; that is, people will always buy the same quantity of a commodity, regardless of its price.

    3. Cases of perfectly elastic demand and perfectly inelastic demand are rare.

C. Calculations of demand elasticity coefficients are simplified by using average values for price and quantity in percentage computations.

$$E_D = \frac{\% \Delta Q}{\% \Delta P} = \frac{\Delta Q}{(Q_1 + Q_2)/2} \div \frac{\Delta P}{(P_1 + P_2)/2}$$

This is called the midpoint formula.

D. The number of units sold of a commodity multiplied by its price is equal to total revenue.

    1. If demand is elastic, total revenue will increase if the price is lowered and will drop if the price is raised.

    2. If demand is inelastic, total revenue will vary directly with price changes. That is, total revenue will increase if price is raised and will drop if price is lowered.

E. The degree of elasticity of demand for a commodity is influenced by the availability of substitutes for the commodity, the number of uses of the product, its degree of necessity, its cost relative to income, and the time available in which people may adjust to price changes.

    1. If a commodity has few substitutes, its demand is likely to be inelastic, and vice versa.

    2. If a commodity has many uses, changes in price will have more of an effect on the quantity demanded than if the commodity has few uses. Commodities with many uses tend to have more elastic demands than commodities with few uses.

    3. The demand for necessities tends to be more inelastic than that for luxury items.

    4. If the cost of an item is large relative to income, demand tends to be more elastic than if the cost is relatively small in comparison to income.

5. The more time people have to respond to price changes, the greater the change in quantity demanded will be. Thus, the demand for a good tends to be more elastic when a long period of time is considered and less elastic when a short period of time is considered.

II.   Other demand elasticities measure responsiveness of quantity demanded to changes in income or changes in the prices of other goods (substitutes or complements).

A. Income elasticity is defined as the ratio:

$$\frac{\% \text{ change in quantity demanded.}}{\% \text{ change in income}}$$

Goods are income elastic if the value of the ratio is greater than 1, and are income inelastic if the value of the ratio is less than 1.

B. Cross elasticity is defined as the ratio:

$$\frac{\% \text{ change in quantity demanded of good } A}{\% \text{ change in price of good } B}$$

where goods A and B are different commodities. Cross elasticity is frequently used to determine the economic relationship between goods.

III.   Supply elasticity is used to measure the responsiveness of quantity supplied to changes in price.

A. Supply elasticity is measured by the ratio:

$$\frac{\text{Percentage change in quantity supplied}}{\text{Percentage change in price}} = \frac{\% \Delta Q}{\% \Delta P}$$

Both the numerator and the denominator of this ratio are expressed as percentages.

1. If the ratio is greater than 1—that is, if the percentage change in quantity supplied is greater than the percentage change in price—supply is elastic.

2. If the ratio is less than 1—that is, if the percentage change in quantity supplied is less than the percentage change in price—supply is inelastic.

3. Supply is unit elastic if the percentage change in quantity supplied is equal to the percentage change in price (the ratio is equal to 1).

B. For most commodities, supply elasticity is determined by time available for adjustments in the market.

1. In the market period (the very short run), it is normally not possible to change the supply available except by small amounts; therefore, supply tends to be inelastic.

2. In the short run, when firms may adjust production by changing the amount used of certain factors of production, supply will tend to be more responsive (more elastic) than it is in the market period.

3. In the long run, when substantial production adjustments may be made by business firms, the supply of a commodity will tend to be quite elastic or responsive to changes in price.

IV. Government may intervene in markets by controlling prices for social purposes.
   A. Price ceilings (maximum prices) may be imposed by government in order to keep commodity prices from rising. If ceilings are established *above* the market-clearing equilibrium price, there will be no effect on the market. However, if ceiling prices are established *below* the market-clearing equilibrium, shortages will result since the quantity demanded will be greater than the quantity supplied. In such a situation prices cannot rise to eliminate the shortage because they are legally set, and shortages persist.
      1. Black markets may arise when government imposes price ceilings below the market equilibrium price. A black market is an illegal transaction between buyers and sellers at prices that are greater than the legally established maximum.
   B. Price supports or minimum prices (price floors) may be imposed by government in order to keep commodity prices from falling. If support prices are established *below* the market equilibrium, there will be no effect on the market equilibrium. If, on the other hand, price supports are established *above* the market-clearing equilbrium price, excess supply (a surplus) will result since at prices above the market equilibrium quantity demanded will be less than quantity supplied. In this situation, prices cannot fall to restore equilibrium, and surplusses persist.
V.   By imposing taxes on consumer goods, government changes the market-clearing equilibrium price and quantity.
   A. If a tax is imposed on the sellers of a commodity, the imposition of the tax has the effect of increasing costs. The supply curve shifts up to the left by the full amount of the tax. When the market adjusts to this supply shift, a new equilibrium is determined.
   B. The extent to which a tax results in an increase in the commodity's price depends, in part, on the elasticity of the demand and the supply for the commodity.

KEY TERMS

You should be familiar with the meaning of the terms listed below. For definition of these terms, please refer to the glossary at the end of your textbook and to the appropriate section in this chapter.

elasticity	perfectly elastic demand
elasticity coefficient	perfectly inelastic demand
price elastic	income elasticity of demand
price inelastic	income elastic
unitary price elasticity	income inelastic
cross elasticity of demand	price ceilings
elasticity of supply	

CONCEPTS AND DEFINITIONS

Fill-in Questions

Complete each sentence by writing in the blank the most appropriate word or words from the terms listed below or by circling the word in parentheses that is correct.

price ceilings   elasticity coefficient
unitary   income elastic
price supports   elasticity
inelastic   perfectly inelastic
elastic   perfectly elastic
cross elasticity   price ceiling
supply elasticity   income inelastic

1. If the price of a good is raised and total receipts from the sale of the good increases, the demand for that good is _____.

2. The relative change in demand for butter resulting from a change in the price of oleomargarine would be measured by _____.

3. A horizontal demand curve would reflect a perfectly (inelastic/elastic) demand for a commodity.

4. In percentage terms, if consumption of steak increases more rapidly than changes in income, demand for steak may be regarded to be _____ _____.

5. _____ elasticity measures percentage change in quantity demanded as a result of percentage changes in price along a demand curve while _____ elasticity or _____ elasticity measures changes in demand resulting from shifts of the demand curve.

6. If government imposes a tax on each unit of a firm's output, that action will result in a (shift in/movement along) the firm's supply curve which will disturb the pretax equilibrium price and quantity.

7. The minimum wage is an example of a _____ where price may rise above the minimum but cannot fall below it.

8. _____ is a measure of responsiveness of quantity demanded to changes in price.

9. At the midpoint on a linear demand curve, the ratio of percentage change in quantity divided by percentage change in price would equal 1, which would indicate _____ price elasticity.

10. If firms were willing to increase production by 12 percent for every 1 percent increase in price, supply would be quite _____.

11. If shortages exist for long periods of time in a certain market, we may be reasonably certain that government has established a(n) _____ _____ which has led to excess demand. On the other hand, if government actions have resulted in continual surpluses, it is probable that a(n) _____ _____ has been established which has held the price above equilibrium.

12. If consumer demand is reflected in a vertical demand curve, demand must be _____.

13. If a 10 percent increase in the price of a commodity causes demand to change by only 5 percent, the commodity has a(n) _____ demand.

14. The value of the ratio that is a measure of the responsiveness of quantity to changes in price is known as the _____.

15. If a demand is _____, supply alone would determine changes in the equilibrium price charged for a commodity.

16. If people do not wish to buy either more or less of a good regardless of its price, their demand must be _____.

17. An elastic demand would be measured by a(n) _____ that is greater than 1.

18. If the percentage change in quantity demanded is twice as large as the percentage change in price, demand must be _____.

19. The demand for a commodity is _____ if a 5 percent change in income results in a less than 5 percent change in consumption.

20. The ratio of percentage change in quantity supplied divided by percentage change in price is a measure of _____.

21. If total revenue increases as price increases, that is an indication of (elastic/inelastic) demand, while if an increase in price causes total revenue to fall, demand would be (elastic/inelastic).

22. If a change in the price of a commodity has no effect on total sales revenue, demand for that good would be of (perfect/imperfect/unitary) elasticity.

Multiple Choice Questions

Circle the correct answer for each of the following questions.

1. If demand is elastic,

   a. the elasticity coefficient is less than 1.

   b. the change in quantity demanded is less than the percentage change in price.

   c. the change in quantity demanded is equal to the percentage change in price.

   d. the elasticity coefficient is greater than 1.

2. If government establishes a minimum wage for labor above the equilibrium price,

   a. a shortage of labor will appear on the market.

   b. an excess supply of labor will appear on the market.

   c. the law will have no market effects.

   d. the law will undoubtedly help people making low wages.

3. In a market with normally shaped (i.e., not vertical or horizontal) demand and supply curves, government levies a sales tax. It is reasonable to predict that

   a. price and quantity demanded will both increase.

   b. the equilibrium price and quantity will both decrease.

   c. price will increase while quantity demanded decreases.

   d. price will decrease while quantity demanded increases.

4. If the sales tax in problem 3 is imposed on a commodity for which demand is elastic,

   a. consumers will spend less on the good after it is taxed than before it was taxed.

   b. consumers will spend more since they are now paying a tax in addition to the commodity price.

   c. total consumer spending on the commodity will not change.

   d. it is impossible to determine what will happen to consumer spending on the commodity based upon the information provided.

5. If the demand for a commodity is perfectly inelastic, a sales tax on the commodity will

   a. be evenly split between consumers and business firms.

   b. be fully paid by consumers.

   c. have no effect on the market price.

   d. result in a change in quantity demanded.

6. The demand elasticity in an industry producing similar products was reported to be 2. One firm in the industry lowered its price by 10 percent and experienced a sales gain of 40 percent. This indicates that

   a. demand elasticity is affected by the availability of substitute products.

   b. the single firm's sales should have increased only by 20 percent.

   c. the firm has an inelastic demand.

   d. the industry elasticity estimate is undoubtedly incorrect.

7. If different values of elasticity are found at different points along a linear demand curve,

   a. the calculations used to derive the elasticities must be incorrect.

b. the law of demand is confirmed.

c. the good must be a necessity.

d. the demand curve is horizontal.

8. In order for a price increase to cause an increase in total revenue

   a. demand must be elastic.

   b. demand must be inelastic.

   c. demand elasticity must equal 1.

   d. price could increase or decrease.

9. If the demand for a commodity is elastic,

   a. its cost may be large relative to income.

   b. the commodity is probably a necessity.

   c. the elasticity coefficient is less than 1.

   d. total revenue will increase if price goes up.

10. The elasticity of supply for a commodity

   a. will change only if the good is a necessity.

   b. will be different in the market period than in the short or long run.

   c. determines the equilibrium price and quantity marketed.

   d. is a measure of the extent to which consumers want the product.

11. If a 10 percent change in income results in a 5 percent change in consumption of a particular service, it can be determined that

   a. demand for the service is income elastic.

   b. the supply elasticity is less than 1.

   c. the result of a shift in the demand curve is being measured.

   d. there are a large number of substitutes for the service.

12. A price ceiling imposed on apartment rents

   a. will always cause excess demand for rental units.

   b. will disrupt the market only if the ceiling is higher than the market equilibrium price.

   c. will result in excess supply in the market for rental units.

   d. may give rise to black market transactions.

APPLICATIONS

1. As a result of record profits during the third quarter of 1979, one oil company announced that gasoline prices would be lowered by a few cents per gallon.

When this policy took effect, the price of regular gasoline dropped from $1.02 to 98¢ per gallon. Shortly thereafter, consumption was observed to increase, on the average, by 3 percent.

a. From the data given above, use the midpoint formula to determine the elasticity coefficient for the demand for regular gasoline.

b. On the basis of the elasticity coefficient determined above, state whether the demand for regular gasoline is elastic or inelastic.

c. On the basis of the elastic coefficient, do you think consumers will spend more or less on regular after the price is lowered from $1.02 to 98¢ per gallon? Justify your answer.

d. If instead of lowering the price of regular by 4¢ per gallon, the oil company had raised its price by 4¢, what impact would that have on the total revenue of that oil company? (Use your estimate of demand elasticity from Part a in answering this problem.)

2. The demand elasticity for residential consumption of natural gas is estimated to be approximately .85. If natural gas prices are deregulated as a part of the president's energy policy, what will happen to consumer expenditures on this commodity assuming that higher prices will result from the deregulation?

3. a. If the supply elasticity coefficient for ball-point pens is 3, by how much should production change as a result of a 5 percent increase in the price of ball-point pens?

b. An individual's income increased from $48 to $52 per day and subsequently, his consumption of oleomargarine declined by 2 percent. From these data, determine the coefficient of income elasticity for the commodity oleomargarine and state whether demand is income elastic or income inelastic.

4. At the present time, American farmers are asking Congress to establish minimum prices for certain agricultural goods. Assume that Congress responds to this call and establishes minimum prices for certain farm commodities above the current equilibrium levels.

a. What effect would you expect to follow the action taken by Congress? Why?

b. If the demand for agricultural products is inelastic, how will the actions taken by Congress affect the incomes of farmers? What will happen to consumer expenditures on farm products subject to the minimum price legislation? Justify your answers.

c. Suppose that consumer advocate groups succeed in influencing Congress to amend the farm bill to read *maximum* prices above equilibrium rather than *minimum* prices above equilibrium. How, if at all, would that change your answer to Part a of this problem?

5. In response to consumer complaints about skyrocketing rental housing costs, the Los Angeles city offficials recently enacted a rent-control law which established maximum prices that can be charged for rental dwellings within the city limits. Assume that the legal ceilings are below the prevailing rents being charged up to the effective date of the act.

   a. Suppose the Los Angeles city officials ask you for your opinion concerning the effects that this law can be expected to have on the rental-housing market in Los Angeles. What is your expert opinion? A graph may help you determine your answers.

   b. What impact, if any, would you expect this law to have on the rental-housing markets in areas surrounding Los Angeles where no rent-control laws are in effect? Again, a graph may help you determine your answer. (Hint: Think about the possibility of demand or supply changes in these nearby markets as a result of actions taken by the Los Angeles city officials.)

ANSWERS

Fill-in Questions

1. inelastic
2. cross elasticity
3. inelastic
4. income elastic
5. price; income; cross
6. shift in
7. price support (or price floor)
8. elasticity
9. unitary
10. elastic
11. price ceiling (or maximum price); price support (or minimum price or price floor)
12. perfectly elastic
13. inelastic
14. elasticity coefficient
15. perfectly inelastic
16. perfectly inelastic
17. elasticity coefficient
18. elastic
19. income inelastic
20. supply elasticity
21. inelastic; elastic
22. unitary

Multiple Choice Questions

1. d
2. b
3. c
4. a
5. b
6. a
7. b
8. b
9. a
10. b
11. c
12. d

APPLICATIONS

1.

   a. The midpoint formula is:

$$E_D = \frac{\% \text{ change } Q}{\% \text{ change } P} = \frac{\text{change } Q}{(Q_1 + Q_2)/2} \div \frac{\text{change } P.}{(P_1 + P_2)/2}$$

The percentage change in price is computed by dividing the change in price, $4^\cent$, by \$1.00, the average price.

$$\frac{.04}{1.00} = 0.4 = 4\%$$

The percent change in quantity is given: 3 percent. Thus, the elasticity coefficient for regular is 3/4.

   b. Demand for regular gasoline is inelastic because the elasticity coefficient is less than 1. When the percentage change in quantity is smaller than the percentage change in price, demand is inelastic.

   c. Consumer spending (price paid per unit times the number of units purchased) should drop since price is being reduced along an inelastic demand curve.

   d. The oil company's total revenue would increase with an increase in price as long as demand remained inelastic.

2. Consumer expenditures will increase since prices are assumed to rise along an inelastic demand curve.

3.

   a. Production should increase by 15 percent. The elasticity coefficient (3) is given, as is the percent change in price (a 5 percent increase). Using the formula

$$E_S = \frac{\% \Delta Q}{\% \Delta P},$$

we come up with the following equation:

$$3 = \frac{\% \Delta Q.}{5\%}$$

By multiplying both sides of the equation by 5 percent, we can solve the problem:

$$3 \times 5\% = \frac{\% \Delta Q}{5\%} \times \frac{5\%}{1},$$

which equals $15\% = \% \Delta Q$.

   b. The percentage change in income is 8 percent. Thus, the elasticity coefficient is 1/4, which indicates that oleomargarine is income inelastic (the percent change in quantity is less than the percent change in income). The answer is arrived at as follows: The formula for income elasticity is

$$E_Y^D = \frac{\% \Delta Q}{\% \Delta \text{ income}}$$

Percent change in income is computed as follows:

$$\frac{\Delta Y}{(Y_1 + Y_2)/2} = \frac{4}{(48 + 52)/2} = \frac{4}{50} = 0.8 = 8\%$$

Percent change in quantity of margarine purchased is given as 2 percent.

$$E_Y^D = \frac{2\%}{8\%} = \frac{1}{4}$$

4.

a. If minimum prices above equilibrium are established by Congress, the market will not clear and surpluses can be expected.

b. If demand is inelastic and prices rise, both incomes for farmers and consumer expenditures on farm goods must increase.

c. A maximum price above equilibrium would have no short-run effect on the market, since the market can reach or remain at equilibrium.

5.

a. It can be expected that the law will create shortages since, at a price below the equilibrium rental, quantity demanded will be greater than quantity supplied. Over time, the problem of shortages should become worse since the supply of rental housing can be expected to decline as a result of the price ceiling. Deterioration of some units will account for some of the reduced supply, and the conversion of rental units to other uses (office space, condominiums) which are not subject to the rent-control law would account for additional supply reduction.

b. Individuals unable to find rental housing in the Los Angeles area will undoubtedly seek shelter in nearby areas. In general, we would expect this to increase the demand for rental housing in the adjacent areas, driving up rental prices and, perhaps, generating political support for rent-control statutes in these areas.

Chapter 21

Consumer Demand

LEARNING OBJECTIVES

This chapter introduces marginal utility and indifference analysis as alternative explanations underlying the law of demand which was first presented in Chapter 3. Although both approaches assume that consumers will maximize their utility, marginal utility analysis requires measurable utility data while the more modern, indifference curve approach is based upon the ability of individuals to identify and express preferences when confronted with choice.

After reading this chapter, you should be able to:

1. explain how the law of diminishing marginal utility influences an individual's demand for economic goods;

2 describe how the law of diminishing marginal utility is used to explain why consumer demand curves are negatively sloped;

3. use indifference curve analysis to analyze problems involving maximizing behavior by consumers;

4. identify and discuss the effects that changing relative prices have on the buying behavior of consumers.

CHAPTER OUTLINE

I. In economics, there are two distinct approaches to the theory of demand: marginal utility theory and indifference theory.
    A. Marginal utility theory assumes that people wish to obtain maximum satisfaction or utility from their expenditures on goods and services. This theory assumes that the satisfaction derived from consuming goods and services is measurable.
        1. Total utility is a measure of the *total satisfaction* obtained from all units of a good consumed.

2. Marginal utility measures the *change in total satisfaction* that results from consuming a little more or less of an item.
   a. According to the law of diminishing marginal utility, beyond some point, additional units of a good consumed in a given time period will yield smaller and smaller additional amounts of satisfaction.
   b. The utility of a marginal unit of a good or service determines the price that a consumer will pay for different amounts of that good or service.
   c. Because of the law of diminishing marginal utility, consumer demand curves are downward sloping; that is, more units will be purchased only if the price is lowered.
   d. If a consumer obtains utility from a commodity that is greater than its price in the market, that difference is known as consumer surplus.
   e. The attempt to balance marginal utility per last dollar spent is called the equal marginal utility principal. Consumers will adjust the quantities of goods and services in order to obtain the greatest total utility. They will adjust their spending until
   $$\frac{MU_1}{P_1} = \frac{MU_2}{P_2} = \frac{MU_3}{P_3}.$$
3. Total utility is maximized when the last dollar spent on each good is equal to the amount of satisfaction received from the additional unit of the good.

B. Indifference theory provides an alternative explanation of consumer demand and does not require explicit measurement of utility or satisfaction. Indifference theory requires that consumers rank commodities and determine which combinations of particular goods yield equivalent satisfaction (are equally preferred).
   1. Alternative combinations of two goods that yield the same amount of satisfaction can be plotted on a graph to form an indifference curve.
   2. Along any indifference curve, consumer satisfaction is the same—since any of the combinations shown on a single indifference curve are equally preferred, the consumer is assumed to be indifferent among them.
   3. The marginal rate of substitution refers to the number of units that a consumer is willing to sacrifice to obtain an additional unit of another good, with total satisfaction remaining the same. Although a movement along an indifference curve indicates that a different combination of goods is consumed, total satisfaction remains constant.
   4. A set of indifference curves that describes the full range of a consumer's preferences is called an indifference map. On any indifference map, indifference curves that are closer to the origin represent lower levels of satisfaction while those further from the origin indicate greater levels of satisfaction.
   5. An individual's income or budget determines the highest level of satisfaction that can be obtained. Optimal, or utility maximizing, consumption is shown by the highest indifference curve touched by the budget-constraint line.

II. The law of demand is formulated by observing the behavior of consumers in the market. Their behavior is affected by a number of determinants.

A. Consumers are influenced by changes in the relative prices of goods. A change in relative prices occurs when the price of one good changes and other prices do not change, or when several prices change but they do not change by equal percentage amounts.

1. As prices change, consumers tend to purchase more units of those goods that become relatively cheaper, and purchase fewer units of those goods whose relative prices have increased. This is known as the substitution effect.

B. Consumer behavior is also influenced by changes in real income or purchasing power. This is known as the income effect.

C. As the price of a good changes, consumer purchasing power also changes so that consumer demand can be influenced both by a substitution effect and by an income effect.

KEY TERMS

You should be familiar with the meaning of the terms listed below. For definition of these terms, please refer to the glossary at the end of your textbook and to the appropriate section in this chapter.

utility	indifference map
marginal utility	marginal rate of substitution
law of diminishing marginal utility	budget-constraint line
consumer surplus	substitution effect
equal marginal utility principle	income effect
indifference curve	

CONCEPTS AND DEFINITIONS

Fill-in Questions

Complete each sentence by writing in the blank the most appropriate word or words from the terms listed below or by circling the word in parentheses that is correct.

budget-constraint line	marginal utility
law of diminishing marginal utility	substitution effect
indifference curve	income effect
indifference map	consumer surplus
marginal rate of substitution	equal marginal utility
utility	

1. A(n) _____ is a collection of indifference curves that displays the full range of consumer preferences.

2. Economists often refer to consumer satisfaction as _____.

3. If the prices of all commodities increase proportionately, but John Fredericks changes his buying habits, economists would classify this as a change in consumption due to a(n) _____.

4. If I obtain 25 units of satisfaction from a single-scoop ice cream cone and 40 units of satisfaction from a double dip, the additional satisfaction from the second scoop is known as _____.

5. In problem 4, the fact that the additional utility obtained from the second scoop of ice cream (15 units) was less than that obtained from the first (25 units) is an example of the _____.

6. Indifference theory avoids the problem of measuring utility by using a(n) _____ to show various combinations of two economic goods that yield equivalent satisfaction to an individual consumer.

7. The high price of diamonds (which are not essential to life) and the low price of water (which is essential) may be explained by using the _____.

8. If the price of one good has increased and subsequently a consumer buys less of that good and more of a closely related good whose price has not changed, this change in consumption would be attributed to a(n) _____.

9. The _____ states that the marginal satisfaction per dollar spent on each and every commodity must be the same if satisfaction is to be at a maximum.

10. Although according to indifference theory individuals are assumed to prefer more to less, their ability to consume more is limited by the _____.

11. Milk costs $1.70 per gallon at the store. However, consumers would be willing to pay $2.50 per gallon rather than do without it. The difference between the market price and the consumer valuation of milk (80¢) is the _____.

12. The gains and losses of economic goods that would be required to move from one point on an indifference curve to another point on the same curve are measured by the _____.

13. According to _____ theory, consumers are able to measure the amount of satisfaction they receive from the consumption of all economic goods.

14. Beyond a certain point, additional units of a good consumed in a given time will yield (greater/smaller) additional amounts of satisfaction.

15. A consumer will maximize her satisfaction by purchasing that combination of goods represented by the the point at which her _____ is tangent to her highest possible _____.

16. In making his purchases, the consumer tries to maximize _____.

17. The difference between the total utility a consumer derives from 10 units of a commodity and the price of the 10 units is called _____.

18. A movement along an indifference curve indicates that total satisfaction is (increasing/decreasing/staying the same).

Multiple Choice Questions

Circle the correct answer.

1. All economic theories of consumer behavior assume that individuals seek to maximize

   a. the amount of goods and services they consume.

   b. satisfaction from goods and services they consume.

   c. income for purposes of consumption.

   d. the sale of their resources in factor markets.

2. If a good provides utility, that means the good

   a. is useful.

   b. must have several different uses.

   c. must be a necessity.

   d. must provide satisfaction.

3. The marginal utility derived from consuming an additional unit of a good is equal to

   a. the total utility obtained from consuming all units of the good divided by the number of units consumed.

   b. the total utility derived from consumption divided by the change in consumption.

   c. the change in total utility divided by the change in consumption.

   d. the total utility associated with consuming all units of the good divided by the price of the good.

4. Consumer surplus is

   a. the difference between price and cost of a good.

   b. the difference between value obtained and the market price of a good.

   c. the amount that different consumers must pay for goods.

   d. the amount of surplus commodities available to individuals on public assistance.

5. To maximize total utility according to the equal marginal utility principle,

   a. the total utility derived from the consumption of each good must be equal.

   b. the marginal utility derived from the consumption of each good must be equal.

   c. an equal amount of money must be spent on each good consumed.

   d. the marginal utility per dollar spent on each good must be equal.

6. If $MU_1 \over P_1$ is greater than $MU_2 \over P_2$, the consumer will be able to increase total utility by

   a. buying less of good 1 and more of good 2.

   b. buying less of goods 1 and 2.

   c. buying less of good 2 and more of good 1.

   d. leaving the amount consumed of each good unchanged.

7. A utility maximizer consuming two goods, 1 and 2, is confronted with a 10 percent increase in the price of good 1. In order for this individual to continue to maximize satisfaction, he should

   a. buy more of both goods.

   b. buy more of good 1 and less of good 2.

   c. buy more of good 2 and less of good 1.

   d. reevaluate the marginal utility of each good.

8. Marginal utility theory has been rejected as a useful way in which to determine consumer demand because

   a. people are rarely satisfied with their purchases of mass-produced goods.

   b. people lack the background in mathematics to perform the calculations (required by the equal marginal utility principle).

   c. individuals have no conception of the worth or value of individual goods.

   d. the satisfaction obtained from consuming goods cannot be measured objectively.

9. An individual is maximizing satisfaction according to indifference theory when the

   a. marginal rate of substitution is constant.

   b. consumer's budget-constraint line intersects an indifference curve.

   c. indifference curve intersects the budget-constraint line in two places.

   d. budget-constraint line just touches but does not intersect the consumer indifference curve.

10. In attempting to maximize his satisfaction the consumer will adjust his purchases between two or more goods until

   a. all marginal utilities are equal.

   b. $\dfrac{MU_1}{P_1} > \dfrac{MU_2}{P_2}$

   c. $\dfrac{MU_1}{P_1} = \dfrac{MU_2}{P_2}$

   d. $\dfrac{P_1}{U_1} = \dfrac{P_2}{U_2}$

11. As the price of any commodity declines,

    a. consumer purchases will change because of a substitution effect and an increase in real income.

    b. consumer purchases will change because real incomes have fallen.

    c. consumers will substitute goods that are more expensive for the one that is less expensive.

    d. the quantity demanded will fall as a result of a change in relative prices and an income effect.

12. The law of demand is confirmed by

    a. the income effect in which an increase in prices raises real income.

    b. the substitution effect in which an increase in the price of a good causes people to seek lower-priced substitutes.

    c. the income effect in which a decrease in price lowers real income.

    d. the substitution effect in which a decrease in the price of a good causes people to seek lower-priced substitutes.

APPLICATIONS

1. After finishing a difficult week at school, John Hill visited his local pub. Assume that John receives satisfaction from consuming pretzels and beer. Shown below are John's *total* utility schedules for pretzels and beer. (The units of satisfaction are expressed in "utils.")

Pitchers of beer per evening	Total utility "utils"	Marginal utility of beer (MU_b)	$\dfrac{MU_b}{P_b}$
0	0		
1	10		
2	19		
3	27		
4	34		
5	40		

Bowls of Pretzels per evening	Total utility "utils"	Marginal utility of pretzels (MU_p)	$\dfrac{MU_p}{P_p}$
0	0		
1	8		
2	13		
3	17		
4	20		
5	22		

a. Compute John's marginal utility schedules for both beer and pretzels.

b. Suppose that the price of beer is $2.00 per pitcher, that pretzels are $1.00 per bowl, and that John only has $9.00 to spend on food and drink. What will the utility-maximizing consumption amounts of beer and pretzels be? (That is, how much of each will he buy?) Assume that all funds are spent on only these two goods.

c. What is the value of the total utility resulting from John's expenditures? (Assume he wants to maximize satisfaction and that he goes home broke.)

2. The figures below represent an individual's demand curve for a commodity.

Price	Quantity
$10	1
9	2
8	3
7	4
6	5
5	6
4	7
3	8

a. If the market price of the good is $4.00, how much will be purchased by the individual?

b. What is the total amount of money that the individual must pay for the goods purchased?

c. What is the total monetary value to the individual of the goods purchased?

d. Is there any consumer surplus resulting from this purchase? If so, how much? If not, why not?

3. Using marginal utility analysis as a basis for your answer, explain why diamonds are expensive and water is cheap—especially since everyone needs water to live while diamonds, under most circumstances, are luxury items.

4. The figure on p. 203 illustrates some indifference curves and a budget-constraint line for an individual. Use this information to answer the following questions.

a. Which line(s) in the figure represent the individual's indifference curves?

b. Which line(s) in the figure represent the individual's budget constraint?

c. Indicate whether the statements below are true or false.

TRUE   FALSE

1. The consumption bundle at point C yields the same satisfaction as the consumption bundle at point E.   _____   _____

2. Consumption bundles C and D yield the same level of satisfaction.   _____   _____

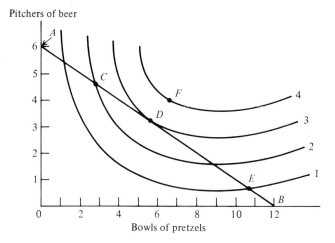

Pitchers of beer

Bowls of pretzels

3. Consumption at point *D* would be preferred to consumption at point *A*.   _____ _____

4. Consumption at point *D* would be preferred to consumption at point *F*.   _____ _____

5. If the consumer wanted to maximize satisfaction, point *A* with 6 units of beer would be most desirable.   _____ _____

6. The price of pretzels according to the information provided must be twice that of beer.   _____ _____

7. If the indifference curves were ranked from least preferred to most preferred, the order would be 4, 3, 2, 1.   _____ _____

8. The consumer cannot buy the consumption bundle represented by point *F* because of the restriction of his budget constraint.   _____ _____

ANSWERS

Fill-in Questions

1. indifference map
2. utility
3. income effect
4. marginal utility
5. law of diminishing marginal utility
6. indifference curve
7. law of diminishing marginal utility
8. substitution effect
9. equal marginal utility principal

10. budget-constraint line
11. consumer surplus
12. marginal rate of substitution
13. marginal utility
14. smaller
15. budget-constraint line; indifference curve
16. utility
17. consumer surplus
18. staying the same

Multiple Choice Questions

1.	b	7.	c
2.	d	8.	d
3.	c	9.	d
4.	b	10.	c
5.	d	11.	a
6.	c	12.	b

APPLICATIONS

1. a.

Pitchers	MU_b	$\dfrac{MU_b}{P_b}$	Bowls	MU_p	$\dfrac{MU_p}{P_p}$
0	—	—	0	—	—
1	10	10/\$2 = 5	1	8	8/\$1 = 8
2	9	4.5	2	5	5
3	8	4	3	4	4
4	7	3.5	4	3	3
5	6	3	5	2	2

b. To maximize utility, increase purchases to the point where $\dfrac{MU_b}{P_b} = \dfrac{MU_p}{P_p}$ and all income is spent. Utility is at a maximum with 3 beers and 3 pretzels.

c. Total utility is 44. This figure can be obtained directly by adding the total utilities of beer and pretzels at the maximizing point. (At 3 pitchers, the total utility of beer is 27; at 3 bowls of pretzels, total utility is 17: 17 + 27 = 44.) This figure can also be obtained indirectly by adding the marginal utilities of the commodities consumed up to the maximizing point (for beer: 10 + 9 + 8 = 27; for pretzels: 8 + 5 + 4 = 17.)

2. a. 7 units.

   b. \$28 (7 units × \$4.00 ea.).

   c. Total value is equal to 10 + 9 + 8 + 7 + 6 + 5 + 4 = \$49.

   d. There is a consumer surplus of \$21 (\$49 − \$28).

3. Although the total utility from the consumption of water is greater than the total utility from the consumption of diamonds, the marginal utility of water is low because of its relative abundance. On the other hand, although the total satisfaction gained from diamonds is lower than that gained from water, their relative scarcity causes the marginal or extra satisfaction from one more diamond to be high. Therefore, people are willing to pay a higher price for an additional diamond and a low price for an additional unit of water. If you are

still uncertain of this explanation, consider the extreme case: If you were stranded in the desert for a long time without water, the marginal value of water would increase enormously so that you would be willing to offer a very high price (perhaps all of your diamonds) for even a small amount of water.

4. a. The indifference curves are represented by the lines 1, 2, 3, and 4.

    b. Line *AB* is the individual's budget-constraint line.

    c. 1. False

        2. False

        3. True

        4. False

        5. False

        6. False

        7. False

        8. True

Chapter 22

The Costs of Production

LEARNING OBJECTIVES

In Chapter 3 we discussed the law of supply, which postulates a direct relationship between the market price of a good and the quantity of that good that a firm is willing and able to sell. In this chapter we will analyze the firm's costs of production and will see why the direct relationship between price and quantity supplied exists. The analysis presented in this chapter is central to an understanding of how a firm will respond to a change in costs of production or a change in the market price.

After reading this chapter, you should be able to:

1. identify the features that distinguish short-run production from long-run production;

2. describe how a firm's short-run output changes as additional amounts of variable factors of production are combined with fixed factors of production;

3. identify how a firm's physical production relationships determine its short-run variable costs of production;

4. describe the relationship between a firm's per unit costs and its total costs of production;

5. analyze both tabular and graphic presentations of cost data for a typical firm;

6. discuss the manner in which firms make long-run decisions about the scale of operations.

CHAPTER OUTLINE

I.   In producing an output, a firm incurs explicit costs (costs of buying and possessing productive resources) and implicit costs (the amount of money needed to bid all necessary resources away from alternative uses). Implicit costs plus explicit costs equal total costs.
A. When a firm's revenues exactly equal its total costs, it earns a normal profit.

    B. Revenue in excess of total costs provides an economic profit.

II. Two types of economic resources are used in producing an output: variable inputs (those resources that can be changed as output changes; that is, changed
in the short run) and fixed inputs (those resources that cannot be changed
quickly in response to a decision to produce more or less output; that is, cannot be changed in the short run).

    A. The alternative levels of output that a firm is able to produce by changing
the amounts of variable resources that are combined with fixed resources is
shown by a total product curve (Fig. 1).

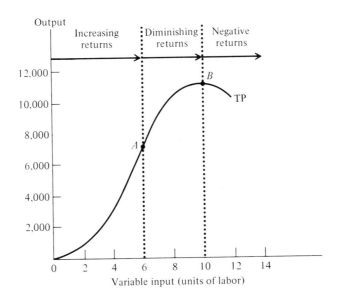

Figure 1.

    1. Usually, a total product curve contains three distinct regions: a region of
increasing returns, a region of decreasing returns, and a region of
negative returns.

       a. Increasing returns usually occur when output is small because so few
variable resources are combined with the firm's fixed resources that
the production process is inefficient. As additional units of a variable
input are used, output increases.

       b. Diminishing returns occur when increased use of variable inputs
begins to result in less than proportionate gains in output. That is,
each additional unit of variable input results in a smaller increase in
output than the previous additional unit.

       c. Negative returns occur when total output actually drops as more and
more variable resources are combined with fixed resources.

    B. The additional output obtained by adding more variable resources to fixed
resources is known as the marginal product. It is defined as the change in

total output divided by the change in the amount of variable input used in production.

C. The average product is the ratio of total product to the total amount of variable resources used. Together with marginal product data, it provides a measure of the efficiency with which the firm utilizes its fixed and variable resources.

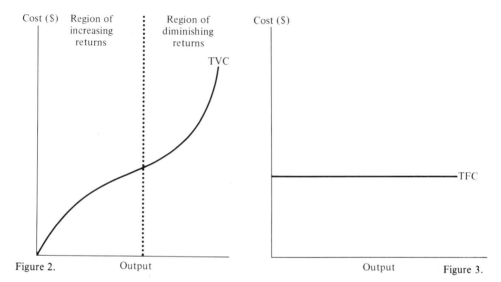

Figure 2.   Output   Output   Figure 3.

III. In the short run, the firm incurs both fixed costs (costs that cannot be increased or decreased in the short run) and variable costs (costs that can be increased or decreased in the short run). The sum of these two costs equals the firm's total cost of production.

A. In order to produce more output, a firm must employ more variable resources. Hence its total variable costs of production will increase as output increases. This can be seen in the total variable cost curve (Fig. 2).

1. In the region of increasing returns, output can be increased by a less than proportionate increase in the amount of variable resources used. Thus, although *total* variable costs go up as more variable resources are used, these costs increase more slowly than output increases.

2. In the region of diminishing returns, ever larger amounts of variable inputs are required to obtain a given increase in output. In this region the increases in total variable costs are much greater than the corresponding increases in output.

B. In the short run, a firm's total fixed costs of production (commonly referred to as overhead costs) will not change as output changes. Graphically, these costs are shown by a horizontal line (see Fig. 3).

C. Short-run production decisions frequently require unit cost data rather than total cost figures.

1. The marginal cost of production is the additional cost incurred by a firm in producing additional units of output. It is defined as *the change* in total cost divided by *the change* in total output.
2. The firm's fixed, variable, and total costs of production may be expressed on a per-unit or average basis.
   a. Average fixed cost is equal to total fixed cost divided by quantity of output.
   b. Average variable cost is equal to total variable cost divided by quantity of output.
   c. Average total cost is equal to total cost divided by quantity of output. Average total cost is also equal to the sum of average fixed cost and average variable cost.

IV. In the long run, a firm can vary the amount of all resources used in production. That is, the size of the plant and equipment which cannot be altered in the short run can be changed over time. Thus, the long run can be regarded as a planning period in which the firm will attempt to find the most economical plant size, the one that provides the lowest unit cost for the level of output the entrepreneur expects to produce.

A. A firm seeks to minimize costs *given* output; it does not select an output according to the minimum ATC of its existing plant. It selects an output and builds the plant in which the output can be produced at the lowest cost.

KEY TERMS

You should be familiar with the meaning of the terms listed below. For definition of these terms, please refer to the glossary at the end of your textbook and to the appropriate section in this chapter.

normal profit	variable costs
fixed inputs	fixed costs
variable inputs	total cost curve
total product curve	marginal cost curve
marginal product	average fixed costs
average product	average variable costs
total cost	average total cost

CONCEPTS AND DEFINITIONS

Fill-in Questions

Complete each sentence by writing in the blank the most appropriate word or words from the terms listed below or by circling the word in parentheses that is correct.

implicit costs   total cost

explicit costs
fixed costs
marginal cost
total fixed cost
average fixed cost
total variable cost
average variable cost

variable inputs
fixed inputs
average product
marginal product
total product curve
average product
normal profit

1. In the long run, a firm will not have any _____ costs.

2. If it costs $5000 to produce 50 units of output and $5200 to produce 51, then the _____ is equal to $200.

3. If total variable costs are subtracted from total costs, the difference is _____.

4. The change in total output divided by the change in the amount of variable inputs used is a definition of the _____.

5. _____ is equal to total variable cost divided by output or quantity.

6. The relationship between a firm's use of variable resources and total output may be shown graphically on a _____.

7. If resources used in production by a firm are earning as much as they could in any alternative use, the firm is making a _____.

8. The _____ curve shows the sum of all costs incurred by a firm in short-run production.

9. The slope of the total product curve measures the _____.

10. If the average fixed cost of production is subtracted from average total cost, the difference is the _____.

11. To determine _____ it is necessary to divide a firm's total output by the total amount of variable resources used in production.

12. In the short run, the amount of _____ used by a firm in production will vary directly with changes in output.

13. As a firm's output gets larger and larger, _____ will always get smaller and smaller since a fixed sum is being divided by an ever-increasing number.

14. The _____ of production is equal to the sum of all implicit and explicit costs incurred in production. It is also equal to the sum of _____ and _____.

15. When the change in total cost is divided by the change in quantity, the resulting number is known as the _____ of production.

16. In the short run, the amount of certain resources used by a firm cannot be changed; consequently, these resources are known as _____.

17. The slope of the total cost curve is equal to _____.

18. _____ is another name for overhead costs or costs that do not vary in the short run with changes in output.

19. The costs to the firm of buying and processing inputs are called _____ .

20. The opportunity costs to the firm of staying in business are called _____ .

Multiple Choice Questions

Circle the correct answer.

1. If a firm's revenues are exactly equal to the sum of implicit and explicit costs,

    a. the firm is making an explicit profit.
    b. the firm is making an implicit profit.
    c. the firm is making an economic profit.
    d. the firm is making a normal profit.

2. The single feature that distinguishes the short run from the long run is

    a. the amount of variable factors used in production.
    b. the amount of time it takes to produce an output.
    c. the existence of fixed costs.
    d. the cost of obtaining capital goods.

3. In the short run, a firm may not

    a. increase its total productive capacity.
    b. increase its use of variable resources.
    c. experience increasing or decreasing returns.
    d. make an economic profit.

4. The total product curve for a typical firm shows

    a. the relationship between production and sales.
    b. a direct relationship between variable inputs and output.

   c. the total amount of output divided by the total amount of input.

   d. the relationship between fixed inputs and output.

5. In the range of increasing returns, a firm could, in the short run,

   a. double output by doubling fixed inputs.

   b. double output by doubling variable inputs.

   c. double output by using less than twice as many variable resources.

   d. double output by using less than twice as many fixed resources.

6. Diminishing returns is a situation in which

   a. the marginal product of variable inputs is negative.

   b. the marginal product of variable inputs is usually positive.

   c. total output is falling.

   d. average output is increasing at a very slow rate.

7. If a firm experiences negative returns,

   a. the total product curve is horizontal.

   b. the firm's marginal product curve is above its average product curve.

   c. the firm's costs of production are lower than if returns were positive.

   d. output could be increased by laying off workers.

8. If a firm can produce 9000 units of output with 7 workers and 10,200 units of output with 8 workers

   a. the marginal product of labor is equal to 9000 + 10,200 divided by 15 workers.

   b. the marginal product of labor is equal to 1290 units of output.

   c. the marginal product of labor is equal to 1200 units of output.

   d. the marginal product of labor cannot be computed from the data provided.

9. If the average product of 3 workers is 600 units of output and of 4 workers is 750, then

   a. the marginal product of labor must be greater than the average product of labor.

   b. the marginal product of labor is equal to 150 units of output.

   c. the firm is experiencing diminishing returns.

   d. the firm's total output is increasing but at a decreasing rate.

10. If the average production of 10 workers is 1100 units, total output is equal to

   a. 110 units.

    b. 1100 units.

    c. 11,000 units.

    d. 110,000 units.

11. The value of the average product for a typical firm will always increase

    a. as long as the firm experiences either increasing or decreasing marginal returns.

    b. regardless of the amount of variable resources used in production.

    c. only while marginal productivity is rising.

    d. up until the point where diminishing returns set in.

12. The total fixed cost of production for a firm in the short run is equal to

    a. variable costs plus total costs.

    b. total cost minus total fixed cost.

    c. the marginal cost of production times the number of units of output produced.

    d. (average total cost minus average variable cost) times quantity.

13. If the average fixed cost of production for a firm is $40 at a production level of 5 units, and if total variable cost is $72, what is the total cost of production for that level of output?

    a. $272.00

    b. $560.00

    c. $400.00

    d. $22.40

14. If a firm's total cost of producing 10 units of output is $570 and the marginal cost of the 11th unit is $150, the total cost of producing 11 units of output is

    a. $207.00

    b. $150 − $57.00

    c. $2277.00

    d. $720.00

15. If a firm's management decides to change the size of the plant and equipment used to produce an output,

    a. that decision would entail long-run analysis since the firm cannot make changes in plant and equipment in the short run.

    b. they will always be able to find a scale of plant that has lower per-unit costs than their present plant.

c. they will first build a plant and then determine the appropriate output to minimize average total costs.

d. they will always find it to their advantage to overutilize a small plant rather than underutilize a larger one.

16. Suppose a friend of yours decides to go into business producing handmade candles. For the level of output she wishes to produce, she estimates that she must pay $200 per month for wax, $500 per month for another worker, $100 per month for her candle-making studio, and $100 per month for miscellaneous decorations. All of these costs are

a. implicit costs.

b. explicit costs.

c. variable costs.

d. total costs.

17. The funds invested in the candle business could earn $200 per year if placed in a savings account. The proprietor is also giving up a salary of $6000 per year if she worked part-time for U.S. Candles, Inc. These costs are

a. implicit costs.

b. explicit costs.

c. variable costs.

d. total costs.

APPLICATIONS

1. In the space provided, write the formula for each of the following:

a. Average fixed cost _____

b. Average variable cost _____

c. Average total cost _____

d. Marginal cost _____

2. Complete each of the following statements by specifying the computations necessary to determine the answer.

a. If you knew average total cost, you could compute total cost by _____

b. If you knew total cost and total fixed cost, you could compute total variable cost by _____.

c. If you knew average variable cost and total fixed cost, you could compute total cost by _____.

3. Supply the missing figures in the table below. All amounts are in dollars.

Quantity	Total fixed costs	Total variable costs	Total costs	Average fixed costs	Average variable costs	Average total costs	Marginal cost
0		0		xxx	xxx	xxx	xxx
1					20		
2			46				
3							8
4						14	
5				2			9

4. a. In a concise statement, explain what is meant by the law of diminishing returns as that "law" pertains to short-run production for a typical firm.

   b. Explain why the law of diminishing returns is not used when dealing with production in the long run.

5. Determine whether the following statement is true or false, and justify your answer: "If the average cost curve is rising, the marginal cost curve must also be rising."

6. Complete each of the following statements:

   a. In the region of increasing returns for the firm, output is increasing at an increasing rate; therefore, total variable cost is increasing at a(n) (increasing/decreasing) rate.

   b. In the region of diminishing (but not negative) returns, output is increasing at a decreasing rate; therefore, total variable cost is increasing at an (increasing/decreasing) rate.

   c. In the region of negative returns, output is falling while total variable cost is (increasing/decreasing).

7. With reference to the law of diminishing returns, explain why the average variable cost curve for a typical firm is "U"-shaped.

8. Explain why the firm's average fixed cost curve will always have a negative slope as output increases.

9. Marginal cost is defined as the change in total cost divided by the change in quantity. In looking at the table in problem 3, it can be seen that marginal cost is also the change in total variable cost divided by the change in quantity. Explain why these two different approaches to determining marginal cost yield the same result.

ANSWERS

Fill-in Questions

1. fixed
2. marginal cost
3. total fixed cost
4. marginal product
5. average variable cost
6. total product curve
7. normal profit
8. total cost
9. marginal product
10. average variable cost
11. average product
12. variable inputs
13. average fixed cost
14. total cost; total fixed cost; total variable cost
15. marginal cost
16. fixed inputs
17. marginal cost
18. total fixed cost
19. explicit costs
20. implicit costs

Multiple Choice Questions

1. d
2. c
3. a
4. b
5. c
6. b
7. d
8. c
9. a
10. c
11. d
12. d
13. a
14. d
15. a
16. b
17. a

APPLICATIONS

1. a. TFC/Q (total fixed cost/quantity)
   b. TVC/Q (total variable cost/quantity)
   c. TC/Q (total cost/quantity)
   d. change TC/change Q (change in total cost/change in quantity)
2. a. multiplying total cost by quantity.
   b. subtracting total fixed cost from total cost.
   c. multiplying average variable cost by quantity, and adding that figure to total fixed cost.

3. Quantity	Total fixed costs	Total variable costs	Total costs	Average fixed costs	Average variable costs	Average total costs	Marginal cost
0	10	0	10	xxx	xxx	xxx	xx
1	10	20	30	10	20	30	20
2	10	36	46	5	18	23	16
3	10	44	54	3.3	14.67	18	8
4	10	46	56	2.5	11.5	14	2
5	10	55	65	2	11	13	9

Total fixed cost is obtained by multiplying the only given average fixed cost ($2) by the quantity (5). Remember that in the short run, fixed costs do not change with changes in output.

Total variable cost is obtained by (1) multiplying average variable cost by quantity; or (2) subtracting total fixed costs from total costs.

Total cost is obtained by (1) adding total fixed and total variable costs; (2) multiplying average total cost by quantity; (3) adding the marginal cost to the previous total cost.

Average fixed cost equals total fixed cost divided by quantity.

Average variable cost equals total variable cost divided by quantity.

Average total cost equals total cost divided by quantity.

Marginal cost equals the change in total cost divided by the change in quantity.

4. a. The law of diminishing returns states that in the short run, a firm may increase output by adding variable resources to fixed inputs, but beyond some point, additional variable inputs will add smaller and smaller additional amounts to total output. This means that the output of a firm in the short run may increase but that the rate of increase will slow down beyond some point as more and more variable resources are used with the available fixed resources.

   b. In the long run, there are no fixed resources since it is possible to vary all inputs to production. Hence, the limitations imposed by the existence of fixed resources in the short run are not present in the long run.

5. False. If the average cost curve is rising, the marginal cost curve can either be rising or falling. For the average variable cost curve to rise, it is necessary only that the marginal cost curve be *above* the average variable cost curve.

6. a. decreasing.
   b. increasing.
   c. increasing.

7. The shape of the average variable cost curve reflects the law of diminishing returns. When the firm's fixed capital is underutilized so that the firm experiences increasing returns, average variable cost of production will drop as output increases. As soon as diminishing returns set in, average variable cost will start to increase.

8. As the same amount of fixed cost is allocated to (divided by) larger and larger amounts of output, the amount of fixed cost per unit of output must drop.

9. The formulas yield identical results because the only way that total cost can change in the short run is through a change in total variable cost. Hence, a change in total variable cost is the same as a change in total cost. The only difference between TVC and TC is total fixed cost, which doesn't change as output changes.

Chapter 23

Price and Output under Perfect Competition

LEARNING OBJECTIVES

This chapter uses the general mode of demand and supply developed in Chapter 3 to analyze production situations in perfectly competitive markets. An understanding of the operation of purely competitive markets enhances our ability to analyze actual market situations.

After reading this chapter, you should be able to:

1. identify the characteristics of a perfectly competitive market;

2. analyze how a firm in competition determines the level of production that yields maximum profit;

3. describe the long-run industry adjustments to the existence of economic profit or loss;

4. evaluate the benefits and problems associated with a perfectly competitive market.

CHAPTER OUTLINE

I. Even though a perfectly competitive market does not exist in reality, economists use the model of perfect competition as an analytical tool to study the determinants of price and output in actual market situations. The perfectly competitive model makes certain assumptions which correspond only occasionally to actual market situations.

A. There are many buyers and sellers in the market.
B. Each seller, because of competition, charges the same price for output.
C. No buyer or seller can influence the market price by individual action.
D. The good sold by every seller is uniform, with no individual brand names or trademarks.
E. All buyers and sellers have complete knowledge of the market.
F. All productive resources in the market are perfectly mobile.

II.   A competitive firm pursuing a goal of maximizing profit must consider both
      revenue and cost. The firm will choose to sell the quantity of output that yields
      maximum profit.
      A. The price of a competitive product is determined by the interaction of
         market demand and supply curves.
         1. By assuming that no firm can individually influence the market price,
            every firm in a competitive market becomes a price taker.
         2. Each firm in a competitive market faces a perfectly elastic demand
            curve. That is, it can sell all the output that it wants at the market price
            without having any appreciable effect on the equilibrium price or quan-
            tity.
      B. Profit is the difference between total revenue and total cost. Thus, any firm
         can compare its total revenue and its total cost at different outputs to deter-
         mine the most profitable level of output.
         1. Total revenue is the price of the product multiplied by the number of
            units sold.
         2. Any positive difference between total revenue and total cost is con-
            sidered to be an economic profit since a normal profit is inclined in the
            firm's costs of production.
      C. Another method of determining the most profitable output is the marginal
         cost-marginal revenue approach.
         1. Marginal cost is the change in total cost divided by the change in quan-
            tity.
         2. Marginal revenue is the change in total revenue divided by the change in
            quantity.
         3. In a competitive market, marginal revenue is equal to the price because
            each unit of output sells for the same market-determined price.
         4. Only where MC = MR will the firm be making the greatest possible
            total profit. This rule holds for all firms, not just firms in perfect com-
            petition.
            a. As long as the cost of producing an extra unit of output is smaller
               than the increase in revenue that the extra unit will bring, a firm will
               expand its production because it can add to its profits.
            b. If a firm produces one more unit beyond the MC = MR point, the
               cost of making the unit becomes greater than the additional revenue
               its sale brings in, and the firm's total profit begins to diminish.
      D. At different prices, the most profitable output for a firm to produce is
         determined by the firm's marginal cost curve.
         1. The segment of the firm's marginal cost curve above the average
            variable cost curve is its supply curve.
         2. The firm's supply curve slopes upward and to the right as a result of the
            law of diminishing returns and the law of increasing costs.
      E. If a firm incurs a short-run economic loss, it must decide whether to con-
         tinue production or shut down.
         1. Losses will be minimized with continued production only if total revenue
            is larger than total variable cost.

2. Losses will be minimized by ceasing operations if total revenue is less than total variable cost.

III. In the short run, adjustments in the competitive market will occur in response to a change in the market price.

    A. The market price may change because of a change in demand or a change in supply.

        1. If the market price changes, firms will seek a new profit-maximizing or loss-minimizing equilibrium quantity.

IV. In the long run, a competitive market will adjust to ensure that firms earn only a normal profit.

    A. If firms in a competitive market are earning an economic profit, new firms seeking profit will enter the industry.

        1. The entry of new firms will increase market supply, lower the market price, and cause quantity adjustments by all firms. In this way, a lower market price will eliminate economic profits for firms in the industry. After these adjustments, only a normal profit will be earned and the industry will be stable.

    B. If firms in a competitive market earn less than a normal profit (incur an economic loss), some firms will leave the industry and seek more profitable opportunities elsewhere.

        1. As firms leave an industry, the market supply will decrease, raising the equilibrium price which will cause all remaining firms to adjust their output. A higher market price will eliminate economic losses for the remaining firms. When firms earn only a normal profit, the market will again be stable with no further tendency for change.

V. The long-run industry supply curve in a competitive market is influenced by the cost of the resources used in production.

    A. In a constant-costs industry (an unusual situation) the entry of new firms has no effect on the price of resources. Therefore, price remains constant regardless of the level of demand and the long-run supply curve is perfectly elastic.

    B. In an increasing-costs industry (a more common situation) the entry of new firms drives up the price of scarce resources and, consequently, increases each firm's costs of production. As output expands, the industry price rises to cover the additional cost of production, and the long-run industry supply curve is positively sloped.

    C. In a decreasing-costs industry, a special situation in which firms have very large capital requirements, additional production results in !ower resource prices and, consequently, lower costs of production.

    D. In a competitive market, long-run equilibrium will be reached when MC = MR = short-run average cost = long-run average total cost.

VI. An assessment of the competitive market must consider both benefits and problems.

    A. There are several benefits of competitive markets.

        1. From an efficiency standpoint, optimal allocation of resources will occur only in competitive markets.

2. Firms in the long run will earn only a normal profit.
3. The product price will equal the marginal cost of production.
B. There are also several problems arising from competitive markets.
   1. Firms have little incentive to develop new or improved products or technologies because any new developments by one firm will be available to all others.
   2. The number and variety of products may be restricted, thus limiting the amount of consumer choice. (Not all economists regard this as a problem.)
   3. The social costs and benefits associated with production by competitive firms are not considered in determining equilibrium output.
   4. Because of the unequal distribution of income and wealth, the price system is not sensitive to the needs of all individuals. Therefore, social welfare goals may not be met by competitive markets.

KEY TERMS

You should be familiar with the meaning of the terms listed below. For definition of these terms, please refer to the glossary at the end of your textbook and to the appropriate section in this chapter.

total revenue   increasing-costs industry
constant-costs industry   decreasing-costs industry

CONCEPTS AND DEFINITIONS

Fill-in Questions

Complete each sentence by writing in the blank the most appropriate word or words from the terms listed below or by circling the word in parentheses that is correct.

MC = MR   constant-cost industry
total variable cost   decreasing-cost industry
total revenue   increasing-cost industry
marginal revenue   marginal revenue-marginal
total cost   cost approach
marginal cost   average variable cost
perfect competition   variable inputs
normal profit

1. If _____ is greater than _____, the short-run economic loss for the firm will be greater than total fixed cost.

2. To compute total profit at any level of output, it is necessary to subtract total cost from _____.

3. _____ is a market situation in which there are a large number of buyers and sellers.

4. If at closing time one evening, a firm were to sell one more unit of output, its _____ would be larger by the amount of _____ _____ associated with the sale of that last unit.

5. A competitive firm's supply curve is the portion of the _____ curve that lies above the _____ curve.

6. If a competitive firm is earning only a normal profit in the short run, _____ is equal to _____.

7. _____ measures the addition to revenue from the sale of additional output while _____ measures the additional cost associated with producing the last unit of output.

8. If a competitive firm incurs a short-run economic loss, its _____ is larger than _____.

9. If the difference between _____ and _____ is zero, the firm in perfect competition must be at the profit-maximizing or loss-minimizing output.

10. If, in response to economic profit, a large number of new firms enter an industry and, subsequently, the price of resources increases, it is reasonable to classify this as a(n) _____.

11. A firm in competition that equates marginal cost with marginal revenue will earn a(n) _____ if average total cost is equal to average revenue.

12. A firm's short-run decision to produce at a loss rather than shut down is based upon the size of _____ and _____.

13. If a(n) _____ were to expand productive capacity, that would result in lower resource prices and, consequently, lower costs of production.

14. If a firm were to subtract total fixed cost from total cost, the difference would equal _____.

15. By following the _____ approach to profit maximization, it is not necessary to determine the largest difference between total revenue and total cost in order to find the profit-maximizing output.

16. In a(n) _____, the long-run supply curve is perfectly elastic.

17. The firm will have to increase its capacity if the market price (increases/decreases).

18. The firm will continue to operate as long as it can cover all the costs for its _____.

19. When firms are making excess profits, new firms will be attracted to the industry. The long-run effect of the entry of new firms is to shift the supply curve to the _____.

20. The point of maximum profit for a firm in a perfectly competitive market would be the quantity for which P = _____ = _____.

Multiple Choice Questions

Circle the correct answer.

1. It is assumed that goods produced under conditions of perfect competition will

   a. sell for low prices.
   b. be agricultural goods.
   c. be standardized products.
   d. have a well-known brand name.

2. To meet the conditions of perfect competition, each firm in an industry must

   a. be willing to undercut the price of all competitors.
   b. be a price taker.
   c. produce only top-quality merchandise.
   d. produce at a profit.

3. Which of the following items is a fixed cost of production for a competitive firm?

   a. payment for raw materials
   b. wage payments
   c. postage on all shipments
   d. insurance premiums on building

4. In the long run, a firm in competition will have

   a. fixed costs that are larger than variable costs.
   b. variable costs that are larger than fixed costs.
   c. only costs of production that are variable.
   d. only costs of production that are fixed.

5. In the short run, a competitive firm can maximize profit or minimize losses by equating

   a. price and marginal revenue.
   b. price and total cost.
   c. price and average revenue.
   d. price and marginal cost.

   Use the following figure to answer questions 6 through 14. It represents a competitive firm's cost and revenue schedules. P_o is the market price.

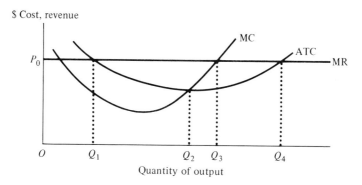

6. The most profitable output for this firm to produce is

    a. Q_1.
    b. Q_2.
    c. Q_3.
    d. Q_4.

7. If output is at Q_1, the firm will be

    a. earning an economic profit.
    b. incurring an economic loss.
    c. unable to pay fixed costs of production.
    d. earning a normal profit.

8. If the firm is producing at Q_2,

    a. average total cost of production is at a minimum and the firm is therefore earning maximum profit.
    b. the firm could reduce output and increase the level of profit.
    c. the level of profit at output Q_2 would be greater than at Q_4.
    d. the firm must be in long-run equilibrium since it is producing at minimum average total cost.

9. If the market price were to drop below P_o,

    a. the firm would necessarily incur an economic loss.
    b. the lower market price would shift the firm's supply curve.
    c. total revenue would be larger than before since price dropped and demand is elastic.
    d. the firm would produce an output smaller than Q_3.

10. If the firm were to produce an output larger than zero but less than Q_1 at the market price P_o,

a. the firm would incur an economic loss.

b. the firm would incur an economic profit.

c. the firm would break even since revenue must cover cost.

d. there is insufficient data to determine if that level of output is profitable.

11. Assume that the competitive firm (whose goal is maximum profit) faces the price P_o for its output. If there were an increase in the market demand for the product supplied by this firm,

a. the market price would rise and, hence, the firm's output would fall.

b. the output of the firm and output in the market would increase.

c. the market price would fall and, hence, the firm's sales would increase.

d. the market price would remain unchanged but the firm would sell more.

12. If the firm were producing output Q_3 at price P_o, and it decided to increase its revenue, it could do so

a. by raising its price and selling quantity Q_3.

b. by lowering its price and selling quantity Q_3.

c. by selling more output at the current price.

d. only if the market price rose.

13. At the profit-maximizing output (Q_3), the firm will be earning an economic profit equal to the difference between

a. average total cost and average revenue multiplied by quantity.

b. average total cost and marginal cost multipled by quantity.

c. marginal revenue and marginal cost multiplied by quantity.

d. price and average revenue multiplied by quantity.

14. Given the cost and revenue situation of the firm in the diagram, we know that the number of firms in the industry will change. Following that change, we can be sure that

a. more firms will be in the industry than before.

b. fewer firms will be in the industry than before.

c. there will be more or fewer firms in the industry, but there is no way from the information given to determine whether there will be more or fewer.

d. the diagrammed firm's profit will get larger.

15. Perfect competition does not necessarily result in optimum allocation of resources when

a. all costs of production are considered to be direct costs.

b. social costs are not borne by the producer.

   c. there are social costs but they are borne by the producer.

   d. there are no social costs of production.

16. The short-run supply curve for a perfectly competitive firm is

   a. its average cost curve.

   b. its average variable cost curve.

   c. the total cost curve for the firm.

   d. the firm's marginal cost curve above the AVC curve.

17. The long-run supply curve for a constant-cost industry

   a. slopes upward to the right.

   b. slopes downward to the right.

   c. reflects the law of diminishing returns.

   d. is a horizontal line over a wide range of output.

18. In a perfectly competitive market, the firm is in long-run equilibrium when

   a. there are excess profits.

   b. MR = ATC = MC = P.

   c. the price is greater than average cost.

   d. the price is stable.

19. If the market price falls, a firm may continue to operate. If it falls below a certain level, however, the firm will shut down. For the firm with the cost curves shown below, which dashed line represents the minimum price at which production will continue in the short run?

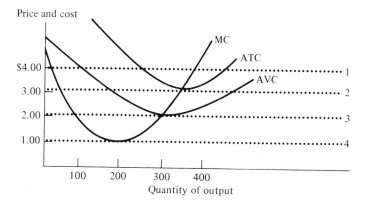

   a. 1

   b. 2

   c. 3

   d. 4

20. The market that would most closely resemble perfect competition is the

    a. automobile industry.

    b. telephone industry.

    c. potato industry.

    d. soft-drink industry.

21. A firm in a perfectly competitive market

    a. has an incentive to raise its price.

    b. has an incentive to lower its price.

    c. can sell any quantity it wishes at the market price.

    d. can lower the market price by offering a larger quantity for sale.

APPLICATIONS

1. A competitive firm is confronted with a price of $4.00 per unit for its output. The marginal cost of production for this firm increases by 50¢ for each additional unit of output produced. That is, the marginal cost of the first unit produced is 50¢; the marginal cost of the second unit is $1.00; of the third, $1.50, etc. It is known that at the profit-maximizing output, this firm has average total costs of production of $2.50. From the information provided, compute total revenue, total cost, and profit at the profit-maximizing output for this firm and indicate the quantity that will be supplied by this firm in profit-maximizing equilibrium.

2. In a brief statement, explain why a firm cannot be maximizing profit if marginal cost is greater or less than marginal revenue.

3. Although it is necessary to equate marginal cost and marginal revenue if the firm in perfect competition is to maximize profits, once MC = MR, that does not guarantee that the firm will earn a profit. Explain why.

4. On the next page is a figure that shows the revenue and cost schedules for a typical firm in a perfectly competitive market. Use this diagram, as necessary, in answering the following questions. The market price is P_o.

   a. What is the profit-maximizing output for this firm? How do you know?

   b. What is the size of total revenue at output Q_1?

   c. What is the size of total cost at output Q_4?

   d. Where is the firm's average revenue curve? Label it AR.

   e. If the firm decided to produce output Q_5, would the firm be making a profit or loss? How do you know?

   f. At what output(s) will the firm break even? How do you know?

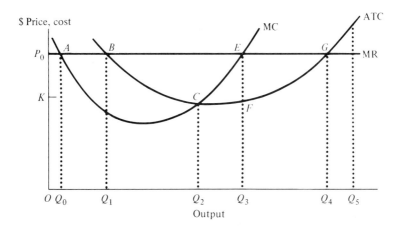

g. At the profit-maximizing output, label the area that corresponds to total profit. If necessary, add lines to the diagram.

h. If the market price were to rise about P_o, would the firm still be able to produce the output you indicated in Part a of this problem and maximize the profit? If not, explain why not and what the firm would have to do to return to a profit-maximizing equilibrium.

ANSWERS

Fill-in Questions

1. total variable cost; total revenue
2. total revenue
3. perfect competition
4. total revenue; marginal revenue
5. marginal cost; average variable cost
6. total cost; total revenue
7. marginal revenue; marginal cost
8. total cost; total revenue
9. marginal cost; marginal revenue
10. increasing-cost industry
11. normal profit
12. total revenue; total variable cost
13. decreasing-cost industry
14. total variable cost
15. marginal cost-marginal revenue
16. constant-cost industry
17. increases
18. variable inputs
19. right
20. MC; MR

Multiple Choice Questions

1. c
2. b
3. d

12. c
13. a
14. a

4.	c	15.	b
5.	d	16.	d
6.	c	17.	d
7.	d	18.	b
8.	c	19.	c
9.	d	20.	c
10.	a	21.	c
11.	b		

APPLICATIONS

1. Marginal revenue is $4.00 at any level of output since that is the amount added to revenue by sale of another unit of output. Since marginal cost increases by 50¢ per unit of output produced, the marginal cost of the eighth unit would be $4.00. At any other output, marginal cost would be greater or less than marginal revenue. Total revenue ($Q \times$ Price) at $Q = 8$ is $32.00; total costs (or average costs, $2.50, multiplied by quantity, 8, is equal to $20.00 at that output. Profit equals total revenue ($32) minus total costs ($20) or $12.

2. If marginal cost is greater than marginal revenue, each additional unit of output produced is adding more to cost than to revenue so that net profit must be shrinking. If marginal cost is less than marginal revenue, each additional unit produced will add more to revenue than to most so that net profit will be growing. Only when MC = MR will all potential net additions to profit be captured by the firm.

3. Finding the output where MC = MR does not guarantee a profit since total profit is the difference between total revenue and total cost. The marginal calculations reflect profit or loss only on individual units and do not measure earlier profits or losses, or fixed costs of production (which are not reflected in the MC figures). Once a maximizing output is found using MC and MR, it is necessary to rely on average cost and revenue data to determine if any particular level of output is profitable.

4. a. Q_3, where MC = MR
   b. Total revenue is represented by the rectangle OQ_1BP_o (or $P_o \times Q_1$).
   c. Total cost is represented by the rectangle OQ_4GP_o (or $Q_4 G$ (average cost) $\times Q_4$.
   d. The price line is the same as the firm's average and marginal revenue curves.
   e. At Q_5, the firm will be making a loss since at that output, average cost is greater than average revenue.
   f. The firm will break even at outputs Q_1 and Q_4 since at these production levels, average total cost is equal to average revenue.

g. The rectangle P_oEFK is the area corresponding to profit at the profit-maximizing output. This is also equal to EF (the difference between average total cost and average revenue) times Q_3 (the profit-maximizing level of output). Remember that profit equals *total* revenue minus *total* cost.

h. If the market price rose above P_o, marginal revenue would exceed marginal cost at output Q_3. Hence, it would be in the firm's interest to expand output until, once again, MC was equal to the new value of MR.

Chapter 24

The Economics of Agriculture

LEARNING OBJECTIVES

Although no market conforms precisely to the model of competition developed in the previous chapter, the closest real-world counterpart in the United States is the market for agricultural goods. In this chapter, we take a close look at agricultural markets to learn about the special characteristics and problems of this sector of the economy, and the history of government policies that have been formulated to deal with the farm problem.

After reading this chapter, you should be able to:

1. describe the economic causes of historically declining farm prices and the sources of instability in farm incomes;

2. describe and evaluate the effectiveness of government policies that attempt to deal with fluctuations in farm prices and farm incomes;

3. describe how the farm problem in the 1970s is different from the more traditional farm problem;

4. discuss and evaluate proposals for dealing with the current problems facing farmers in the United States.

CHAPTER OUTLINE

I. The farm problem in the United States has traditionally been one of abundant production combined with low incomes for most of those who produce the abundance.
    A. With rapid advances in technology, farm production has grown rapidly. Because of the inelastic demand for farm commodities, however, increased production has resulted in low commodity prices.
    B. Because of this price inelasticity, low farm prices result in low incomes for the majority of farm families in the United States.

1. Except for brief periods, particularly wartime, the per-capita income of the farm population has been below the per-capita income of the non-farm population. Although the per-capita incomes of both groups have grown over time, farm incomes have grown more slowly because of the income inelastic demand for farm commodities.
2. Largely as a result of natural phenomena, farm prices have tended to fluctuate dramatically in the short run. This fluctuation has contributed to variation in farm incomes and to instability in the agricultural sector of the economy.

C. Changes in farm technology which have increased farm productivity have primarily benefitted large-scale farm operations because smaller farms frequently lack the capital to take advantage of improved production techniques.

D. Even though the monetary returns from farming are slight for many individuals, some are unwilling to leave the farm sector because of cultural or non-monetary reasons, or because the costs of relocating in urban areas are viewed as excessive.

II. Government farm policy from the 1920s to the 1970s has consisted of information and technical-aid programs aimed at boosting farm production and programs to support farm prices and the incomes of farmers.

A. Direct subsidies have been given to farmers since the 1930s through a system of parity prices.
1. Parity entails a system of price supports whose purpose is to increase the revenues received by farmers from the sale of their products.
2. At full parity, government price supports for agricultural commodities would be maintained at a level that would ensure an equivalence between current purchasing power and purchasing power during a base period (initially the years 1909-1914).
3. Since parity did not apply to all farm products, however, farm incomes failed to keep pace with nonfarm incomes even with government supports.
4. Even with modifications in the parity formula following World War II, the goal of maintaining equivalence between farm and nonfarm incomes was not realized because the parity formula was too rigid in the face of changing market conditions.

B. When parity prices were above market-clearing prices, surplus farm production was purchased from farmers and stored by government.
1. The bulk of government support payments went to large farms with relatively high incomes and not to low income farms for which the program was designed.
2. The cost of storing surplus commodities and the problems associated with the disposal of stored goods prompted the government to seek alternative ways of assisting farmers.
3. The primary program designed to curtail production involved restrictions on the acreage that could be planted.
a. Although acreage under cultivation was reduced, production often rose because the remaining land was cultivated more intensively.

      b. Because acreage restrictions failed to limit production, many people proposed a revamping of support programs: some people argued for a return to free markets while others favored the provision of direct income subsidies to low income farmers.

III. In the early 1970s the traditional farm problem of overproduction was replaced by one of increased worldwide demand for United States farm products, sharply rising costs of production for farm goods, and higher prices for farm output.

    A. Increased foreign demand for American farm products, which was stimulated by crop failures abroad as well as by the devaluation of the United States dollar, resulted in higher domestic farm prices.

      1. As a result of higher prices, the per-capita income of farmers surpassed the per-capita income of the nonfarm population in 1973. By 1974, however, net farm income declined once again as a result of the rising costs of production necessities such as fuel and fertilizers.

      2. While market conditions improved during the late 1970s, the real income of farmers in 1978 was no higher than in 1969.

IV. In the 1970s farm legislation was no longer focused on restrictive policies and parity pricing but, instead, encouraged all-out production.

    A. Price supports were abandoned in favor of target or guaranteed prices on basic agricultural commodities.

    B. Increased reliance on market forces in the agricultural sector in the mid-1970s was tempered somewhat as farm prices fell in the late 1970s.

      1. Legislation in 1977 and 1978 emphasized the use of target prices and of authority by the government to restrict production. This legislation reflects a compromise between strict government regulation, which has a long history in agriculture, and a return to the forces of demand and supply to determine price in the farm sector.

KEY TERMS

You should be familiar with the meaning of the terms listed below. For definition of these terms, please refer to the glossary at the end of your textbook and to the appropriate section in this chapter.

parity pricing
target prices

CONCEPTS AND DEFINITIONS

Fill-in Questions

Complete each sentence by writing in the blank the most appropriate word or words from the terms listed below or by circling the word in parentheses that is correct.

acreage
farm problem
perfect competition
economies of scale
parity pricing
income elasticity of demand
technological improvements

normal good
surpluses
income inelastic
target prices
price inelastic
resources
golden age of agriculture

1. Historic overproduction of agricultural products and low income in the farm sector are chief symptoms of the _____.

2. Undifferentiated products, a large number of firms, and an inability by any one firm to change the market price are characteristics of _____.

3. The variability of farm incomes in the short run is attributed primarily to the _____ demand for most farm commodities.

4. Large-scale farms are often more efficient than smaller farms because they take advantage of _____.

5. Farm legislation in the 1970s replaced _____ programs with _____ or guaranteed minimum prices on basic agricultural commodities.

6. A long-run factor that has influenced the level of farm income is the low _____ for farm products.

7. Recent legislation providing _____ for agricultural commodities also makes provision for the government to control the number of acres under cultivation.

8. If the percentage change in income is greater than the percentage change in consumption of agricultural goods, these products should be classified as _____.

9. An increase in the supply of wheat will result in reduced expenditures on wheat if the demand for wheat is _____.

10. A program of _____ attempts to achieve equivalence between current purchasing power of farmers and their purchasing power in a selected base period.

11. One of the main reasons that changing weather and, consequently, variable harvests drastically affect farm incomes is the _____ demand for farm commodities.

12. Government maintenance of _____ schemes relied on government purchases of surplus farm products and on the imposition of production and acreage controls.

13. The years 1909-1914 are often referred to as the _____ because farm prices were stable during those years and farm income was comparable to income in other sectors of the economy.

14. Since most farm commodities are _____ goods, an increase in incomes will result in an increase in consumption.

15. A characteristic of _____ demand is that if agricultural prices fall by 10 percent, the quantity demanded will increase by less than 10 percent.

16. The individual farmer is almost powerless to affect his or her economic position because the market for most farm goods is almost one of _____ .

17. Because of the character of the demand curve for most agricultural products, a drop in the market price for agricultural products means that total revenue to the farmer will (increase/decrease).

18. Some of the causes of the dramatic increases in agricultural productivity in this century are _____ and _____ .

Multiple Choice Questions

Circle the correct answer.

1. Until the 1970s, the traditional farm problem consisted of
   a. agricultural abundance and parity pricing.
   b. low farm incomes and mechanization of farms.
   c. parity pricing and mechanization of farms.
   d. agricultural abundance and low farm incomes.

2. The first government aid to agriculture was provided to farmers
   a. following World War II.
   b. following the Great Depression.
   c. prior to World War I.
   d. immediately following the golden age of agriculture.

3. Parity pricing is a concept that entails
   a. farmers selling crops to government for subsequent resale to the public at higher prices.
   b. government selling goods to farmers at subsidized prices.
   c. government setting prices for farm goods above the market equilibrium level.
   d. the establishment of farm cooperatives to restrict production and sale of farm goods.

4. The "family farm" in agriculture is often less profitable than larger scale farming operations because small farms cannot take advantage of
   a. significant economies of scale.
   b. significant diseconomies of scale.

    c. the law of diminishing returns.

    d. the law of variable proportions.

5. For years the market for agricultural goods was regarded as an example of perfect competition because

    a. the concept of parity and fairness was applied throughout the agricultural sector.

    b. of the coexistence of small farms along side many large-scale, highly mechanized farms.

    c. prices fluctuate drastically from year to year depending on weather and crop conditions.

    d. farmers cannot individually raise prices in order to increase their incomes.

6. Parity prices for farm goods are similar to

    a. minimum prices established by government above the market equilibrium.

    b. maximum prices established by government above the market equilibrium.

    c. minimum prices established by government below the market equilibrium.

    d. maximum prices established by government below the market equilibrium.

7. Since the demand for farm goods is price inelastic

    a. the percentage change in quantity demanded will always be greater than the percentage change in price.

    b. the percentage change in quantity supplied will always be less than the percentage change in price.

    c. the percentage change in quantity demanded will be greater than the percentage change in income.

    d. the demand elasticity coefficient will always be less than 1.

8. The majority of farms in the United States

    a. are small-scale operations with excess profits as a result of government subsidies.

    b. are large-scale operations with sales in excess of $10,000.

    c. are responsible for producing more than 50 percent of all farm output.

    d. face a highly inelastic demand for their output and, therefore, their incomes are low.

9. The government program designed to limit the amount of land under cultivation by farmers did not reduce output because

    a. the program was in effect only a short time and was never given a fair trial.

    b. the government had no way to check if farmers actually planted fewer acres.

    c. each farmer was free to choose what acreage to leave unplanted.

d. acreage not subject to production controls was farmed less intensively and thus provided higher yields.

10. The agricultural problem of the 1970s is different from the farm problem before the 1970s because

    a. it is now possible to store commodities more cheaply than before as a result of new technology such as freeze drying.

    b. of the increased worldwide demand for food and sharply higher farm production costs.

    c. per-capita consumption of food in the United States dropped from 1965 to 1974 adding yet another source of instability to farm incomes.

    d. farm income has consistently surpassed nonfarm income thus creating cries for relief from high farm prices by consumers.

11. A paradox that confronts farmers as a group is that

    a. more production means less income and vice versa.

    b. less production means less income and vice versa.

    c. weather and growing conditions are likely to change from year to year.

    d. shifts in demand are closely related to shifts in supply.

12. The parity concept did not always have the desired results because

    a. the formulas were too complicated for farmers and consumers to understand.

    b. prices of supported products were held below those of unsupported products.

    c. the price received by farmers did not keep pace with the prices paid by farmers.

    d. black markets developed to counteract the government-established parity pricing policies.

13. The period 1909-1914 is referred to as the golden age of agriculture because

    a. farm incomes and farm prices were at record high levels and climbed steadily throughout the period.

    b. demand for farm products was high as people stockpiled food in anticipation of shortages during World War I.

    c. the purchasing power of farmers was comparable to that of workers in other sectors and farm prices remained stable.

    d. the wave of European immigrants to the United States during that period sharply increased the demand for foodstuffs.

14. Increased growth and productivity in the farm sector have been responsible for lowering farm income in the long run because the demand for farm products

    a. is income elastic.

    b. is price elastic.

c. is income inelastic.

d. has over time shifted more than the supply of farm goods.

15. If the demand for foodstuffs is income inelastic, then an increase in income would result in the demand for food

   a. increasing in the same proportion as income.

   b. increasing by a smaller proportion than the change in income.

   c. remaining constant since demand is income inelastic.

   d. increasing by a larger proportion than the change in income.

16. The parity pricing program for agricultural goods was most successful in

   a. raising overall farm income.

   b. solving the persistent problem of oversupply.

   c. dealing with the problem of too many resources in agriculture.

   d. lowering consumer prices for foodstuffs.

17. Parity support was not given to all agricultural products but to those that could be easily

   a. sold abroad.

   b. stored for long periods of time.

   c. distributed to needy households.

   d. used as animal feed and fertilizer.

APPLICATIONS

1. a. If the price elasticity of demand for wheat is .75, by how much would consumption be expected to change following an increase in the price of wheat by 8 percent?

   b. Will the price increase referred to above raise or lower the incomes of wheat farmers? How do you know?

   c. Assume that the market demand for wheat is a straight diagonal line, and that the initial increase in price raised the incomes of wheat farmers. Would it be possible to continue to raise the price of wheat week after week by the same amount and still have the incomes of wheat farmers increase? Use the concept of demand elasticity in formulating your answer.

2. Assume that the market for hayseed is perfectly competitive. If the government were to subsidize fertilizer purchases for a single hayseed farmer in Mishawaka, that farmer would benefit. Yet if government subsidized fertilizer purchases for all hayseed farmers, the benefit to the farmer in Mishawaka would disappear. Explain why.

3. The text suggests that during the Kennedy administration farmers faced a choice of high support prices for their crops coupled with production quotas, or lower support prices and only acreage restrictions. Congress, responding to farm lobbyists, voted for the lower support prices. What economic justification might be offered for their action?

4. Suppose the price of a pound of butter in 1909-1914 is the basis for the parity price of butter. By checking the various price indexes for nonfarm goods, you determine that the price of nonfarm goods has risen 320 percent. If the average price of a pound of butter was 20 cents over the period 1909-1914, the parity price of butter would be _____.

5. Suppose that the market for corn is represented by the curves below.

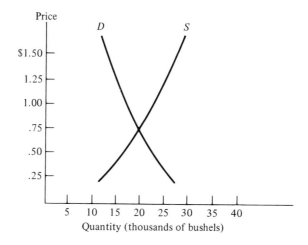

Assume that the prices of nonfarm goods have risen by 250 percent since the base period and the price of corn during the base period was 50 cents per bushel. The government wishes to support the price of corn to the parity price.

a. Compute the parity price.

b. If government makes a commitment to purchase any surplus production, how many bushels of corn is it obliged to buy?

c. If it costs 10¢ per bushel to store corn, what will be the amount of storage costs incurred by government?

ANSWERS

Fill-in Questions

1. farm problem
2. perfect competition
3. price inelastic

10. parity prices
11. price inelastic
12. parity pricing

4. economies of scale
5. parity pricing;
        target prices
6. income elasticity of demand
7. target prices
8. income inelastic
9. price inelastic

13. golden age of agriculture
14. normal
15. price inelastic
16. perfect competition
17. decrease
18. technological improvements;
        economies of scale

Multiple Choice Questions

1. d
2. b
3. c
4. a
5. d
6. a
7. d
8. c
9. c

10. b
11. a
12. c
13. c
14. c
15. b
16. a
17. b

APPLICATIONS

1. a. Consumption would drop by 6 percent
    $$\left(E = \frac{\% \text{ change in price}}{\% \text{ change in quantity}} = \frac{8\%}{x} = .75; x = 6\%\right)$$

    b. A price increase in the inelastic region of the demand curve (elasticity coefficient is less than one) will cause total expenditures (and, therefore, total revenues to farmers) to increase.

    c. At some point, the price increases would move past the midpoint on the demand curve and into the elastic portion of the curve. Any price increase beyond that point would cause total expenditures on farm goods to drop because the demand would be elastic.

2. Initially, the subsidy to the single farmer would lower his costs and increase profitability. Price would remain unaffected since the single competitive firm cannot change the market price. If the subsidy were provided to all farms, however, it would affect profitability in the industry. New resources would be drawn into agriculture to take advantage of the profit possibilities; price would drop and the advantage that resulted from the subsidy would disappear.

3. With a production quota in effect, there is an upper limit on income. Without a production quota, farmers are able to increase incomes by increasing production.

4. 64¢ ($.20 × 3.20).

5. a. $1.25 [$.50 (the base price) × 2.50 (percent increase in price)]
   b. 10,000 (At $1.25, farmers would supply 25,000 bushels. However, at $1.25 consumers would demand only 15,000 bushels. Therefore the government would have to buy 10,000 bushels of corn.)
   c. $1,000 (10,000 bushels × $.10 per bushel)

Chapter 25

Price and Output under Monopoly

LEARNING OBJECTIVES

This chapter describes the model of a pure monopoly market and the power over price and output that the monopolist is able to exercise. The purchase monopoly is in sharp contrast to the model of competition presented earlier in the chapter on perfect competition where the individual firm was unable to influence the market price and was able to make decisions only about the level of output to produce. Both of these models are used to analyze and evaluate real-world resource allocation decisions and to formulate public policy to deal with situations involving the exercise of monopoly power.

After reading this chapter, you should be able to:

1. describe the characteristics of a monopoly market and the circumstances under which a monopoly may arise;

2. describe how the profit-maximizing price and level of output are determined under monopolistic conditions;

3. identify the conditions that must exist in order for price discrimination to occur;

4. demonstrate how economic inefficiency arises in a monopolistic industry;

5. discuss the methods of government intervention in monopoly markets and show why intervention rarely results in the optimal allocation of resources.

CHAPTER OUTLINE

I.   A pure monopoly exists when a single firm is the only producer of a product or service for which there are no close substitutes. There are many characteristics of a monopoly.

    A. A monopoly can exist only when there is no near substitute for the product traded in the market.

        1. The number of substitutes available for a product depends on how markets are defined. The public's perception and consequently their

definition of a market is frequently influenced by advertising which attempts to narrow the public's definition of the market and thus create a monopolistic market.

B. Taxes, duties, and tariffs may be imposed at the federal level to protect some industries and firms from foreign competition, thus possibly giving rise to a monopoly.

C. Monopolies may exist as a result of certain barriers that prevent other firms from entering a market.

  1. High set-up costs in certain capital-intensive industries inhibit competition.

    a. In these markets, the government may intervene and guarantee a monopoly when one firm can produce enough output to satisfy market demand at a lower average total cost than would be possible with more than one firm in the market. One example of such an industry is an electric power company.

  2. A firm may also become a monopoly through ownership and control of the total supply of particular raw materials that are essential in a production process.

  3. Patent and copyright laws can provide innovative firms with short-term monopoly power.

    a. The purpose of granting patent and copyright monopolies is to encourage and reward innovation and product improvement.

  4. Most barriers to entry are short-run problems for would-be competitors. In the long run, it is possible to overcome most barriers.

II. A monopolist equates marginal cost and marginal revenue to maximize short-run profit.

A. Unlike a perfect competitor, who faces a perfectly elastic demand curve, the demand curve faced by a monopolist is downward sloping. The demand curve faced by a monopoly is also the market demand curve for a product since the monopoly is the only seller of the product.

  1. Since the market demand curve is downward sloping, a monopolist must lower the price of all goods sold in order to increase sales.

  2. At any level of output, marginal revenue (MR) is always less than price (or average revenue). Since marginal cost (MC) must equal MR in order to maximize profit, MC is always less than price at the profit-maximizing output.

B. Although there is no assurance that a monopoly will make a profit, if a short-run profit is made, it may persist due to barriers to entry.

  1. Since other firms are prevented from entering an industry that is a monopoly there is no competitive pressure to eliminate long-run profit. Hence, the long-run equilibrium output may be the same as short-run equilibrium output.

III. The existence of a monopoly (which may result in a lack of incentive for innovation) results in misallocation of resources.

A. To achieve efficiency in the allocation of resources, a firm must operate where price is equal to marginal cost as is the case in perfect competition.

B. A monopolist pursuing a goal of profit maximization equates marginal cost with marginal revenue. Since marginal revenue is less than price, the firm's goals of profit maximization is inconsistent with the social goal of allocational efficiency.

   1. When price is greater than MC, this indicates that society places a higher value on consuming an additional unit of that good than on the marginal cost of producing that extra unit. The monopoly will not produce the extra unit (because it is maximizing its profits) and the resources will be allocated to some other use less preferred by consumers.

IV. The existence of monopoly creates the possibility of successful price discrimination—that is, charging different prices to different groups of consumers for the same product or service.

   A. There are two necessary conditions for successful price discrimination.

      1. The original purchaser of a product must not be able to resell the product or service.

      2. The monopolist must be able to sort the entire market into well-defined groups or submarkets, and the elasticity of demand at any price must differ among the submarkets.

         a. Most commonly, submarkets are defined for price discrimination according to sex, income, geographic location, and time of day.

   B. In order to maximize profit, the marginal cost of production must be equal in each submarket.

V. Since efficiency in the allocation of resources is not a goal of monopoly, it is in the interest of society to restrict the use of monopoly power if such efficiency is a goal of society.

   A. Regulation of monopoly may take two forms.

      1. The government can encourage competition through legislation that prevents deliberate monopolization of an industry or that eliminates barriers that prevent other firms from entering the market.

      2. The government may regulate the price charged by a monopolist and, from time to time, the level of output produced.

   B. Even with government regulation of price and output, a monopoly will continue to misallocate resources as long as the price charged is greater than the marginal cost of production.

KEY TERMS

You should be familiar with the meaning of the terms listed below. For definition of these terms, please refer to the glossary at the end of your textbook and to the appropriate section in this chapter.

patent laws
price discrimination

CONCEPTS AND DEFINITIONS

Fill-in Questions

Complete each sentence by writing in the blank the most appropriate word or words from the terms listed below or by circling the word in parentheses that is correct.

perfect competition
monopoly
patent laws
copyright
price
marginal revenue
market demand curve

indivisible
price discrimination
barrier(s) to entry
tariffs and duties
marginal cost (MC)
law of demand

1. The government may restrict foreign competition with American goods by imposing _____ which raise the price of imports relative to American goods.

2. The government will frequently sanction the existence of a monopoly if the product or service is _____ or if initial capital costs are very large.

3. _____ make it difficult for prospective producers to join markets that are monopolized.

4. Because most consumer goods may be resold, _____ is usually practiced by the sellers of services.

5. As long as a monopolist is maximizing profit, _____ will be greater than _____ which is an indication that resources are misallocated.

6. In _____ long-run adjustments will eliminate economic profit because new firms may enter the market; in _____ markets, the absence of competition allows economic profit to persist in the long run.

7. _____ exists when different prices are charged to different consumers of a product for reasons other than differences in the cost of production.

8. Prior to World War II, Alcoa was able to monopolize the market for new aluminum because its control of the world's supply of bauxite constituted a _____ to other firms.

9. A _____ exists when a single firm is the only producer of a product or service for which there are no close substitutes.

10. _____ grant a producer the exclusive right, for a limited period of time, to produce, use, transfer, or withhold a product or process from the market.

11. A type of government-sanctioned monopoly is created for literary works, songs, and trademarks through the issuance of a _____.

12. The demand curve facing a monopolist is the same as the _____ _____ since the firm controls the entire supply of a product or service.

13. In order to maximize profit, a monopolist must equate _____ with _____.

14. A monopolist attempts to influence the _____ for a product through advertising or innovation which changes the nature of the product.

15. The assertion that monoplies are free to set any price and sell any quantity of output that they wish ignores the _____ which states that there is an inverse relationship between price and quantity demanded.

16. A product that is useful only when the consumer has access to a whole system is called a(n) _____ product.

17. Under monopoly conditions, production is at a level above the lowest point on the ATC curve. The monopolist produces (more/less) output than is required for maximum efficiency.

Multiple Choice Questions

Circle the correct answer.

1. A profit-maximizing monopolist

   a. follows the same rules for profit maximization as the perfectly competitive firm.

   b. follows different rules for profit maximization than does the perfectly competitive firm.

   c. will set price equal to marginal cost in order to determine the maximizing output.

   d. will set marginal cost equal to average revenue in order to determine the maximizing output.

2. Marginal revenue is less than the price charged by a monopolist

   a. because a monopolistic firm can sell a larger quantity of output only by lowering the market price of all units sold.

   b. in order for economists to distinguish between markets that are competitive and those that are monopolized.

   c. as a result of consumer-protection legislation which requires marginal revenue to be less than the price charged to consumers.

   d. because the monopolist faces an infinitely elastic demand curve.

3. A monopoly is said to misallocate resources

   a. when it fails to operate at maximum average total cost or the point of greatest productive efficiency.

   b. because, without competition, there is no pressure on the firm's management to be efficient.

   c. because under certain circumstances, different consumers are charged different prices for the same product or service.

   d. because the market price under monopoly is greater than the marginal cost of additional output.

4. A monopoly may engage in price discrimination

   a. because some groups in society such as children and senior citizens cannot afford to pay the same price as everyone else for certain goods and services.

   b. in order to increase revenues without a corresponding increase in production costs.

   c. in order to determine how many submarkets exist for the product.

   d. because the cost of serving some markets is greater than the cost of serving others.

5. A monopolist does not have a supply curve because

   a. a monopolist can sell any amount of output at a price of its choosing, as long as the price is not unreasonable.

   b. when there is only one seller, any information regarding supply can be obtained from a single source; hence, a supply curve is unnecessary.

   c. any level of output may be produced at different prices, depending on the shape and location of the market demand curve.

   d. data regarding supply might reveal trade secrets to potential competitors of the monopoly.

6. A pure monopoly will always exist

   a. whenever a firm has many direct competitors.

   b. when consumers cannot find any close substitutes for a product.

   c. when the federal government imposes taxes, duties, and tariffs on imported goods.

   d. whenever an industry is capital intensive.

7. All things being equal, an increase in the variable costs of production for a monopolist

   a. will result in a higher profit-maximizing price and a smaller level of output being produced.

   b. will result in a lower price being charged and a higher level of output produced.

c. will result in consumers paying a higher price for the same level of output.

d. will have no effect on price or quantity sold, but rather will reduce the profitability of the firm's operations.

8. Market equilibrium for a monopolist seeking to maximize profit

   a. is determined by the "invisible hand" of market forces.

   b. is determined solely by the firm's costs of production.

   c. is not defined since the monopolist is the only seller of a product or service.

   d. is determined by product demand and the firm's costs of production.

9. Advertising is undertaken by a monopolist

   a. to create a strong product image and broaden the public's definition of the market.

   b. in order to ensure that a firm's product is evaluated fairly with all competing products.

   c. to create a strong product image and narrow the public's definition of the market.

   d. to convince the public that its product is superior to that of its competitors.

10. A monopoly is similar to a competitive firm in that it

    a. faces a horizontal demand curve.

    b. must equate MC and MR to maximize profits.

    c. is a price taker.

    d. cannot influence the market price by its own actions.

11. It would be difficult for a monopolist to practice price discrimination if

    a. the product could not be resold.

    b. the total market could easily be divided according to age and income.

    c. there were only one firm from whom the product or service was available.

    d. the demand curve in each submarket were identical.

12. A monopolist and a single competitive firm are similar in that

    a. both are able to influence the market demand via advertising.

    b. over time, profits for both are eliminated by competition.

    c. both are likely to be capital intensive with high set-up costs.

    d. their cost curves reflect the law of diminishing returns.

13. Government usually controls the actions of a monopoly by

    a. legislation or court action.

    b. urging consumers to boycott monopoly products.

c. installing public officials on the board of directors of the monopoly.

d. urging corporate compliance with social goals.

14. Government sanctions the existence of monopoly

a. through patent and consumer-protection laws.

b. by removing duties on imports.

c. in the case of natural monopoly.

d. through vigorous antitrust actions.

15. For price discrimination to be successful, there must be

a. elastic demand.

b. the possibility of reselling the product.

c. the means for distinguishing different groups of potential purchasers.

d. a horizontal MR curve.

APPLICATIONS

1. A monopoly is generally seen as a bad thing. Explain why. If a part of your answer is that a monopoly misallocates resources, explain what "misallocates resources" means.

2. Since monopoly is generally regarded as bad, why do we allow public officials to create monopoly conditions for some firms like utility companies by providing exclusive franchises or licenses that exclude all other competition?

3. The following table shows a demand schedule facing a monopolist.

Quantity:	0	1	2	3	4	5	6	7	8	9	10
Price:	26	25	24	23	22	21	20	19	18	17	16

The marginal cost of production is always $13.00, and at the profit-maximizing output, average total cost is $20.00.

a. What is the profit-maximizing (or loss-minimizing) output for this monopolist?

b. What is the price at which that output will sell in the market?

c. Compute total cost, total revenue, and profit (or loss) at the maximizing output.

4. a. Define price discrimination.

b. (1) Explain why it is feasible to use price discrimination in establishing the fare structure for a public transit system. (2) Explain why it is not feasible to exercise price discrimination in selling used buses once owned by the transit company.

5. If a public utility confronted with decreasing average costs were forced by a regulatory agency to equate price and marginal cost, would that utility make an economic profit? Why or why not?

ANSWERS

Fill-in Questions

1. tariffs and duties
2. indivisible
3. barriers to entry
4. price discrimination
5. price; marginal cost
6. perfect competition; monopoly
7. price discrimination
8. barrier to entry
9. monopoly
10. patent laws
11. copyright
12. market demand curve
13. MC; MR or MR; MC
14. market demand curve
15. law of demand
16. indivisible
17. less

Multiple Choice Questions

1. a
2. a
3. d
4. b
5. c
6. b
7. a
8. d
9. c
10. b
11. d
12. d
13. a
14. c
15. c

APPLICATIONS

1. Monopoly is often regarded as a bad thing because it restricts output and charges a higher price than the same firm would charge under condition of perfect competition. (This assumes, of course, that any economies of scale enjoyed by the monopoly would also be available to competitive firms if the monopoly were broken up.) Monopoly also misallocates resources because the price charged for its output is greater than the marginal cost of production. Efficiency of resource allocation is achieved only when price is equal to marginal cost.

2. In an industry (such as utilities) where fixed costs represent a very large component of total costs, average total costs will decline over a substantial range of output. Only if competition is restricted will the firm be able to produce a large enough output to take advantage of economies of scale that are evident in decreasing unit costs. By their actions, politicians recognize the need to limit competition in these decreasing-cost industries. At the same time, to limit the exercise of monopoly power by these firms, public regulation of price is required.

3. From the information regarding demand, compute total revenue and then marginal revenue at the levels of output shown. Then equate marginal cost with marginal revenue.

   a. $Q = 7$ [At 7 units of output, marginal revenue (the change in total revenue = the change in $P \times Q$) is $13.00—6 $\times$ $20 = $120; 7 $\times$ $19 = $133; $133 − $120 (the change in total revenue from 6 to 7 units of output) = $13.]

   b. Price = $19 at 7 units of output.

   c. Total cost = $140 (ATC $\times$ Q = $20 $\times$ 7 = $140); total revenue = $133 ($P \times Q$ = $19 $\times$ 7 = $133); loss = 7 (Profit = total revenue minus total cost = $133 − $140 = $−7, or a loss of $7)

4. a. Price discrimination involves charging different prices to different customers for the same good or service for reasons not associated with differences in cost.

   b. The demand for bus or other public transit meets the two necessary conditions for price discrimination: (1) The original purchaser of the transit company's service is not able to resell the product and the transit company is able to distinguish clearly the different groups of demanders (such as senior citizens; children under 5, and so on. (2) Since used buses may be obtained from several sources and may be resold once purchased, they do not meet one of the conditions required for price discrimination.

5. As long as the average total cost curve declines, the marginal cost curve must be below it. Thus, at any level of demand where P = MC, average revenue (price) is less than average cost. Consequently, total revenue is less than total cost and the utility sustains an economic loss.

Chapter 26

Price and Output under Imperfect Competition

LEARNING OBJECTIVES

Most American businesses face market conditions that do not conform fully to the assumptions of the economic models of competition or monopoly. Instead, these firms achieve some degree of monopoly power by marketing products that are perceived as unique, yet, at the same time, they experience competition from other firms selling similar products. To help analyze the economic behavior of firms in these markets economists have developed two models of imperfect competition, the *oligopoly model* and the model of *monopolistic competition*. These two models enable us to better analyze and understand a variety of market structures and to formulate sound economic policy.

After reading this chapter, you should be able to:

1. identify the characteristics that distinguish each of the four basic economic models (competition, monopolistic competition, oligopoly, and monopoly) from one another;

2. describe how price and output are determined under market conditions of oligopoly and monopolistic competition;

3. state the purpose of nonprice competition (advertising and product differentiation) in imperfectly competitive markets and provide an assessment of its effectiveness;

4. assess the costs and benefits associated with imperfect competition from the perspective of economic efficiency.

CHAPTER OUTLINE

I.   In an oligopolistic market, a small number of large firms produce identical or, more commonly, similar products that constitute the bulk of the output within an industry. The market for domestically produced automobiles is an example of an oligopoly.

A. Since only a few firms dominate the industry, the actions of any one firm will affect the behavior of its competitors. As a result, there is a special interdependence among firms in oligopoly that is absent in perfect competition or monopoly.

B. An oligopolistic industry is usually capital-intensive and heavily dependent on advanced technology.

   1. As a result of these conditions, only a large firm can produce sufficient output to take advantage of the economies of scale that permit profitable operation.

   2. The large amount of capital required to enter an oligopolistic industry serves as a barrier to entry by new firms.

   3. In American industry, some oligopolies have been created because a competitor has managed to enter a market that was previously monopolized. Others have arisen as the technological requirements within an industry eliminated smaller firms, leaving only the larger ones to compete with one another.

C. Like perfect competitors and monopolists, an oligopolist must equate marginal cost and marginal revenue to maximize short-run profit.

   1. As a result of differentiated products, each firm in an oligopoly faces a negatively sloped demand curve, and, therefore, the marginal revenue curve is located below the demand curve.

      a. In order to sell more units, the oligopolist (like the monopolist)must lower the per-unit price. To sell one more unit, the firm must lower the price of all units on the market. Therefore, the marginal revenue of each successive unit will be smaller than the one before it.

D. Because of the interdependence among firms in an oligopoly, when one firm changes its price, the demand curves of other firms in the industry are affected.

   1. It is assumed that if one firm raises its price, other firms will not raise their prices. By keeping their prices lower, other firms will increase their sales to previous customers of the firm with the higher price.

   2. It is further assumed that if one firm lowers its price, others in the industry will follow its lead. Consequently, any short-term advantage of price cutting is diluted as other firms reduce their prices.

   3. Because changes in price offer little long-term benefit to an oligopolist, prices within an oligopolistic industry tend to be more rigid than prices in other markets.

   4. The assumptions about the reaction of firms in an industry to price changes give rise to a kinked demand curve for each firm. For prices above the current price, demand is elastic. If the price is reduced, however, demand is inelastic.

   5. As a result of the kinked demand curve, the firm's marginal revenue schedule contains a discontinuous vertical segment at the currently marketed quantity and the current price. This vertical segment indicates that small changes in marginal cost will not affect equilibrium output or price.

E. Because of the kinked demand curve, individual oligopolistic firms rarely change their price. Instead, when a price change occurs all firms in the industry make similar changes.
   1. The characteristic of all firms changing price simultaneously suggests that the firms might be engaging in collusion (price-rigging, or secretly setting industry-wide prices).
   2. Instead of direct collusion, which is illegal, the accepted practice within an industry may call for one firm to be the price leader and for other firms to follow any changes that are made by that firm.
II. The economic model of monopolistic competition describes a market structure characterized by a large number of small firms that sell slightly differentiated products and compete with each other in an industry.
   A. The market demand faced by any firm is downward sloping, and the elasticity of the curve reflects the degree of product differentiation and the availability of substitute products. Because the demand curve is negatively sloped, the marginal revenue curve is located below the demand curve.
   B. Since products are differentiated in monopolistic competition, buyers will no longer automatically seek the commodity with the lowest price.
   C. Monopolistically competitive firms are not interdependent and do not, in general, react to one another's pricing and output decisions as do firms in oligopolistic industries.
   D. It is easy for firms to enter an industry that is monopolistically competitive because the capital requirements are usually not large.
   E. Like firms in all the other market models we have discussed, firms in monopolistic competition maximize short-run profits by producing the level of output where marginal cost equals marginal revenue.
   F. The existence of short-run economic profit will attract new firms into a monopolistically competitive industry. In the long run, however, competition will eliminate economic profit.
      1. At the long-run equilibrium level of output, each firm will charge a price greater than marginal cost, which indicates that resources are not being allocated in the most efficient way.
      2. Furthermore, in long-run equilibrium, firms are producing a level of output that is smaller than the optimal, or least-cost level of output. This indicates that monopolistically competitive firms underutilize plant and equipment and possess excess productive capacity.
III. Nonprice competition, which includes product differentiation and advertising, is used by oligopolistic and monopolistically competitive firms in an attempt to make their individual demand curves less elastic and thereby enhance the firm's control over product price and output.
   A. Advertising is used by firms in imperfectly competitive markets to create a product image, capture a segment of a market, and obtain a larger share of a market.
   B. There is disagreement about the economic value of advertising.
      1. Some argue that advertising provides information to consumers,

enhances the utility derived from consumption, stimulates spending in an economy, and expands the market for a product, thereby permitting a firm to take advantage of economies of scale.

2. Critics of advertising say that it is wasteful, it misrepresents products, it has little effect on a firm's share of the market, and it causes people to prefer private to public goods.

IV. In markets characterized by monopolistic competition or oligopoly, resources fail to be allocated in their most efficient manner.

KEY TERMS

You should be familiar with the meaning of the terms listed below. For definition of these terms, please refer to the glossary at the end of your textbook and to the appropriate section in this chapter.

oligopoly   collusion
monopolistic competition   price leader

CONCEPTS AND DEFINITIONS

Fill-in Questions

Complete each sentence by writing in the blank the most appropriate word or words from the terms listed below or by circling the word in parentheses that is correct.

collusion   price leader
product differentiation   economies of scale
oligopoly   perfect competition
nonprice competition   monpoloy
advertising   economic profit
monopolistic competition   marginal cost
kinked demand curve   marginal revenue
mutual interdependence   product development
capital intensive

1. Monopolistic competition is similar to the economic model of _____ _____ in the sense that it is easy to enter an industry and, within any market, there is a large number of small firms.

2. Oligopolists are said to face a(n) _____ because if they raise their price, demand is elastic and if they lower price, demand is inelastic.

3. An example of _____ would be when two airlines charge identical fares to travel from Ontario to San Jose, but one provides a snack lunch and complimentary champagne and the other makes more leg room available for passengers in the coach section of the airplane.

4. As a result of _____ consumers might be willing to pay more for Superclean Soap with Secret Ingredient XJ3 than for Smith's Plain Old Soap.

5. The small number of firms in an oligopolistic industry allows each firm to take advantage of _____ which result in lower production costs than if many firms were to compete.

6. The model of _____ would be most appropriate to use in analyzing a market in which there are a large number of small firms, each providing a somewhat differentiated product or service.

7. The elasticity of a firm's demand curve reflects the degree of _____ _____ as well as the availability of substitutes.

8. A characteristic of _____ is that firms are mutually interdependent so that each firm is aware of the actions taken by its competitors.

9. If all firms in an industry change price simultaneously, they might be engaging in _____. The firms in the industry might also be following the example set by a(n) _____.

10. An oligopolistic firm usually prefers to engage in _____ rather than in price competition since it faces a kinked demand curve.

11. Monopolistically competitive firms do not exhibit _____ and thus do not in general react to one another's pricing and output decisions.

12. The economic model of _____ is used to analyze markets in which a few large firms produce most of the output.

13. Economies of scale are normally found in oligopolistic industries where production is _____.

14. The presence of _____ induces new firms to enter a monopolistically competitive industry where capital requirements are modest.

15. The model of oligopoly is similar to that of _____ because firms in both market structures can exercise discretion in determining level of output and price.

16. Two major ways of establishing product differences are through _____ _____ and _____.

17. An oligopolist and a firm in monopolistic competition must equate _____ _____ with _____ in order to maximize profit.

18. For each case described below, indicate whether it applies to perfect (P) or imperfect (I) competition.

   a. Long-run equilibrium occurs when firms are operating at the lowest point on the average cost curve.

b. There is idle capacity when firms operate at the maximum profit point.

c. There is greater differentiation of products.

d. There will be some inefficiencies of resources allocation.

19. For each of the characteristics below, indicate whether it applies more closely to the model of oligopoly (O) or monopolistic competition (MC).

   a. Entry into the industry is likely to require large investments.

   b. Entry into the industry is relatively easy.

   c. One firm does not have to respond immediately to the pricing decisions of competitors.

   d. It is relatively common for nonprofitable firms to simply leave the industry.

   e. One firm must respond quickly to the pricing decisions of its competitors.

Multiple Choice Questions

Circle the correct answer.

1. Oligopolies may form when

   a. some firms manage to overcome the entry barriers to an industry dominated by a monopoly.

   b. small firms gradually leave the market.

   c. firms within the industry merge.

   d. all of the above.

2. Which of the following industries does not fit the stereotype of an oligopolistic industry?

   a. automobile-manufacturing industry

   b. aircraft-manufacturing industry

   c. TV repair industry

   d. Aluminum industry

3. At one time, the capital required to enter the automobile-manufacturing industry was not large and many different suppliers were in the market. Today, three American firms supply well over half of the domestic car market. This shows that

   a. an industry that once was oligopolistic may become monopolistically competitive over time.

   b. the creation of an oligopoly may depend in part on the capital requirements in an industry.

   c. the three largest automobile manufacturers in America engage in collusive practices.

   d. firms in this industry are large enough to ignore the actions of competitors.

4. Nonprice competition is preferred to price competition by oligopolists because

   a. each firm faces a kinked demand curve.

   b. nonprice competition is less expensive than price competition.

   c. price competition is infeasible with uniform products.

   d. nonprice competition increases the elasticity of demand for a firm's product.

5. If a firm has a kinked demand curve, that means

   a. the firm is unable to change price or quantity.

   b. demand is elastic if price is reduced and inelastic if price is raised.

   c. it is a monopolistically competitive industry.

   d. the marginal cost curve may change somewhat without affecting the equilibrium price or quantity.

6. In oligopolistic markets, prices are usually

   a. high.

   b. low.

   c. flexible.

   d. inflexible.

7. Collusive agreements among oligopolists not only eliminate the uncertainty each firm has about others' behavior but also

   a. permit firms to reap most advantages of a monopoly.

   b. are encouraged by government in order to give consumers information about products.

   c. are easy to maintain since these agreements are a matter of public record.

   d. ensure that each firm will produce the same product or service as all others.

8. If Cal's Stereo advertises "We'll beat any deal" and Leo's Stereo promises the lowest prices in town

   a. both firms are using price and nonprice competition to attract customers.

   b. both firms are using nonprice competition to increase the elasticity of their individual demand curves.

   c. each firm is trying to consolidate rather than fragment the total market demand curve for stereos.

   d. one or both firms must be guilty of false advertising since there can be only one lowest price for a stereo.

9. Critics of advertising argue that

   a. expenditures on advertising add to the utility consumers gain from products.

   b. resources spent on advertising could be better used for other purposes.

    c. advertising stimulates spending, thus returning national income to the circular flow.

    d. advertising expands the market, thus promoting the sale of public goods.

10. If firms in a monopolistically competitive industry are in long-run equilibrium making zero excess profits, we can be sure that

    a. resources are being allocated efficiently since firms are not earning economic profits.

    b. each firm in the industry must be producing at its most efficient level of output.

    c. new firms will be seeking entry into this industry because capital requirements are modest.

    d. the equilibrium price and output for most firms is to the left of minimum average total cost.

11. The shape of a kinked demand curve faced by an oligopolistic firm indicates that if one firm lowers its price

    a. other firms will keep their prices constant because rigid prices are typical in oligopoly.

    b. its demand curve will become much more elastic than if price remained constant.

    c. other firms will also lower their prices or face a decline in sales.

    d. it is not adhering to the collusive agreement signed by all participating firms.

12. If one firm in an oligopoly raises its price and other firms fail to take similar action, it is safe to conclude that the firm raising its price will have

    a. increased revenues because demand is elastic.

    b. decreased revenues because demand is elastic.

    c. increased revenues because demand is inelastic.

    d. decreased revenues because demand is inelastic.

13. If American Motors Corporation, the smallest of the domestic automobile producers, wants to increase its share of the domestic automobile market, the *least* likely method of accomplishing that goal would be to

    a. decrease the price it charges for its automobiles.

    b. launch an ambitious advertising campaign showing that AMC cars get better gas mileage than their competitors.

    c. extend their "Buyer Protection Plan," which covers normal repairs to the auto, from five years to the life of the car.

    d. make AM/FM radios and air conditioning standard equipment on all AMC models without increasing sticker prices.

14. Which of the following is a unique characteristic of oligopoly?

    a. production of a standardized product.

    b. mutual interdependence among firms in the industry.

    c. the use of advertising and product development.

    d. the existence of barriers to entry including patents and copyrights.

APPLICATIONS

1. Oligopolists prefer to engage in nonprice competition as opposed to price competition. Define and provide examples of nonprice competition, and explain why in oligopolistic markets, nonprice competition might be preferred to price competition. Be specific.

2. How do the long-run results of monopoly and monpolistic competition differ? Be specific.

3. Why doesn't freedom of entry in monopolistic competition lead to the same results as those that characterize pure competition?

4. With as much *relevant* detail as you can provide, describe accurately and completely the features that characterize each of the four major market forms: perfect competition, monopolistic competition, oligopoly, and monopoly, from one another.

5. Assume a market study indicates that an oligopolist faces an elastic demand curve. In general, what prevents the oligopolist from lowering price and thereby increasing total receipts from the sale of its product?

ANSWERS

Fill-in Questions

1. perfect competition
2. kinked demand curve
3. nonprice competition
4. product differentiation
5. economies of scale
6. monopolistic competition
7. product differentiation
8. oligopoly
9. collusion; price leader
10. nonprice competition
11. mutual interdependence
12. oligopoly
13. capital-intensive

14. economic profit
15. monopoly
16. product development; advertising
17. *MC*; *MR* or *MR*; *MC*
18. a. P
    b. I
    c. I
    d. I
19. a. O
    b. MC
    c. MC
    d. MC
    e. O

Multiple Choice Questions

1.	d	8.	a
2.	c	9.	b
3.	b	10.	d
4.	a	11.	c
5.	d	12.	b
6.	d	13.	a
7.	a	14.	b

APPLICATIONS

1. Nonprice competition is competition by firms that is aimed at increasing sales by using tactics other than price changes. Advertising, promotional campaigns, trading stamps, product differentiation, and gifts are all examples of nonprice competition. In oligopolistic markets, the actions taken by one firm to increase sales will evoke reaction from other firms in the industry. For example, if one firm decreases its price to gain a larger share of the market, others will react with price cuts of their own causing profits of all firms in the industry to fall. Since price competition adversely affects profits, nonprice competition tends to be preferred as a way to attempt to increase sales and to gain a larger share of the market.

2. In the long run, a monopolist can earn an economic profit because other firms are prevented from entering markets that are monopolized. In monopolistic competition, short-run profits will attract other firms into the industry. New firms will enter the industry until economic profits are eliminated. In the long run, each firm in monopolistic competition will have excess capacity since the equilibrium output is smaller than that at which average total cost (ATC) is at a minimum. Whether or not a monopolist will have excess capacity depends on the position of its ATC curve at the profit-maximizing output.

3. Since each firm in monopolistic competition faces a downward-sloping demand curve, the long-run profit-maximizing price for any firm in the industry will be higher and the corresponding output will be smaller than they would be in perfect competition, where each firm faces a perfectly elastic demand curve. Moreover, as noted in Problem 2, monopolistically competitive firms will have long-run excess capacity where, in the long run, perfectly competitive firms will operate at the minimum on their ATC curve.

4. The most important characteristics of each of the four market forms we have discussed are summarized below.

Type of market	Type of product	Slope of firm's demand curve	Firm's ability to influence price	No. of firms in industry	Ease of entry into industry
Perfect competition	Uniform	Horizontal at market price	None	Large number of small firms	Easy
Monopolistic competition	Differentiated	Downward sloping	Limited	Large number of small firms	Easy
Oligopoly	Differentiated	Downward sloping	Yes	Few large firms	Barriers
Monopoly	Differentiated	Downward sloping	Yes	One	Barriers

5. An oligopolistic firm may decrease price and increase revenues only if other firms in the industry do not react to the price change. If other firms react by decreasing their prices, the first firm's demand curve will become inelastic. In that situation, the lower price results in reduced rather than increased revenues.

Chapter 27

Big Business in the American Economy

LEARNING OBJECTIVES

In this chapter we look at the impact of big business on the American economy. As noted in the previous two chapters, there are conflicting viewpoints regarding the costs and benefits of monopoly and oligopoly. Some argue that big business is primarily responsible for developments that contribute to the high per-capita GNP enjoyed in the United States. Others indicate that oligopolies and monopolies in the United States economy restrain competition and trade and pursue goals that are not in the public's interest.

After reading this chapter, you should be able to:

1. identify the ways in which large corporations restrain free competition through the exercise of economic power;

2. identify the beneficial effects associated with large-scale enterprise;

3. trace the history of antimonopoly legislation in the United States and assess the effectiveness of that legislation in encouraging competition in the economy;

4. speculate about the future course of public policy toward big business.

CHAPTER OUTLINE

I. Big business can be defined according to the absolute size of the firm (total sales revenue, assets, market value) or according to the firm's control of the market.
   A. Market control may be independent of the size of a firm. For example, a general store in a small town may possess considerable economic power in the market it serves.
   B. As used in this chapter, big business refers to the firms in the United States economy that sell their products in monopolistic or oligopolistic markets.
   C. There is continuing growth in corporate assets, which indicates a trend toward bigness among American companies.

1. The percent of total output produced by the four largest firms in an industry is called the concentration ratio and is one indication of bigness.
2. The United States has the largest GNP in the world, and a significant portion of that output comes from large corporations.

II. One of big business' impacts on economic activity is the restriction of competition. This restriction can be accomplished in several ways.

A. If a firm is a monopsonist, the only buyer of a product or service, it may have the power to insist on discounts from suppliers that will lower its production costs, but will not necessarily lower the prices charged to consumers. Monopsony also acts as a barrier to small firms which might attempt to enter an industry.

B. A large corporation can also reduce competition by extending its control over the supply of raw materials and intermediate goods (vertical integration) or by limiting competition from other firms in the product market through the purchase of competing companies that produce substitute products.

C. Large manufacturing firms can restrict competition by exercising control over distributors of manufactured goods.

D. A large corporation may also use legal and political means to restrain competition. Large corporations have the funds and ability to influence election outcomes which may yield subsequent benefits to the firm. They also have the financial ability to bear the cost of product litigation, lobby for favorable legislation, hire the most qualified employees, and take other actions that restrict a smaller firm's ability to compete.

E. Big business may erect psychological barriers to prevent entry of smaller firms into a market.

III. In addition to restricting competition, big business also has other effects on the economy.

A. Big business can take advantage of economies of scale. Even though a firm has the power to charge a price greater than marginal cost (MC), economies of scale may result in product prices that are lower than would result from competition.

1. Although a single plant may have to be large to take advantage of economies of scale, there is little evidence that justifies the existence of multi-plant firms on grounds of efficiency.

B. Generally, only large firms are able to afford expensive product research and development, marketing studies, and the advertising that is necessary to launch new products in the market.

1. While big business can afford to be progressive, it has been suggested that large firms may resist technological advances because new advances may make existing production processes obsolete and would therefore necessitate substantial outlays for retooling.

C. Big business may be necessary to compete with other large firms, labor unions, and government. Galbraith's theory of countervailing power explains how large and powerful groups give rise to other large and powerful groups. For example, large corporations may give rise to large unions.

Collectively, these large organizations in competition with one another limit the ability of each to restrict competition.

IV. Legislation to control big business first appeared in the late nineteenth century. Its objective was to preserve and protect market competition in industries where large corporations had acquired considerable economic power.

    A. The Sherman Antiturst Act (1890) makes it illegal to monopolize an industry or to conspire to restrain trade.

        1. Early court interpretation of this act held that there were good trusts and bad trusts, and, under the "rule of reason," only the latter were viewed as having violated the law.

        2. The decision in the *Alcoa* case in 1945 repealed the "rule of reason" and stipulated that all trusts are illegal.

    B. The Clayton Act (1911) outlaws specific activities that are held to be restraints of trade.

        1. The Robinson-Patman Act (1936) amends the Clayton act to make price discrimination illegal.

        2. The Celler-Kefauver Antimerger Act (1950) further amends the Clayton Act to prevent mergers that would weaken or reduce competition.

    C. The Federal Trade Commission Act (1914) establishes a federal agency to make and enforce rules regarding acceptable business conduct.

V. Although big business has prospered in the 1970s, increased concern regarding the potential abuses of economic power has provided an impetus for strengthening enforcement of antitrust statutes. However, since it is recognized that many benefits accrue to consumers from big business, stricter enforcement will be selective in nature.

KEY TERMS

You should be familiar with the meaning of the terms listed below. For definition of these terms, please refer to the glossary at the end of your textbook and to the appropriate section in this chapter.

concentration ratios	conglomerate mergers
monopsony	countervailing power
vertical integration	trust
horizontal integration	Sherman Antitrust Act

CONCEPTS AND DEFINITIONS

Fill-in Questions

Complete each sentence by writing in the blank the most appropriate word or words from the terms listed below or by circling the word in parentheses that is correct.

horizontal integration
Sherman Antitrust Act
factor
concentration ratios
vertical integration

monopsony
conglomerate mergers
trust
countervailing power

1. The idea embodied in the concept of _____ is that a concentration of economic strength in one group will stimulate development of other groups with similar, perhaps offsetting, economic strength.

2. When a company such as Mobil Oil purchases a controlling interest in a department-store chain, that is a(n) _____.

3. The _____ makes it illegal for a company to monopolize trade or to conspire with others to restrain trade.

4. If many firms compete in an industry, the industry's _____ would likely be low.

5. Since the United States government is the sole domestic purchaser of tanks and certain other forms of military equipment, a(n) _____ exists in the military-equipment industry.

6. The first federal legislation specifically designed to curb the economic power of trusts was the _____, which was passed by Congress in 1890.

7. One reason that _____ are undertaken by companies is to help ensure that they will make a profit even if one or more of the markets in which they sell goods may be temporarily depressed.

8. An example of _____ is the formation of a consumer cooperative to counteract a firm's monopolistic selling practices. In effect, the cooperative obtains economic power by acting as a buyer's monopoly or a(n) _____.

9. An industry's _____ is obtained by dividing the amount of output produced by the four largest firms in an industry by total industry output.

10. The merger of many independent sugar refining companies in 1892 into the American Sugar Refining Company represented _____ within the sugar industry and the formation of a sugar _____.

11. _____ exists when one company owns all of the resources necessary to produce and market a product. _____ occurs when one company monoplizes one stage of production or product distribution.

12. A collection of corporations under the control of an individual or a few individuals is called a _____.

13. If General Motors purchased Chrysler Corporation and AMC, that would be an example of _____.

14. If a single hospital were the only source of employment for nurses in a small town, the hospital would be a _____ in the labor market for nurses.

15. Studies of market _____ have shown that, currently within consumer-goods industries, there is a tendency toward larger and larger firms and less competition.

16. Standard Oil Company created an economic _____ when, through acquisition of various companies, it was able to dominate the production, refining, and distribution of oil in the United States.

17. Large corporations tend to have monopsony power in _____ markets.

18. For each of the statements below, indicate whether it is made for (F) or against (A) the existence of big business.

   a. The sales price of goods is above the marginal cost of production.

   b. The firm is able to produce at the lowest point on its long-run average cost curve.

   c. There are incentives to devote resources for research and quality control.

   d. The firm pays lower wages than labor's marginal revenue product.

   e. Market power is a necessary part of the incentive system of the economy.

   f. There is competition between departments and functions within a firm.

   g. Firms can afford to enter industries formerly dominated by monopolies.

Multiple Choice Questions

Circle the correct answer.

1. If big business is defined in terms of market control, a single bank in a small, isolated community in Wyoming may have relatively more market control than General Motors since

   a. the small bank must belong to the Fed, which gives great economic strength to its member banks.

   b. General Motors faces competition of other automobile firms while the small-town bank has no direct competition.

   c. the bank is capable of creating money and thus has greater influence over market activity than a firm that cannot create money.

   d. a larger fraction of the town's residents must work for the bank than for the local GM dealer.

2. In the United States, the peak years for merger activity occurred in the

   a. early 1960s.

   b. later 1960s.

    c. early 1970s.

    d. later 1970s.

3. One explanation of a high industry-concentration ratio would be that

    a. significant economies of large-scale production exist.

    b. the law of demand is particularly important in that industry.

    c. many firms in the industry work intensively on their production.

    d. the production processes of firms in this industry are labor-intensive.

4. One of the most compelling arguments against the existence of big business is that

    a. economies of large-scale production are realized within a plant and not among the plants of a large-scale enterprise; thus, large multi-plant firms are unnecessary.

    b. only small firms or independent inventors have been responsible for all of the most important inventions of the twentieth century; thus large firms are unnecessary for progress.

    c. gains in production efficiency will always accompany a move toward purely competitive conditions; thus, there should be many small firms in every industry.

    d. nearly every market can support enough firms to assure competition; hence, markets should be competitive.

5. If a firm producing automobile bumpers acquired the assets of other companies producing such diversified products as sugar, cigars, zinc, fertilizer, wire and cable, and musical instruments, that would be an example of

    a. horizontal merger.

    b. conglomerate integration.

    c. conglomerate merger.

    d. vertical integration.

6. By contributing substantial sums of money to the campaigns of candidates for political office, a firm hopes to

    a. provide a public service to American voters.

    b. reduce the need for others to contribute.

    c. set an example so that others are motivated to contribute large sums.

    d. help elect individuals who may be sympathetic to the firm.

7. Which of the following is *not* a tactic generally used by big business to restrict competition?

    a. Lobbying for favorable legislation.

    b. Hiring the most-qualified empolyees.

    c. Erecting psychological barriers to entry in an industry.

    d. Initiating class-action lawsuits against competitors.

8. As a result of economies of scale in large enterprise,

    a. product prices are always lower than they would be under competitive conditions.

    b. production is greater than it would be under conditions of competition.

    c. within a certain range of production, unit costs are reduced as output is increased.

    d. a firm will earn substantial economic profits because average cost will be less than average revenue.

9. Product improvement and technological advance

    a. are synonymous since both have the same meaning.

    b. may mean different things since product improvement may involve only superficial changes.

    c. require enormous capital outlays and therefore are usually undertaken only by the largest firms.

    d. will generate increased profits for firms who provide funding for these activities.

10. The concept of countervailing power as applied to economic situations involving large-scale economic enterprise is prominent in the writings of

    a. Joe Bain.

    b. Adam Smith.

    c. John Galbraith.

    d. Joan Robinson.

11. The "rule of reason"

    a. was first applied in 1920 in the case of *U.S.* v. *U.S. Steel.*

    b. was used to broadly define the scope of the Sherman Antitrust Act.

    c. stipulated that a distinction should be made between large and small trusts, and that only large trusts should be prosecuted.

    d. was established by the Federal Trade Commision (FTC) in its standards for acceptable conduct of business.

12. The Clayton and Federal Trade Commission Acts were passed by Congress

    a. to end unfair competition by big business.

    b. as a result of limitations in the Celler-Kefauver Act.

    c. as a result of a Supreme Court decision regarding a trust that pooled the railroad interests of J.P. Morgan and J.D. Rockefeller.

d. to deal explicitly with the problem of price discrimination and its effects on small, independent businesses.

13. A firm engaged in price discrimination violates the

a. Sherman Antitrust Act.

b. The Clayton Antitrust Act.

c. The Robinson-Patman Act.

d. The Celler-Kefauver Act.

14. Many experts believe that the government should prevent any mergers between two firms that already have a large market share. That approach to mergers reflects the philosophy embodied in

a. original court interpretations of the Sherman Act.

b. recent court opinions that all monopolies should be prevented.

c. the belief that government should prevent unfair competition arising from mergers.

d. the "rule of reason" which came out of the 1920 *U.S. Steel* case.

15. The primary purpose of the Robinson-Patman Act is to

a. establish an agency to enforce rules of business conduct.

b. encourage certain business practices which otherwise might be regarded as restraints of trade.

c. prohibit a firm from buying stock of a competitor when that reduces competition.

d. prohibit price discrimination by manufacturers in their dealings with retailers.

APPLICATIONS

1.   *"The Justice Department filed a civil antitrust suit charging two Texas trade associations with conspiring to fix shipping rates of fresh fruits and vegetables from the Rio Grande Valley."*

"The suit was filed in federal district court in Brownsville against the Texas Citrus and Vegetable Growers and Shippers of Harlingen, and the Greater Texas Motor Transportation Broker Association of Pharr."

"It charges that since early 1969 both associations and their members prepared and circulated rate schedules for the interstate transportation of fresh produce by truck and encouraged adherence to the rate schedules. As a result, the complaint contends, shipping rates have been fixed at 'artificial and noncompetitive levels' and competition in the market for truck services has been restrained."

According to the above passage, it would seem most likely that the produce shippers involved are being charged with violating the

a. Celler-Kefauver Act.

b. Federal Trade Commission Act.

    c. Sherman Act.

    d. Robinson-Patman Act.

2. If the nation's second-largest producer of cans tried to merge with the third-largest producer of glass containers, that would constitute

    a. vertical integration.

    b. horizontal integration.

    c. an economic trust.

    d. countervailing power.

3. In 1962, the Supreme Court ruled against a merger between the Brown Shoe Company and the Kinney Shoe Company. Brown was the country's fourth-largest shoe manufacturer and Kinney was the largest individual shoe retailer. If it had been permitted, the merger between Brown and Kinney would constitute

    a. vertical integration.

    b. horizontal integration.

    c. conglomerate merger.

    d. countervailing power.

ANSWERS

Fill-in Questions

1.	countervailing power	13.	horizontal integration
2.	conglomerate merger	14.	monopsony
3.	Sherman Antitrust Act	15.	concentration ratios
4.	concentration ratio	16.	trust
5.	monopsony	17.	factor
6.	Sherman Antitrust Act	18.	a. A
7.	conglomerate mergers		b. F
8.	countervailing power; monopsony		c. F
9.	concentration ratio		d. A
10.	horizontal integration; trust		e. F
11.	vertical integration;		f. F
	horizontal integration		g. F
12.	trust		

Multiple Choice Questions

1.	b	6.	d	11.	a
2.	b	7.	d	12.	a
3.	a	8.	c	13.	c
4.	a	9.	b	14.	b
5.	c	10.	c	15.	d

APPLICATIONS

1. c
2. b
3. a

Chapter 28

Demand in the Resource Market

LEARNING OBJECTIVES

Up to this point, we have focused on the transactions that take place between households and firms in the product market. We will now investigate another set of transactions: those that occur when businesses purchase resources. In this chapter we will find out how the demand for productive resources is determined and will discuss the elements that affect the elasticity of demand for factors of production.

After reading this chapter, you should be able to:

1. distinguish between derived and direct demand;

2. explain how a firm's demand and the market demand for variable factors of production are obtained;

3. estimate a factor demand schedule from data regarding resource productivity and a firm's product demand curve;

4. explain how an entrepreneur determines the optimal amount of resources to use and how that leads to a profit-maximizing level of production;

5. identify the determinants of factor demand and of demand elasticity;

6. explain how a firm determines the optimal mix of resources to be used in production.

CHAPTER OUTLINE

I. To determine a firm's demand for a resource or factor of production, it is necessary to determine the factor's marginal physical product (MPP—the change in total output brought about by a change in one unit of a variable factor of production) and the factor's marginal revenue product (MRP—the change in total revenue that results from the addition of one unit of a variable factor of production).

    A. Because of the law of diminishing returns, a graph of the MPP schedule is negatively sloped.

    B. A firm's marginal revenue product schedule for a resource is also the firm's demand curve for that factor.

        1. Since the MPP schedule declines as additional output is produced, the MRP schedule is also negatively sloped.

        2. Adding the MRP schedules for individual firms provides an estimate of the market demand curve for a factor of production.

    C. In order to maximize profit, a firm will continue to hire additional units of a variable resource as long as its marginal resource cost (MRC—the cost of an additional unit of a variable resource) is less than the additional revenue produced by that resource (MRP). Therefore, profit maximization occurs at that level of output where MRC = MRP. The output at which MRC = MRP is the same output at which MC = MR.

    D. Under imperfectly competitive conditions, a firm's factor demand curve will be steeper, or less elastic, than that of a perfectly competitive firm since marginal revenue declines as output increases for imperfectly competitive firms.

II. A firm will produce a given level of output at the least cost, that is, it achieves its optimum resource mix when the MRP per dollar spent on each resource is the same ($\dfrac{\text{MRP}_1}{P_1} = \dfrac{\text{MRP}_2}{P_2} = \dfrac{\text{MRP}_3}{P_3}$, and so on). This is analogous to the equal marginal utility principle in consumption.

III. The demand for a resource is *derived* from the demand for the final product that can be manufactured with the resource. Therefore, resource demand changes with changes in demand for the final product.

    A. If demand for a product increases, the demand for the resources used to manufacture the product increases. If product demand decreases, resource demand will also decrease.

    B. The more productive a resource, the greater the demand for the resource.

    C. If the price of a *substitute* resource increases the demand for a resource will increase. If the price of a *complementary* resource increases, the demand of a resource will decrease as well.

IV. There are several factors that influence the elasticity of demand for a resource.

    A. If MPP declines slowly as additional variable resources are used, factor demand will be more elastic than if MPP declines rapidly.

    B. If final product demand is elastic, a small change in product price will have a greater effect on sales and, consequently, on factor demand. If product demand is inelastic, factor demand is likely to be inelastic.

    C. The elasticity of a factor demand curve will increase as the number of substitutes for the factor increases.

    D. Elasticity of resource demand also will depend on the amount of total production cost attributed to a factor. If the cost of some resource represents only a small fraction of total production cost, any change in the cost of the resource will have only a small effect on product demand and, consequently, on factor demand. Conversely, if a factor accounts for a substantial amount of total production cost, its demand is likely to be elastic.

KEY TERMS

You should be familiar with the meaning of the terms listed below. For definition of these terms, please refer to the glossary at the end of your textbook and to the appropriate section in this chapter.

marginal physical product (MPP)   optimal resource mix
marginal revenue product (MRP)   derived demand

CONCEPTS AND DEFINITIONS

Fill-in Questions

Complete each sentence by writing in the blank the most appropriate word or words from the terms listed below or by circling the word in parentheses that is correct.

direct demand   marginal physical product (MPP)
total product   derived demand
optimal resource mix   marginal revenue product (MRP)
marginal resource cost (MRC)

1. The demand for a resource used in production is a _____ while the demand for a final product is a _____.

2. The additional output that a firm produces as a result of hiring one more worker is known as the _____ of labor.

3. The value of additional output produced as a result of hiring one more worker is the _____ of labor.

4. If as a result of hiring an additional worker, total output increases from 2000 to 2100 units, then the _____ of the additional worker is 100 units.

5. The _____ indicates that beyond some point, total output increases at a decreasing rate as more variable factors of production are combined with fixed factors of production.

6. The _____ of successive workers ultimately declines as a result of the _____.

7. An entrepreneur determines the _____ for the production of a firm's product by equating the MRP per dollar spent on each input used in production.

8. In order to maximize total profits, a firm must equate _____ and _____ when hiring resources.

9. If _____ were greater than _____, a firm would be able to increase profits by hiring more resources.

10. In the market for labor under perfectly competitive conditions, the _____ _____ is equal to the wage rate.

11. If a firm faces a positively sloped factor supply curve, the factor price will be less than the factor's _____.

12. Because resource demand is a _____, any change in product demand will result in a change in demand for resources used to produce the product.

13. If the _____ of labor declines slowly as additional workers are employed, resource demand will tend to be relatively _____; if the decline is rapid, resource demand will tend to be relatively _____
_____.

14. If product demand is inelastic, resource demand is expected to be _____
_____.

15. If the total cost of a resource is a large portion of the total cost of production, resource demand will be relatively _____; if the resource cost represents only a minor part of total cost, demand will be relatively
_____.

16. If a firm hires resources to the point where $\dfrac{MRP_1}{P_1} = \dfrac{MRP_2}{P_2} = \dfrac{MRP_3}{P_3}$,
then the firm has achieved its _____.

17. If the price of a resource increases, the demand for its substitutes can be expected to (increase/decrease).

18. Consider the case of the derived demand for nails. For each of the cases described below, indicate whether the demand for nails is likely to increase (+) or decrease (−).

    a. The demand for housing and furniture rises rapidly.

    b. There is a slump in construction activity.

    c. There is a new, low-cost glue that may be used in the place of nails for both furniture and interiors of buildings.

    d. There is a new machine replacing the hammer that drives nails much more accurately and quickly.

19. For each of the descriptions below, indicate whether there will be an increase (+) or decrease (−) in the demand for the factor.

    a. Consumer demand for the final product produced with the factor increases.

    b. There has been a change in technology that increases the productivity of the factor.

    c. The price of a close substitute for the factor falls.

    d. Consumer demand for the final product falls.

20. For each of the conditions below, indicate whether the factor demand is likely to be elastic (E) or inelastic (I).

   a. There are a large number of close substitutes for the factor.

   b. The marginal physical product curve is relatively flat. That is, it has a gentle downward slope.

   c. The demand for the final product is elastic.

   d. There are no substitutes for the input.

   e. The resource represents only a very small proportion of total input expenditures.

Multiple Choice Questions

Circle the correct answer.

1. As long as the marginal cost of a resource is less than its marginal revenue product, a firm

   a. may benefit from using less of the resource.

   b. is not maximizing profit at the current level of output.

   c. should decrease production to maximize profit.

   d. faces an elastic factor demand curve.

2. Under conditions of perfect competition in the resource market, a firm will maximize profits by hiring workers up to the point where the wage rate is equal to

   a. MRC.

   b. MRP.

   c. MPP.

   d. MC.

3. Resource demand usually increases when

   a. consumer demand declines for a final product produced with the resource.

   b. the price of a close substitute for the resource falls.

   c. there is a change in technology that increases the productivity of the resource.

   d. the supply of the resource increases.

4. If the market demand for a product increases, the demand curves for factors used in the production process

   a. shift to the right.

   b. shift to the left.

   c. are unaffected.

   d. do not change, but the quantity demanded of each resource increases.

5. If a firm is a monopsonist in the labor market

   a. the average cost of labor is less than the marginal cost of labor.

   b. its labor supply curve is horizontal.

   c. its labor supply curve is elastic.

   d. the marginal cost of labor is less than the average cost of labor.

6. The MRP per dollar spent on each resource must be the same if a firm is to obtain an optimal resource mix. This implies that

   a. a firm with an optimal resource mix will use identical amounts of all factors of production.

   b. the total expenditure on each factor of production is the same.

   c. the price of each resource must be the same if a firm is to achieve an optimal resource mix.

   d. the amount of each resource used will depend on resource productivity and price.

7. The sum of each firm's demand curve for an input

   a. is equal to the market demand curve.

   b. is an approximation of the market demand curve.

   c. will show a direct relationship between quantity demanded and price.

   d. can be used to represent the market supply curve.

8. The MRP schedule shows a firm's demand for a resource because

   a. it shows the number of units of a resource the firm is able and willing to purchase at various prices.

   b. it specifies the amount of product that each resource has produced.

   c. it is a schedule that shows the amount of resources available to a firm.

   d. it shows a direct relationship between the number of units of a resource used and the cost of that resource.

9. The demand for a factor of production depends largely upon

   a. the supply of the factor.

   b. the supply of other factors of production.

   c. the demand for other factors of production.

   d. the demand for the product that the factor helps produce.

10. If the MPP of labor declines slowly as additional workers are used in production,

    a. factor demand tends to be relatively inelastic.

    b. the marginal revenue product will be small.

    c. the marginal resource cost will decline slowly.

    d. factor demand tends to be relatively elastic.

11. An entrepreneur determines the optimal resource mix to produce a given level of output by equating

    a. MRC per dollar spent on each input used in production.

    b. MRP per dollar spent on each input used in production.

    c. marginal cost with price.

    d. marginal factor cost per dollar spent on each input used in production.

12. In imperfect competition, the MRP schedule will fall at a faster rate than in competitive markets because

    a. resources are less productive under imperfectly competitive conditions than in competitive markets.

    b. imperfectly competitive firms use fewer resources than competitive firms.

    c. in imperfectly competitive markets, the firm faces a negatively sloped product demand curve.

    d. resource demand is inelastic in imperfectly competitive markets.

APPLICATIONS

1. A firm produces a product with a fixed amount of capital and one variable resource, labor. The daily production capability of this firm is shown below.

Number of workers	Total daily output	MPP
0	0	
1	100	
2	220	
3	300	
4	360	
5	400	

   a. Compute the marginal productivity of the first through fifth workers.

   b. If labor costs $40/worker/day and output sells for 50¢/unit, how many workers should the firm hire to maximize profit? Show your computations.

   c. If the price of output increases to $1.00/unit and labor costs remain at $40/worker/day, how, if at all, will the firm's demand for labor be affected?

   d. If the price of output increases to $1.00/unit as a result of a doubling of wage costs to $80/worker/day, what effect will these changes have on the firm's demand for labor?

2. The ACME Transmission Co. uses three variable factors of production in its assembly operations. The cost of each factor and their respective marginal productivities at the current level of utilization are shown in the table below.

Factor no.	MPP	Factor price/unit
1	10	$20
2	20	$30
3	50	$50

To cope with rising costs, the company management ordered a study of all phases of company operations to see if the current level of output could be produced at a lower total cost. As consultant to ATC, can you recommend a change in the resource mix used by the assembly division that could make the firm more cost-effective in production? Justify your answer.

3. The diagram below shows the situation confronting a monopsonist in the market for one factor of production.

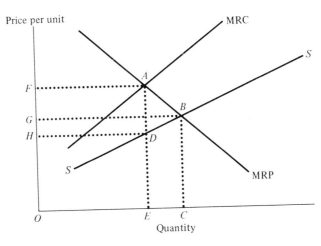

a. According to the diagram, how much of the resource would the firm use in profit maximizing equilibrium? Why?

b. What price/unit must the firm pay to secure its desired amount of resources?

c. Why does the MRC schedule lie above the supply curve for a monopsonist?

ANSWERS

Fill-in Questions

1. derived demand; direct demand
2. MPP
3. MRP
4. MPP
5. law of diminishing returns

16. optimal resource mix
17. increase
18. a. +
    b. –
    c. –

6. MPP; law of diminishing returns	d. +
7. optimal resource mix	19. a. +
8. MRP; MRC	b. +
9. MRP; MRC	c. −
10. MRP	d. −
11. MRC	20. a. E
12. derived demand	b. E
13. MPP; elastic; inelastic	c. E
14. inelastic	d. I
15. elastic; inelastic	e. I

Multiple Choice Questions

1.	b	7.	b
2.	b	8.	a
3.	c	9.	d
4.	a	10.	d
5.	a	11.	b
6.	d	12.	c

APPLICATIONS

1. a.

Number of workers	MPP = change in total output / change in variable resource
0	0
1	100
2	120
3	80
4	60
5	40

b. To maximize profit, the firm should equate MRC or $40 with MRP.

Number of workers	MRP	MRC = wage rate
0	0	
1	$50	$40
2	$60	40
3	$40	40
4	$30	40
5	$20	40

The firm is in equilibrium hiring three workers.

c . As the price of output increases from 50¢ to $1.00, the MRP of each worker will double. At the new price, the firm should hire five workers. At this point, the new MRP ($20 × 2 = $40) is equal to MRC.

d. There should be no change from the original quantity demanded.

2. An optimal resource mix is achieved where the MPP of each factor divided by the factor price is equal for all resources used in production. In this case, although factor 3 is more expensive than 1 or 2, it also is more productive so that the firm could maintain current production and lower variable costs by laying off some of factors 1 and 2 and hiring additional units of factor 3. Adjustment of the factor mix used in the assembly division should continue until the desired equalities are obtained.

3. a. The monopsonist would use quantity E of the resource, since at that level of utilization, MRC = MRP.

   b. Once the firm decides on the appropriate quantity to hire, the supply curve indicates the price at which the resource is available. In this case, the firm will pay an amount H per unit.

   c. The supply curve is an average cost curve for this particular resource. Since the average cost increases as more of the resource is used, the marginal cost must be greater than the average cost. (Remember, for any average to rise, the corresponding marginal figure must be *greater* than the average.) Another way of looking at this situation is as follows: As the firm increases its utilization of the resource, the price of all units of the resource is increased. Hence the cost of an additional unit, the marginal cost, includes the cost of that unit plus the increase in cost for all previous units. Consequently, the MC curve lies above the supply curve.

Chapter 29

Supply in the Resource Market

LEARNING OBJECTIVES

This chapter examines the determinants of the supply of land, labor, and financial capital in the market for resources. Except for certain individual labor supply decisions, the law of supply introduced in Chapter 3 applies in resource markets as it does in product markets.

After reading this chapter, you should be able to:

1. identify the determinants of individual labor supply and derive an individual labor supply schedule using indifference curve analysis;

2. explain how wages are determined in labor markets and why occupational wage differences exist;

3. explain why the supply of land is regarded as fixed and how the concept of economic rent applies to any resource in fixed supply;

4. identify the circumstances under which the supply of land may be regarded as adhering to the law of supply, and the pros and cons of using the price system to allocate the stock of land;

5. identify the factors and institutions that influence the supply of financial capital (loanable funds) to business.

CHAPTER OUTLINE

I. The labor market is the largest and most important of the resource markets.
    A. In making labor supply decisions, individuals consider self-interest which often involves factors in addition to the wage rate (such as job satisfaction). This means that the quantity of labor supplied by individuals does not necessarily increase as the wage or price of labor increases.
    B. Indifference curve analysis is used to analyze individual decisions to work or to use time in nonwork or leisure pursuits.

      1. The line of wage constraint, analogous to the line of budget constraint in the market for consumer goods, shows the rate at which time may be transformed into income for an individual.

      2. The points at which various lines of wage constraint are tangent to an individual's indifference curves tell us how many hours of labor an individual will supply at certain wage rates. From this information we can construct a supply of labor curve.

      3. An individual's labor supply curve may bend backward at high wages indicating that at wages above some level, leisure time is preferred to additional income from working.

      4. The market supply curve for labor (consisting of the sum of all individual labor supply schedules) is probably positively sloped because every individual schedule does not bend backward at the same wage rate.

  C. In labor markets, wages are determined through the interaction of demand and supply.

      1. Occupational differences in wages persist because of differences in job-related skill requirements and because of differences in the skills and abilities possessed by individual workers.

      2. Differences in wages also exist to compensate for differences in working conditions.

II. The supply of land, unlike other productive resources, is more or less fixed. On the other hand, the known quantity of natural resources is continually expanding and with changes in technology, natural resources are becoming more accessible and productive.

  A. When the supply of a resource is fixed, a change in price, either up or down, does not influence supply.

      1. The price paid for the use of land, or any other resource that is fixed, is known as economic rent.

        a. Economic rent is called a pure surplus since it does not create or encourage productivity.

        b. Proposals to redistribute land rent are based on the idea that redistribution of land ownership would have no effect on productivity; the only change would be in the distribution of the income from land.

      2. The price paid for land, as for other resources, serves to ration the stock of land and allocate it to its most productive uses.

        a. Although payments for land allocate land to its most productive uses, the price system fails to take account of the social costs and benefits of alternative uses of land and so may result in a less-than-optimal allocation.

III. The supply of financial capital consists of loanable funds that businesses can borrow and use to purchase capital goods.

  A. Financial capital can be obtained by firms through borrowing from financial intermediaries such as banks and life insurance companies, or through the sale of stocks and bonds.

B. The amount of loanable funds available to business will vary directly with the rate of interest (the price of loanable funds).
   1. The higher the interest rate is, the more savings will be supplied to the financial capital market. Low interest rates mean less savings is supplied.
C. Equilibrium in the market for financial capital is determined by the supply of and demand for loanable funds.
D. The Federal Reserve influences, to a considerable extent, the supply of loanable funds and, hence, the rate of interest.

KEY TERMS

You should be familiar with the meaning of the terms listed below. For definition of these terms, please refer to the glossary at the end of your textbook and to the appropriate section in this chapter.

economic rent	interest
financial capital	interest rate

CONCEPTS AND DEFINITIONS

Fill-in Questions

Complete each sentence by writing in the blank the most appropriate word or words from the terms listed below or by circling the word in parentheses that is correct.

financial capital	interest rate
law of supply	elastic
labor market	inelastic
interest	economic rent
labor supply	indifference curve analysis

1. Although the total supply of land is perfectly _____, the supply of land for any one use is probably _____ since individual parcels of land may be converted from one use to another.

2. The payment of _____ is necessary to induce individuals to forgo current consumption in favor of increased consumption in the future.

3. A negatively sloped _____ curve will exist if the number of hours an individual is willing and able to work decreases as the wage rate increases.

4. According to the _____, more of a resource will be supplied at a high price than at a low price.

5. Since no change in price can affect the total supply of land in the short run, the supply curve for that resource will be perfectly _____ and will be illustrated by a (horizontal/vertical) line on a graph.

6. The price of loanable funds also is known as the _____.

7. The largest and most important of the resource markets is the _____
_____.

8. The price paid for land is referred to as _____ to indicate that
the supply of land cannot be altered.

9. The supply schedule for personal savings indicates the amount of money that individuals are willing and able to save at alternative rates of _____.

10. Through the mechanism of the price system, _____ helps
allocate land to the most profitable of all alternative uses.

11. _____ is used by economists to analyze an individual's choices
between work and leisure.

12. The demand for _____ arises from the desires by businesses to
maintain and increase productive capacity.

13. The supply of loanable funds and, hence, the _____, are influenced by actions of the Federal Reserve System.

14. An individual's _____ curve may be backward-bending when
the marginal utility of additional leisure time is greater than the marginal utility
of additional income from working.

15. _____ is a pure surplus because it does not create or encourage productivity and it does not serve an incentive function.

Multiple Choice Questions

Circle the correct answer.

1. Equalizing differences in wages compensate for differences in

    a. working conditions.
    b. hours worked.
    c. education and training.
    d. labor supply.

2. A single tax on land as proposed by Henry George in *Progress and Poverty* is
based upon the idea that

    a. income taxes discriminate against the rich and favor the poor.
    b. redistribution of payments for land would have no effect on productivity.
    c. simple tax systems are preferred to complex ones; hence a single tax is most
    desirable.
    d. taxes on land can be passed on to consumers; hence, they are preferred to
    other forms of tax.

3. The supply of labor from an individual is not responsive solely to the wage rate since

    a. individuals are profit maximizers.

    b. individual labor supply decisions are based on self-interest.

    c. individuals value income more than nonwork pursuits.

    d. the marginal utility of income, at some point, exceeds the marginal utility of leisure time.

4. The shape of the supply curve of land for public housing is

    a. probably more elastic than the supply curve for all land.

    b. a vertical line since only a limited amount of land is available for public housing.

    c. either vertical or horizontal but cannot be exactly determined without further information.

    d. probably backward-bending, indicating that at a high price, land will be bid away from public housing projects by private developers.

5. While an individual's labor supply curve above some wage may be backward-bending, the aggregate labor supply curve is probably positively sloped because

    a. a market supply schedule must always show a positive relationship between quantity and price.

    b. there is always a large pool of unemployed workers who may be called upon to go to work if the market supply starts to bend back.

    c. the wage rate at which individual labor supply schedules turn back will vary from person to person.

    d. it is not possible to determine equilibrium wages if the market supply curve is negatively sloped.

6. If the supply of a resource is unaffected by changes in the price paid, then

    a. the supply of the resource will be shown by a straight, horizontal line on a graph.

    b. economic rents will be paid to those who consume the resource.

    c. the market price of the resource will be determined solely by forces of supply.

    d. the payment must be a pure surplus for the resource owner.

7. Even if the market supply of land is vertical so that payments for land constitute economic rent, the price system still serves an important economic function. That function is one of

    a. resource allocation.

    b. economic stabilization.

    c. ensuring resource productivity.

    d. providing economic incentives.

8. In the market for land, if the supply curve is vertical, an increase in demand will

    a. cause the equilibrium price and quantity of land to increase.

    b. cause an increase in the payment of economic rent to landowners.

    c. result in a shortage of land since the quantity supplied remains unchanged while the demand for land has increased.

    d. leave the equilibrium price and quantity of land unaffected.

9. The demand for financial capital is

    a. determined by the supply of financial capital.

    b. directly related to the rate of interest.

    c. different from the demand for loanable funds.

    d. a derived demand.

10. If an individual is in the backward-bending region of his or her labor supply schedule, that means

    a. the desired number of hours of leisure will decline if the wage rate is increased.

    b. fewer hours will be supplied in the labor market if the wage rate is lowered.

    c. fewer hours will be supplied in the labor market if the wage rate is raised.

    d. the desired number of hours of leisure will increase if the wage rate is lowered.

11. Wage differences among occupations to compensate for different working conditions are called.

    a. economic rent.

    b. overtime payments.

    c. equalizing differences.

    d. salary differentials.

12. The price system serves to ensure that

    a. all externalities are accounted for in land transactions.

    b. social costs associated with land use are paid by landlords.

    c. social benefits associated with land use are paid to landlords.

    d. land is allocated to its most highly valued uses.

13. The individual's labor supply curve can be drawn from

    a. the wage-constraint line.

    b. the indifference curves.

c. the intersection points of various wage lines with the highest possible indifference curve.

d. none of these.

APPLICATION

1. Assume the market for unskilled labor is shown in the diagram below. The market-clearing wage is $2.50 per hour.

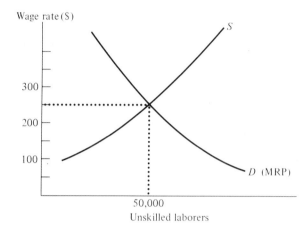

Wage rate ($)

a. What effect will a minimum wage of $2.00 per hour have on this market?

b. If the minimum wage is raised to $3.10 (the current federal minimum wage), how will the demand for and supply of unskilled labor be affected?

c. One Republican presidential candidate recently indicated that he would support the repeal of the minimum-wage law in order to alleviate the problem of youth unemployment. Considering only the market for unskilled labor, does that recommendation make sense? Why or why not?

ANSWERS

Fill-in Questions

1. inelastic; elastic
2. interest
3. labor supply
4. law of supply
5. inelastic; vertical
6. interest rate
7. labor market
8. economic rent
9. interest
10. economic rent
11. indifference curve analysis
12. financial capital
13. interest rate
14. labor supply
15. economic rent

Multiple Choice Questions

1.	a	8.	b
2.	b	9.	d
3.	b	10.	c
4.	a	11.	c
5.	c	12.	d
6.	d	13.	c
7.	a		

APPLICATION

1. a. There should be no effect since the market can reach equilibrium at a wage above the legal minimum.

    b. At a minimum wage of $3.10, there are more individuals willing to work than there are firms that desire to hire unskilled workers. The excess supply of labor constitutes unemployment.

    c. In this market, the only wage that will equate the quantity of labor supplied with that demanded is $2.50. From the standpoint of efficiency, the proposal to eliminate the minimum wage makes sense.

Chapter 30

General Equilibrium

LEARNING OBJECTIVES

Up to this point, the discussion of microeconomic theory has focused on individual, presumably unrelated markets for goods, services, and factors of production. Each market has been assumed to be a closed system and, thus, changes in one market have not affected other sectors of the economy. While that assumption is useful for certain kinds of analysis, the interrelationships among markets must be considered when undertaking certain kinds of analyses and investigations of the economy as a whole.

In this chapter, two approaches to general equilibrium analysis are presented. After reading the chapter, you should be able to:

1. distinguish between partial and general equilibrium analysis and identify the strengths and shortcomings associated with each of these methods of analysis;

2. analyze the effects of a change in one market on another by using the product-market/resource-market approach;

3. explain how the input-output approach to general equilibrium analysis is used to analyze and measure how a change in one market affects other markets;

4. use a simple input-output table to answer questions about economic relationships in a hypothetical economy.

CHAPTER OUTLINE

I. The relationships between various product and resource markets in an economy are investigated using the concept of general equilibrium analysis.
    A. General equilibrium analysis eliminates the *all-other-things-equal* assumption used in partial equilibrium analysis and examines the effects of changes in one market on other markets.
    B. General equilibrium analysis may be used to study an entire economy, as opposed to one segment or market in an economy.

1. General equilibrium analysis provides a connecting link between the microeconomic analysis of individual markets and macro-economic analysis (the analysis of the operation of the entire economic system).
2. As a field of inquiry, general equilibrium analysis is comparatively new and fully accurate models of the economy have not yet been formulated. However, models have been used successfully to follow and anticipate certain economic phenomena.

II. The product-market/resource-market approach to general equilibrium analysis is useful for showing how a change in one market affects other markets. This type of analysis is not as precise as input-output analysis which attempts to measure explicit economic relationships and to predict the magnitude and the extent of economic changes as a result of disturbances in one or several markets.
   A. To analyze the effect of a change in demand in one market, it is necessary to examine the effects of that change on related product and resource markets.

III. The input-output approach to general equilibrium analysis shows, in quantitative terms, the interrelationships between different industries in an economy.
   A. In using input-output analysis, there is no clear distinction between inputs and outputs since one industry's output may also be an input in that and other industries.
   B. The value of each input that is required to produce the total output of each industry is shown in vertical *columns* of an input-output table. The horizontal *rows* of the table measure the value to total industry output and show how the output of each industry is distributed throughout the economy.
   C. A table of input coefficients may be calculated from the data in an input-output table. These input coefficients show the value of the inputs needed to produce one dollar's worth of output in each industry.
      1. The overall economic impact of a change in demand and output in one industry may be estimated from the input coefficients.
         a. If the demand for the products of one industry increases, those industries producing inputs used by that industry will have to expand in order to meet the additional demand. There will be successive rounds of expansion in the relevant industry sectors until the entire increase in demand is met.

KEY TERMS

You should be familiar with the meaning of the terms listed below. For definition of these terms, please refer to the glossary at the end of your textbook and to the appropriate section in this chapter.

partial equilibrium analysis   input-output table
general equilibrium analysis   input coefficient

CONCEPTS AND DEFINITIONS

Fill-in Questions

Complete each sentence by writing in the blank the most appropriate word or words from the terms listed below or by circling the word in parentheses that is correct.

horizontal row   input-output analysis
input coefficient   general equilibrium analysis
Product-market/Resource-   Walras
   market approach   input-output table
partial equilibrium analysis   Leontief
vertical column

1. In studying an economic problem, it frequently is useful to simplify the analysis by assuming that all things not directly involved remain unchanged. This is known as _____ inasmuch as equilibrium is assumed to exist in all markets except those under investigation.

2. _____ entails both the study of the interrelationships between markets in an economic system and the functioning of the economic system itself.

3. Wassily Leontief, a Nobel Prize-winning economist was instrumental in the development of _____ as a method of economic inquiry.

4. A(n) _____ shows the interrelationships between different industries within a single economy.

5. _____ was the economist who first suggested general equilibrium analysis while _____ was a pioneer in doing empirical work on the American economy using this method of investigation.

6. A method that helps to make clear why changes in one market create changes in other markets is the _____ but this method is not particularly useful when measurement of these changes is important.

7. In an input-output table, the figures in each _____ describe the inputs to each industry in an economy while the _____ values specify the distribution of an output from each producer.

8. The ratio of the dollar value of inputs from one industry to the dollar value of all inputs required to produce a specified level of output is known as a(n) _____.

9. _____ shows how the production of one industry may be used in further production by that industry itself and by other industries as well as how it may serve the needs of consumers.

10. An _____ shows the value of each resource used by an industry in order to produce one dollar's worth of output.

11. _____ drops the all-other-things-equal assumption.

Multiple Choice Questions

Circle the correct answer.

1. The study of general equilibrium is primarily concerned with the effects of changes in

   a. a single market.
   b. resource markets.
   c. product markets.
   d. one market on other markets.

2. Although the term "equilibrium" is defined as a state of rest, it is also used in the context of general equilibrium analysis to mean

   a. a process of constant adjustment.
   b. absolute stability.
   c. full utilization of all resources.
   d. operation on the production-possibility curve.

3. In the model of input-output analysis

   a. the output from one industry cannot be an input for other industries.
   b. many outputs from one industry are inputs for other industries.
   c. the output from an industry cannot be an input for that same industry.
   d. inputs and outputs are distinct and separate categories of production.

4. The concept of partial equilibrium

   a. means the economy is in equilibrium at less than full employment.
   b. is used primarily in reference to studies that use general equilibrium as a method of analysis.
   c. is a central assumption in much of microeconomic analysis.
   d. is used only when an economy cannot reach full equilibrium.

5. The pathbreaking empirical work in the development of an input-output model of the American economy

   a. dealt with monetary theory and the permanent income hypothesis.

b. was used to help develop the concept of gross national product.

c. dealt with the theory of money and economic fluctuations.

d. was involved in a study of the economic effects of disarmament.

6. General equilibrium analysis

    a. is a relatively new area of economic inquiry which has not been perfected.

    b. is undertaken with sophisticated models which accurately describe all facets of the economy.

    c. may be used only when an economy is at full employment.

    d. views each sector of the economy as a closed system.

7. Assume an economy produces two goods, lace and felt-tip pens, using two resources, labor and capital. Starting from an initial equilibrium in all markets, if the demand for lace declines, that will initially cause

    a. an increase in the price of lace and a decrease in the quantity sold.

    b. a reduction in the wage rate and in the number of workers employed in the lace industry.

    c. a decline in the demand for felt-tip pens.

    d. a reduction in the price of felt-tip pens.

8. The vertical columns of an input-output table describe

    a. the distribution of the output from each industry.

    b. all of the economic relationships that exist in an economy.

    c. the value of all of the different inputs each industry needs to produce its total output.

    d. the value of total output in an economy.

9. The input coefficients for any industry are ratios which

    a. are obtained by dividing the total value of inputs in an industry by the value of each input required in production of the industry's output.

    b. indicate the percent of total output in an economy that is produced by each industry.

    c. are obtained by dividing the value of each input requirement by the total value of inputs in an industry.

    d. specify the exact quantity of each input that is used in producing an output.

10. The concept of general equilibrium analysis was first suggested by an economist who lived during the

    a. seventeenth century.

    b. eighteenth century.

    c. nineteenth century.

    d. twentieth century.

APPLICATIONS

1. Examine the input-output table below.

(Dollar values)

Industry	A	B	C	Final consumption
A	30	60	70	20
B	100	100	200	50
C	10	50	40	50

a. Add a total output column to the table and supply the values for that column.

b. What is the amount of output of Industry A that is also used by Industry A?

c. According to the table, what is the total value of inputs for Industry B?

2. Look at the input coefficients in the input-output table below.

Industry	A	B	C
A	.22	.44	.40
B	.33	.10	.24
C	.45	.46	.36
Total	1.00	1.00	1.00

a. According to this table, Industry A can expand production by $1.00 only if it purchases inputs from Industry B. What is the value of resources it must purchase from Industry B in order to expand production by $1.00? by $50? by $100?

b. Each of the decimals in the table was obtained as a ratio of two numbers. What element belongs in the numerator of such a ratio, and what belongs in the denominator?

3. Assume that an economy produces only TV's and houses. The TV industry is capital-intensive while the housing industry has not yet managed to convert to mass-production techniques. Now suppose that there is a spurt in the growth of the population among people in their early twenties and therefore an increase in the demand for new housing.

a. The price of housing is likely to (increase/decrease).

b. This change would affect the MRP of labor in the housing industry by ____

_____

c. Since much of the labor employed in the housing industry has a specialized skill and there are not many laborers to be gained from the TV industry, wages in the housing industry are likely to _____.

4. Examine the input-output table shown below.

(Dollar value)

	Chemi-cals	Drugs	Transpor-tation	Final consump-tion	Total output
Chemicals	100	600	100	100	900
Drugs	50	100	50	700	900
Transportation	50	50	20	100	220
Labor	50	50	20	(120)	
Total value of inputs	250	800	190		(2020)

a. Which industry is the biggest user of chemicals as an input in production?

b. Consumers use by far the largest percentage of output of which industry?

c. What is the amount of output of the transportation industry used by the transportation industry itself as an input?

5. From the input-output table in Question 4, compute a table of input coefficients. The first column has been supplied.

	Chemicals	Drugs	Transportation
Chemicals	.40		
Drugs	.20		
Transportation	.20		
Labor	.20		
Total inputs	1.00		

a. Based upon the table values, compute the amount of chemicals that would be required if the drug industry were to expand output by an additional $1.00.

b. Suppose the chemical industry expands output by $100.00. Determine the amount of increased production that is required by the drug and transportation industry to permit the chemical industry to expand.

ANSWERS

Fill-in Questions

1. partial equilibrium analysis.
2. general equilibrium analysis
3. input-output analysis
4. input-output table
5. Walras; Leontief
6. product-market/resource market approach
7. vertical column; horizontal row
8. input coefficient
9. input-output analysis
10. input coefficient
11. general equilibrium analysis

Multiple Choice Questions

1.	d	6.	a
2.	a	7.	b
3.	b	8.	c
4.	c	9.	c
5.	d	10.	b

APPLICATIONS

1. a. Total output (the sum of all figures in a horizontal row)

    A $180

    B $450

    C $150

    b. $30

    c. $210 (the sum of all figures in the vertical column under B)

2. a. $.33; $16.50 (50 × $.33); $33.00 (100 × $.33)

    b. An input coefficient is a ratio of the value of an input divided by the value of all inputs.

3. a. increase

    b. increasing it or shifting the MRP schedule to the right

    c. rise

4. a. drug industry

    b. drug industry

    c. $20

5. Input coefficient $= \dfrac{\text{value of inputs}}{\text{value of all inputs}}$

	Drugs	Transportation
Chemicals	$.75 \left(\dfrac{600}{800}\right)$	$.53\left(\dfrac{100}{190}\right)$
Drugs	$.125\left(\dfrac{100}{800}\right)$	$.27\left(\dfrac{50}{190}\right)$
Transportation	.065	.11
Labor	.06	.11
Total inputs	1.00	1.00

    a. 75¢

    b. $20; $20. (100 × $.20)

Chapter 31

Labor Unions: Collective Bargaining and Wage Determination

LEARNING OBJECTIVES

This chapter examines the history, structure, and functions of labor unions in the United States, describes the process of collective bargaining, and investigates the impact of unions on labor supply and labor demand and on commodity prices and inflation. To a large extent, this chapter represents an extension and elaboration of the material introduced in Chapters 28 and 29 which deal with labor supply and demand.

After reading this chapter, you should be able to:

1. identify significant events in the history of organized labor in the United States;

2. describe the process of collective bargaining, how each of the participants formulates a bargaining position, and the role of government in collective-bargaining activities;

3. analyze the impact of unions on wages by using models of supply and demand;

4. describe the impact of organized labor in the United States on resource allocation, and on prices and the price level;

5. speculate about the future of unions in the United States.

CHAPTER OUTLINE

I. Early attempts by workers to strengthen their bargaining position with employers by forming a union were met with hostility and legal sanctions.
    A. During the early nineteenth century union efforts to raise wages and impose other conditions on employers were viewed as conspiracies in restraint of trade.
    B. In the decade of the 1860s additional production demands caused by the Civil War and by increased industrialization in the United States gave workers in growing industries the opportunity to organize.
II. In the 1870s and 1880s national labor oganizations appeared to coordinate

the activities of local unions and to seek social and political change through federal legislation.

    A. The Knights of Labor, the first national union, emphasized social change as the organization's goal.

    B. The American Federation of Labor (AFL), founded in 1886, used collective bargaining and strikes to pursue short-run economic goals such as higher wages and better working conditions.

        1. The AFL consisted entirely of craft unions, collections of skilled workers with a common trade or craft.

        2. Organization of all workers in manufacturing plants did not occur on a widespread basis until 1938 when the Congress of Industrial Oarganizations (CIO) was founded as a national federation to promote and encourage labor unions on an industry—rather than craft—basis. The AFL and CIO merged in 1955.

III. Employers resisted formation and growth of labor organizations by firing and blacklisting individuals associated with a union, by using lockouts to keep union workers from reporting to work, and by forcing potential employees to sign yellow-dog contracts (pledges not to participate in union activities).

    A. In the 1930s prolabor legislation such as The Norris-La Guardia Act of 1932 was enacted in an attempt to increase the earnings of industrial workers, as well as their bargaining power with powerful employers.

    B. After World War II legislation such as the Taft-Hartley Act of 1947 and the Landrum-Griffin Act of 1909 sought to curb some of the power of unions.

IV. Modern labor unions engage in collective bargaining on economic issues, provide a variety of benefits for members such as insurance and retirement programs, and engage in educational and political activities. There are three levels of union organization in the United States.

    A. Local unions are directly involved in collective bargaining with individual employers.

    B. National unions are parent organizations for local unions, and are responsible for formulating broad policy and for providing assistance to local organizations.

    C. A federation is an organization (such as the AFL-CIO) of national unions that serves to promote union legislative goals.

V. Collective bargaining is the process by which union and management arrive at a mutually acceptable contract that spells out the privileges and obligations of both parties for an agreed-upon period of time.

    A. If a suitable agreement is not reached when the old contract expires, a union may strike.

        1. A collective-bargaining agreement usually covers the following topics: wages and hours of work, job security and seniority, grievance procedures, and status of the union on the job. It also may address other issues such as job safety, supplementary benefits, and penalties for breach of contract.

    B. Government participation in contract negotiations and in labor disputes is relatively common, particularly in large industries that have a significant impact on the economy.

VI. In pursuit of the goal of higher wages, a union may attempt to influence the demand for and supply of labor.

VII. The inflationary trend in the United States since the end of World War II is often considered a result of the ability of unions to secure unreasonably high wage increases in excess of productivity, a pattern which is then followed in nonunion sectors of the economy.

    A. Union officials blame inflation on firms that raise prices following an increase in demand and pass all costs along to the consumer rather than give up income.

VIII. Although union membership has gradually increased in the past few decades, the size of the labor force has increased much more rapidly so that the percentage of workers who belong to unions has declined.

    A. The relative decline in importance is a result of a decreasing number of blue-collar workers, to whom the labor movement in the United States traditionally has been geared.

    B. Although white-collar workers have traditionally been unorganized, many now seek to enhance their income, working conditions, and job security through professional or union organizations. The greatest gains for unions among white-collar workers have been in the public sector.

    C. Unions have failed to appeal to large groups in the labor force, particularly women and minority workers who see union seniority provisions as a barrier to advancement.

KEY TERMS

You should be familiar with the meaning of the terms listed below. For definition of these terms, please refer to the glossary at the end of your textbook and to the appropriate section in this chapter.

strike	union shop
lockout	collective bargaining
yellow-dog contract	escalator clauses
protective injunction	right-to-work laws
closed shop	featherbedding

CONCEPTS AND DEFINITIONS

Fill-in Questions

Complete each sentence by writing in the blank the most appropriate word or words from the terms listed below or by circling the word in parentheses that is correct.

protective injunction
Knights of Labor
closed shop
lockout
inflationary
union shop
skill or craft

right-to-work laws
industries
yellow-dog contract
collective bargaining
escalator clauses
featherbedding
strike

1. The Taft-Hartley Act states that the President of the United States may intervene in labor-management relations if a(n) _____ threatens national health and safety.

2. In states that have passed _____ it is illegal to require membership in a union as a condition of employment.

3. An employer seeking to resist union activities or demands may resort to a(n) _____ which deprives workers supporting a union of employment.

4. The difference between a union shop and a closed shop is that an individual must join a union before he or she can be hired in a(n) _____ while in a(n) _____ one must join the union within a designated period of time after being hired.

5. _____ assure that wages will be increased according to some formula which is tied to the cost of living.

6. A central purpose of the National Labor Relations Act is to legally support and encourage _____.

7. Employers used _____ to inhibit union activities since any drive to organize workers, for example, could be viewed as encouraging a breach of contract which is illegal.

8. In the early 1900s, employers were able to secure a(n) _____ against union-sponsored product boycotts or strikes by claiming that irreparable damage would result from the union's actions.

9. _____ required an employer to hire more labor than is actually necessary to complete a particular job.

10. _____ is the name given to the process by which management and labor arrive at a mutually agreeable contract.

11. The first national union in the United States was the _____.

12. The AFL was a federation of unions, each organized for a different _____.

13. The practice of closing down a plant for a few weeks to discourage workers from joining a union is called a(n) _____.

14. Some employers required workers to sign a pledge stating that they would never join a union. This document was called a(n) _____.

15. The CIO is organized on the basis of _____.

16. For each item below, indicate whether it is the responsibility of the local union (L), the national union (N), or the federation (F).

    a. Main function is to gain public support for union interests.

    b. Responsible for extending membership into those areas that have not previously been organized.

    c. Collects dues and enrolls new members.

    d. Negotiates new contracts with the local employer.

17. For each of the descriptions below, indicate whether the policy is likely to stimulate an increase (+) or decrease (−) in the demand for labor.

    a. Provision for a closed shop in which the company may hire only union members.

    b. The union will sponsor programs designed to increase the demand for the employer's final product.

    c. The union will sponsor programs to increase the skill level of its members.

    d. The contract requires featherbedding.

    e. The union makes suggestions concerning the most efficient way to organize and operate the business.

18. The main criticism of unions is that because they are able to get wage increases in the absence of increases in productivity, the wage increases are _____.

Multiple Choice Questions

Circle the correct answer.

1. Yellow-dog contracts required that individuals

    a. join a union as a condition of employment.

    b. join a union within the first few weeks after being employed.

    c. abstain from participation in union activities.

    d. sign an authorization to deduct union dues from their pay.

2. Protective injunctions were issued under provisions of the

    a. Sherman Act.

    b. Norris-La Guardia Act.

    c. Wagner Act.

    d. Taft-Hartley Act.

3. A central purpose of the Landrum-Griffin Act is to

   a. give any employee the right to bargain collectively with his or her employer.

   b. prohibit the issuance of injunctions against union activities.

   c. permit states to pass right-to-work legislation.

   d. regulate union finances.

4. Featherbedding is a practice that is undertaken

   a. primarily by workers in the bedding and blanket industry.

   b. to modify the labor supply schedule and, consequently, raise the wages of union workers.

   c. to make work easier so that employees are more productive.

   d. by unions to increase demand for their services.

5. In the late 1930s the Congress of Industrial Organizations (CIO)

   a. consisted of a group of management officials and other representatives of workers with a common skill or craft.

   b. was established to form a national federation of industrial unions.

   c. was established to compete with the AFL for control of craft unions.

   d. was created by Congress to help unions counter antiunion employers and a hostile judiciary.

6. The AFL and the CIO

   a. are, respectively, the first and second largest labor federations in the United States.

   b. are national labor federations whose central purpose is to conduct contract negotiations with management.

   c. receive financial support for their activities from the United States Department of Labor.

   d. merged in 1955 to combat growing public hostility toward unions.

7. During 1978, strikes in the United States were responsible for the loss of about 27 million work days, which is about

   a. 1/700th of one percent of the total working time of the labor force during that year.

   b. 1/7th of one percent of the total working time of the labor force during that year.

   c. about 7 percent of the total working time of the labor force during that year.

   d. about 17 percent of the total working time of the labor force during that year.

8. Current data show that fringe benefits including pay for time not actually worked constitute

   a. 10-15 percent of most payroll costs.

b. 15-20 percent of most payroll costs.

c. 20-25 percent of most payroll costs.

d. 25-30 percent of most payroll costs.

9. Right-to-work laws have been enacted by several states

  a. to prevent discrimination against certain groups of workers such as the handicapped.

  b. to specify the degree of recognition that a union may obtain from an employer through collective bargaining.

  c. to ensure that every citizen who desires work will be able to find it.

  d. to ensure that job training and high quality performance will be forthcoming from all individuals who exercise their right to work.

10. According to provisions of the Taft-Hartley Act,

  a. government may intervene in labor-management relations if a strike is judged to constitute a threat to national health or safety.

  b. compulsory arbitration is required if a strike or strike threat constitutes a threat to national health or safety.

  c. government may not intervene in labor-management relations except in wartime or in periods when wage and price controls are necessary.

  d. government's role in collective bargaining is vaguely defined in order to permit the government maximum flexibility in dealing with each situation that warrants attention.

11. Studies researching the effects of unions on wages show

  a. a growing difference between union and nonunion wages as compared to the 1930s.

  b. that unionized industries, on the average, pay higher wages than nonunion industries and this difference is fully attributed to the efforts of unions.

  c. the union-nonunion wage difference tends to narrow during recession and grow during periods of prosperity.

  d. there is less difference today in the wages of union and nonunion workers than there was during the Depression.

12. A closed shop

  a. differs from a union shop in that workers in a closed shop must join the union within a specified period after being hired.

  b. differs from a union shop in that workers in a closed shop must belong to a union before they may be hired.

  c. is a manufacturing plant in which all positions are filled.

  d. was declared to be illegal in provisions of the Wagner Act.

13. The first major piece of federal legislation to permit and provide government support for union activities is the

     a. Sherman Act.

     b. Norris-La Guardia Act.

     c. National Labor Relations Act.

     d. Labor Management Reporting and Disclosure Act.

14. The amount of working time lost to strikes in 1978

     a. was greater than the average time lost to strikes since 1946.

     b. was less than the average time lost to strikes since 1946.

     c. was about the same as the average time lost to strikes since 1946.

     d. cannot be compared to time lost in earlier years because the size of the labor force, the number of union members, and the number of strikes vary from year to year.

15. The Labor Management Relations Act which was passed in 1947

     a. received strong bipartisan support in Congress as well as the support of both labor and management.

     b. stipulated that a closed shop is illegal although a union shop is permissible.

     c. contains provisions which allow the president to dissolve a union if union activities represent a threat to national health or safety.

     d. sought to achieve a balance of power between unions and management by strengthening national unions and labor federations such as the AFL and CIO.

16. The American Federation of Labor (AFL) which was founded in 1886 by Samuel Gompers was initially a national labor organization

     a. of craft unions.

     b. of industrial unions.

     c. of craft and industrial unions.

     d. whose central purpose was to effect social change.

17. An escalator clause in a collective-bargaining agreement

     a. requires that workers who must perform their job on several floors of a building have access to escalators or elevators.

     b. ensures that wages go up during inflation and down during recession.

     c. stipulates who is to be promoted when a job vacancy occurs in a manufacturing establishment.

     d. is designed to protect a worker's real wage.

18. Union activities in the United States in the first half of the nineteenth century were

     a. viewed by the courts as illegal criminal conspiracies.

b. enjoined under provisions of the Sherman Antitrust Act.

c. primarily for the purpose of organizing workers in industrial plants.

d. supported at the national level by the Knights of Labor.

19. The Fair Labor Standards Act

a. historically has been opposed by unions who feel that the right to set labor standards rests with unions and not government.

b. received the support of trade unions when it was passed but now receives little support from the labor movement.

c. is currently supported by the labor movement as a means to protect union employment from competition by cheap labor.

d. does not affect union members and, hence, has never received their support or opposition.

20. If a union is successful in increasing demand for union labor and reducing the labor supply, that action will

a. increase the equilibrium wage and the number of union workers employed.

b. increase the equilibrium wage and decrease the number of workers employed.

c. increase the equilibrium wage but the effect on employment is uncertain.

d. have an effect on the equilibrium wage and level of employment but the direction of both changes is uncertain.

APPLICATIONS

1. The schedule below shows the demand for labor in a manufacturing plant. Assume that a union will determine the wage in this establishment.

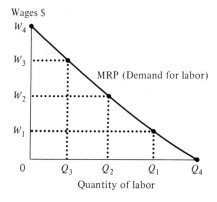

a. What wage would the union select if its goal is to maximize the sum of wage payments (that is, to obtain the largest total payroll)? Why? (Hint: Consider demand elasticity in formulating your answer.)

b. If the union's only goal is to maximize employment of union members in this firm what wage would they accept? Would they set this goal? Why or why not? Do your answers indicate a tradeoff? If so what is it?

c. If the union had a goal of obtaining close to the maximum wage, how, if at all, would that affect the number of workers hired by the manufacturing plant?

d. In view of the employment effects associated with high wages, is it reasonable to expect that a union will always pursue the single goal of high wages?

ANSWERS

Fill-in Questions

1. strike
2. right-to-work laws
3. lockout
4. closed shop; a union shop
5. escalator clauses
6. collective bargaining
7. yellow-dog contracts
8. protective injunction
9. featherbedding
10. collective bargaining
11. Knights of Labor
12. skill or craft
13. lockout
14. yellow-dog contract
15. industries
16. a. F
    b. N
    c. L
    d. L
17. a. −
    b. +
    c. +
    d. +
    e. +
18. inflationary

Multiple Choice Questions

1. c
2. a
3. d
4. d
5. b
6. d
7. b
8. c
9. b
10. a
11. d
12. b
13. c
14. a
15. b
16. a
17. d
18. a
19. c
20. c

1. a. The appropriate wage to maximize the total payroll is W_2. At the price and quantity corresponding to the midpoint on a straight demand (MRP) curve, total revenues (to workers) or total expenditures (by the firm on payrolls) are at a maximum. The value of demand elasticity at this midpoint is 1.

   b. To obtain maximum employment of union members (Q_y), the union would have to accept a zero wage. From a practical standpoint, this would not occur. Therefore, the union faces a tradeoff between higher wages and less employment.

   c. The closer the union sought to be at the maximum possible wage (W_4), the closer it would be to the zero level of employment. As wages got closer to W_4, the employment of union members would be at a minimum.

   d. It is unlikely that a union will pursue the goal of high wages without considering the employment effects of that action.

Chapter 32

The Economics of Environmental Problems

LEARNING OBJECTIVES

This chapter examines the economic aspects of environmental problems such as how to reconcile the conflicting objectives of economic growth and environmental protection and how to deal with the hidden costs of production and consumption. The tools of demand and supply are used to show how externalities may be accounted for in the pricing of goods and services, and in the determination of socially desirable and economically efficient levels of production.

After reading this chapter, you should be able to:

1. provide examples of cost and benefit externalities, show how externalities may arise in production and consumption, and describe the economic consequences of their existence;

2. identify at least three ways in which externalities may be handled and discuss the pros and cons associated with each;

3. describe the problems that confront economists and others in their attempts to measure the costs associated with environmental problems and the benefits that occur as a result of the solution of such problems;

4. indicate how an economist determines the socially desirable and economically efficient level of pollution.

CHAPTER OUTLINE

I.   Growing concern about environmental problems has prompted investigation of their underlying economic causes and a search for ways to remedy them.
   A. Environmental problems arise from the failure to consider hidden costs of production and consumption. By ignoring these costs, commodity prices are lower and output is larger than they otherwise would be.
      1. Hidden costs of production include costs that arise from pollutants discharged into the atmosphere and waters and from the damage to the

environment when resources are extracted from the land. Other costs are imposed on society when products are not fully and completely consumed. For example, waste paper, packaging materials, and other by-products of consumption often must be disposed of at a cost to society.

    3. Individuals in the United States and elsewhere are showing an increased willingness to bear the opportunity cost of reducing pollution and environmental damage.

II.   Economic externalities occur when the use of resources by some individuals has unintended side effects (either positive or negative) on the welfare of others and when there is no economic mechanism to record the change in welfare.

   A. If an economic externality is harmful to others, it is called an external diseconomy. If it is beneficial, it is called an external economy.

   B. An economic externality is also defined as the difference between the private costs of production (producer costs) and the social costs of production (the costs to society, such as the damage caused by water pollution).

     1. One effect of this divergence of private and social costs is that a much larger quantity of a good will be demanded than would be demanded if *all* costs were considered in the price of a good with an external diseconomy. Therefore, resources are misallocated.

III. Most of the solutions proposed for the problem of external diseconomies can be sorted into one of three categories: moral persuasion, regulation, and use of the price system.

   A. Moral persuasion is commonly used to urge consumers and producers to act against their own short-run self-interest in order to promote social welfare.

     1. This approach is often ineffective because people tend to put their own self-interest above society's and because it is difficult to determine what is best for society.

   B. In spite of expense and difficulty of enforcement, government regulation has become increasingly popular over the past decade as a means to deal with external diseconomies.

     1. Government regulations may curtail production of goods that create external diseconomies or may specify production methods and product standards which must be met by all producers.

     2. Even though regulation is expensive and difficult to enforce, it tends to be favored by politicians as a remedy for external diseconomies because it may produce immediate, predictable results.

   C. The price system may also be used to deal with the problem of externalities as long as prices reflect both private and social costs of production. With this approach, people may continue to make production and consumption decisions based upon self-interest.

     1. One way to implement the price system approach would be to charge each firm a fee for wastes discharged into the earth's atmosphere or waters.

      a. Some firms would pay the fee and continue to pollute since it would be cheaper to do so while others would reduce harmful emissions by installing pollution-control equipment, or by changing their production technology. The added cost of the fees or equipment would be reflected in higher prices for goods which would cause some decrease in quantity demanded.

      b. The price system solution might bring about a recession since it could entail a significant reduction in employment and output.

  2. Another way to price externalities is to have the producer of the externality compensate each victim. This approach requires definition of individual property rights and is frequently used in lawsuits where one person alleges that another's actions are damaging.

      a. If a company is forced to compensate those injured by its externalities, the price of its product increases, thus reducing quantity demanded and, consequently, the production of externalities.

  3. Although some people feel that the price system is ineffective in reducing externalities because results aren't immediately apparent, it is superior to other methods for controlling externalities from an efficiency standpoint.

IV. The optimal level of pollution control is reached when the marginal costs and marginal benefits of abatement are equal.

  A. Since clean air and water are economic goods, other goods must be sacrificed to obtain larger quantities of clean air and water. Consequently, it rarely will be desirable to reduce pollution to zero, since the marginal utility of zero pollution is lower than the marginal utility of other economic goods.

  B. Direct measurement of the benefits from reducing pollution is difficult since these are not normally measured in the market. An alternative is to compute an estimate of the damage caused by pollution which would yield information about the benefits to be gained from pollution abatement.

  C. Measuring the cost of pollution control is also difficult. While some of the cost figures are readily available (such as those for emission-control equipment) others must be estimated (such as the costs that arise when workers are laid off because of reduced product demand).

KEY TERMS

You should be familiar with the meaning of the terms listed below. For definition of these terms, please refer to the glossary at the end of your textbook and to the appropriate section in this chapter.

economic externality	external economy	social costs
external diseconomy	private costs	

CONCEPTS AND DEFINITIONS

Fill-in Questions

Complete each sentence by writing in the blank the most appropriate word or words from the terms listed below or by circling the word in parentheses that is correct.

the price system
external economy
compensation
government regulation
external diseconomy
moral persuasion

private costs
hidden costs
social costs
economic goods
economic externality

1. When _____ is used to address environmental problems, economic efficiency is achieved since people are forced to make behavorial adjustments which reflect the opportunity cost of resources used.

2. If there is a divergence between the _____ and _____ _____ of production, quantity demanded will be greater than if price reflects all costs of production.

3. The _____ approach to the problem of externalities requires that a polluter pay each victim for damages suffered.

4. Three methods of addressing the problem of external diseconomies are _____, _____, and _____.

5. One of the more serious defects with using the _____ to curtail externalities is that the desired results are not achieved immediately.

6. Resources are misallocated when a(n) _____ exists.

7. Many economists argue that _____ is an inefficient approach to the problem of externalities because individual producer differences are rarely considered.

8. Class-action lawsuits are one manifestation of the _____ to the problem of externalities.

9. A strong argument in favor of _____ as a means of dealing with hidden costs of production and consumption is that it produces immediately visible results.

10. _____ are not normally included in the price of a product because property rights are absent.

11. _____ asks people to ignore their own short-run self-interest in order to promote social welfare.

12. A(n) _____ exists when an act of production or consumption has unintended side-effects on the welfare of others that the market is incapable of measuring.

13. Air pollution is a(n) _____ or _____ because property rights to air are not well-defined.

14. Since clean air and clean water are _____, the consumption of other goods must be sacrificed to obtain larger quantities of each.

15. In extreme cases, _____ forces producers to curtail production of certain goods because they have a very high social cost.

16. A(n) _____ occurs when a producer's actions have a beneficial effect on others and payment cannot be extracted from the beneficiaries.

17. The only approach that successfully deals with externalities and yet encourages people to act in their own self-interest is _____.

Multiple Choice Questions

Circle the correct answer.

1. Pollution is an externality
   a. because it affects the environment.
   b. since most of the damage from pollution occurs outside.
   c. because pollution costs are not included in the price of goods.
   d. for lack of a better term.

2. When the actions of a producer have a harmful effect on others and no compensation is paid to the affected individuals, the outcome is called an
   a. external economy.
   b. external diseconomy.
   c. individual economy.
   d. individual diseconomy.

3. Studies indicate that the greater the amount of pollution curtailed, the higher is the
   a. marginal cost.
   b. fixed cost.
   c. social cost.
   d. hidden cost.

4. If hidden costs of production are ignored,
   a. production is greater and price is lower than if these costs are included in the product price.

b. production is smaller and price is lower than if these costs are included in the product price.

c. production is greater and price is higher than if these costs are included in the product price.

d. production is smaller and price is higher than if these costs are included in the product price.

5. One of the primary advantages of using the price system to remedy a pollution problem is

a. it will completely eliminate the causes of the problem.

b. it deals quickly with the problem using a mechanism that everyone understands.

c. people are able to follow self-interest in seeking solutions to the problem.

d. it places the cost of abatement on firms where it belongs rather than on consumers.

6. The socially optimal amount of pollution abatement is the point at which

a. all pollution is eliminated from the environment.

b. the government standards for factory and auto emissions have been met.

c. the marginal net benefit from abatement is zero.

d. the total cost of pollution abatement equals the amount of damage caused by pollution.

7. Air and water pollution

a. represent problems unique to capitalistic economies.

b. occur because of the greed of most business people in their search for profit.

c. may be eliminated if the government has public support.

d. exist because the air and most waterways are publicly owned.

8. It is difficult to compute the marginal benefits gained from pollution abatement because

a. the benefits per person are very small.

b. inflation causes the value of benefits to change constantly.

c. it is impossible to place a value on human life and health.

d. the costs of negative externalities are not directly priced in the market.

9. Curtailing or regulating production to eliminate or reduce external diseconomies is advocated because

a. with well-defined standards, enforcement is easy and inexpensive as compared to other approaches.

b. this approach will help a society achieve socially optimal resource allocation.

c. having every firm meet the same standards is less costly than having each firm pursue its own approach to the problem.

d. this approach produces immediate, visible results while the results from other strategies are less predictable.

10. The compensation approach to pollution abatement is to have each polluter

a. charge each of the victims for damages.

b. pay each of the victims for damages.

c. curtail production of goods that pollute.

d. increase production of nonpolluting goods.

11. Attitudes of environmentalists toward pollution are largely a reflection of a high standard of living in which the marginal cost of correction seems

a. higher than the marginal benefit of consuming additional goods.

b. the same as the marginal benefits from increased production.

c. lower than the marginal benefits derived from consuming other goods.

d. unrelated to the marginal benefits from consuming other goods.

12. The effect of charging a price that reflects only private costs is to

a. artificially decrease the quantity demanded.

b. artificially increase the quantity demanded.

c. move society toward an optimal resource allocation.

d. shift the supply curve up and to the left.

13. If a producer's price were changed to reflect both private and social costs, that would

a. decrease quantity demanded by consumers.

b. increase quantity demanded by consumers.

c. increase the supply of the product.

d. increase the equilibrium quantity and price.

14. One problem with the use of moral persuasion to deal with social costs is

a. determining production levels.

b. defining social interest.

c. computing private costs.

d. determining self-interest.

15. When a price is placed on externalities

a. consumers and producers may continue to make decisions on the basis of self-interest.

b. consumers and producers must act according to their understanding of the social interest.

c. producers will refuse to produce goods or services that cause externalities.

d. consumers will refuse to buy any products that cause externalities.

16. One way to estimate the costs of pollution is to

a. measure the value of sales in pollution-producing industries.

b. compute the total amount paid in fines by industries that pollute.

c. determine the market value of each substance that makes up pollution.

d. ask people to estimate what they would pay to have the pollution removed.

APPLICATIONS

1. Negative externalities occur when a firm is able to ignore some portion of production costs. Consider the diagram below in which the private marginal cost of the Johnson Shortblock Company is shown by curve PMC, and the social marginal cost is shown by curve SMC. Demand for the firm's output is shown by curve *D*.

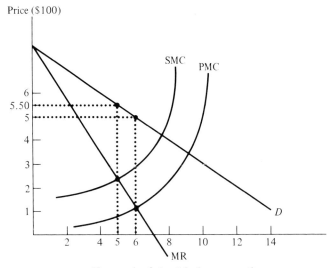

Thousands of shortblocks per month

a. What is the profit-maximizing output for this firm if the social costs of the operation are ignored? What price would be charged at this level of output?

b. What is the socially optimal level of output for this firm to produce? Why is it different from the output which maximizes private profits? How, if at all, is price affected as the firm moves from the profit-maximizing level of output to the socially optimal level of output?

c. A tax on each unit of output has been suggested as one way to force this firm to internalize (take account of) the negative externalities it creates. What is the amount of tax per unit of output that will result in socially optimal behavior?

d. Assume that the negative externalities generated by this firm are limited to a precise geographic area, and that the firm buys all of the land, buildings, and other assets in that area. How, if at all, does the fact that Johnson Shortblock now owns this area affect its decision regarding the profit-maximizing level of output? (Ignore the tax mentioned in Part c of this problem.)

ANSWERS

Fill-in Questions

1. the price system
2. private costs; social costs (or vice versa)
3. compensation
4. moral persuasion; government regulation; the price system. (Any order of answers is acceptable.)
5. price system
6. economic externality
7. government regulation
8. compensation approach
9. government regulation
10. social costs or hidden costs
11. moral persuasion
12. economic externality
13. economic externality or external diseconomy
14. economic goods
15. government regulation
16. external economy
17. the price system

Multiple Choice Questions

1. c
2. b
3. a
4. a
5. c
6. c
7. d
8. d
9. d
10. b
11. c
12. b
13. a
14. b
15. a
16. d

APPLICATIONS

1. a. Profit-maximizing output for the firm is where PMC = MR at $Q = 6$, $P = 5 (at $Q = 6$ on the demand curve, $P = 5).
   b. Socially optimal output is where SMC = MR at $Q = 5$, $P = 5.5 (at $Q = 5$ on the demand curve, $P = 5.5).

The output is different from that at which private profits are maximized because the previously hidden costs are now accounted for. When the firm takes account of the social costs of its actions, its marginal cost curve will correspond to SMC which intersects MR at a smaller output. Since the demand curve is negatively sloped, a smaller level of output will command a higher price.

c. To insure that the firm produces the socially optimal output, government must impose a tax per unit equal to the difference between PMC and SMC at the socially optimal output ($Q = 5$).

d. In this case, what previously were negative externalities to the surrounding community are now costs to the company itself. Its private marginal costs of production are represented by SMC once it owns the entire affected area. Consequently, its profit-maximizing output is now the same as the socially optimal output in Part b ($Q = 5$).

Chapter 33

The Economics of
Urban Problems

LEARNING OBJECTIVES

Using supply and demand analysis, this chapter analyzes contemporary urban problems (including transportation, land use, and public safety) and examines some proposed solutions. In addition, the more general problems of falling tax revenues and increasing demands for public services are discussed.

After reading this chapter, you should be able to:

1. identify why large cities seem to be unable to take further advantage of economies of scale in providing public services;

2. identify the root causes of urban transportation problems and evaluate the proposed solutions to those problems;

3. present economic reasons underlying population movements out of and into central cities, and the effects of these flows on land use and provision of public services;

4. identify the relevant economic considerations which may be used to determine an appropriate level of expenditure on public safety and other public services;

5. explain the causes of the fiscal crisis currently confronting cities, describe ways in which the problem is being addressed, and identify alternatives that would make the true cost of city services apparent to consumers.

CHAPTER OUTLINE

I.   Economies of scale have historically permitted large cities to provide a full range of services at a lower cost than small cities or rural areas. At present, however, many cities are beset with economic and social problems that affect their ability to meet the demand for public services.
   A. The current inability of many large cities to offer adequate services at low cost seems to be caused, in part, by a growing scarcity of trained personnel to coordinate and manage public services.

B. The size of some city governments and public agencies seems, in many cases, to be too large to permit efficient management.

II. An adequate and reliable urban transportation network is essential to transport goods and services to and from cities, and to provide residents with a high degree of mobility.

A. Even though the cost and inconvenience associated with auto users are mounting, private cars are preferred by many to alternatives such as public transit which is often slow, unreliable, and crowded.

1. The true cost of automobile use is actually even higher than consumers realize because certain hidden costs such as pollutants, noise, and hazards are not included.

B. Many solutions to the urban transportation problem share the common feature of including more of the social (hidden) costs of auto use in the price paid by the user (user charges).

1. Tolls and fees reflecting social costs could be charged to commuters with the highest fees being charged at periods of peak use.

2. Parking permits could be sold with the fee directly related to traffic density.

3. Pollution taxes for automobiles many be based upon the amount of automobile exhaust fumes emitted.

C. Another approach to the transportation problem is to improve public transit and lower the cost of this alternative for potential users.

D. Some solutions to the urban transportation problem that do not rely directly on price include staggering work hours to alleviate traffic congestion during peak periods and designating special traffic lanes for buses and carpools.

III. From the end of World War II to the mid 1970s, middle-income families moved from central cities to the suburbs because of the high urban taxes.

A. This population shift resulted in a smaller tax base and less revenue for cities while at the same time, demand for public services by the remaining residents has increased.

B. With dwindling revenues and increasing demands for services for low income residents, cities are unable to finance the kind and level of services to attract and retain middle-income residents.

IV. In recent years, renewed interest in the central city has generated additional demand for urban real estate. A socially optimal pattern of land use will occur if the private and social costs of urban land use are equal.

A. New construction in a city requires police and fire protection, sewage disposal, transit, and other facilities and services that are hidden costs of development.

B. Two solutions to the external diseconomies created by urban land use are zoning codes and imposition of taxes and fees.

1. Zoning prohibits certain kinds of land use and encourages other kinds in designated urban areas so that external diseconomies are minimized.

2. User fees often supplement the effects of zoning. When these fees are

included in the price paid for land, resources are available to compensate for diseconomies and inconveniences associated with new development.

V. Since public safety is not a free good, additional goods and services must be sacrificed if safety is to be increased in urban areas.

   A. The public cost of crime is measured in terms of outlays for police, courts, public prosecutors, jails, and so on.

   B. Private costs of crime include the value of stolen and damaged property, injuries suffered by victims, and the loss of revenue by shops and stores when the public is afraid to venture outside after dark.

   C. Currently, demand for crime prevention is probably artificially low because the social cost of crime is not included in the cost benefit analysis of crime prevention programs.

      1. If cities were liable to compensate victims of crime for their losses, there would probably be a reallocation of resources away from other public services toward crime prevention.

VI. The fiscal crisis in urban areas has been caused by a growing demand for public services coupled with a declining ability to pay for them as a result of a dwindling tax base.

   A. In addition to the middle-income flight to the suburbs, many firms have moved from older, established areas to new ones. This increases the problem of lost tax revenues and of unemployment for those who remain in the central city.

   B. Problems also arise because many suburban residents use city facilities and services but do not pay direct taxes to fund these services.

   C. The fiscal problems of cities may be dealt with by raising taxes, seeking new sources of revenue, or cutting expenditures.

      1. Most cities have raised taxes to meet increased demand for services. However, higher taxes often increase the flight of individuals and firms to the suburbs.

      2. Since 1972, unconditional revenue-sharing funds have been available to cities from the federal government to augment conditional grants (grants for specific programs and purposes).

      3. Politically, it is difficult to reduce expenditures, even on those services and facilities which are wastefully duplicated in adjoining political entities.

VII. The demand for public services in cities seems artificially high because there is no visible link between taxes paid and most public services provided by local government.

   A. Local government can make the cost of certain public goods and service more apparent to the public by using specific fees and charges rather than taxes.

KEY TERMS

Although no new terms are introduced in this chapter, you should be familiar with the meaning of the terms listed below which are used in this chapter.

elasticity of demand
external diseconomies
factors of production
free goods
economic good
user charge

high taxes
managerial skill
revenue sharing
social costs
tax base
zoning laws

CONCEPTS AND DEFINITIONS

Fill-in Questions

Complete each sentence by writing in the blank the most appropriate word or words from the terms listed above or by circling the word in parentheses that is correct.

1. To achieve economies of scale in providing city services, all _____ must be increased proportionately.

2. Exhaust fumes, noise, and congestion are _____ caused by private automobiles.

3. The primary purpose of _____ and building codes is to minimize _____ that might arise from conflicting uses of adjacent land.

4. Since public safety is an _____, it is necessary to sacrifice alternative goods if the quantity of public safety is increased.

5. Whether user charges would significantly reduce the number of automobiles driven in urban areas depends upon the _____.

6. Individuals can be made aware of the _____ of using private automobiles if government charges tolls and fees on automobile use.

7. One factor that prevents cities from taking advantage of economies of scale is the limited availability of _____.

8. _____ frequently are cited as a primary cause of the exodus of middle-income households from urban areas.

9. Since 1972, the federal government has provided funds for urban areas through a program of _____.

10. A general problem facing most American cities is that the demand for city services has increased while the urban _____ has decreased.

11. The quantity of city services demanded is artificially high if residents regard such services as being _____.

12. The price system yields an optimum allocation of land if land prices are based upon the private and _____ of land use.

13. A tax or fee paid by the recipient of a particular service is called a(n) _____.

Multiple Choice Questions

Circle the correct answer.

1. If the demand for public transit is elastic and transit fares are increased, revenues will

   a. increase.

   b. decrease.

   c. stay the same.

   d. change, but the nature of the change cannot be determined.

2. The optimum expenditure on public safety occurs when the

   a. private cost of safety is equal to the social cost.

   b. marginal utility from safety expenditures is greater than that which would be obtained if the funds were spent elsewhere.

   c. total utility from outlays on safety is equal to the total cost of public safety programs.

   d. marginal utility from expenditures on safety is equal to the marginal cost of providing those services.

3. Zoning laws are often used to

   a. prevent diseconomies.

   b. raise revenues.

   c. increase the social cost of land use.

   d. include social costs of land in the price system.

4. A problem that results from charging higher rates for public transit during rush hours is

   a. everyone will want to use public transit during non-rush hours.

   b. the use of private automobiles is made more attractive.

   c. the use of private automobiles is made less attractive.

   d. no one will want to use public transportation during rush hours.

5. The amount of money provided annually by the federal government for urban aid programs and social programs aiding people who live in cities is approximately

   a. $60 billion.

   b. $80 billion.

    c. $100 billion.

    d. $120 billion.

6. If the demand for a given service is inelastic, higher fees will cause city revenues to

    a. increase.

    b. drop.

    c. stay the same.

    d. drop for a while, then increase.

7. According to the text, the most common solution used by cities to remedy financial problems is to

    a. combine local governments.

    b. reduce city services.

    c. increase city revenues.

    d. determine tax rates by referendum.

8. Cities may reduce the quantity of public services demanded by

    a. raising property and sales tax rates.

    b. seeking additional funds from federal and state governments.

    c. cutting back on services that are inefficient.

    d. collecting more revenues in the form of user fees.

9. Wasteful duplication of governmental facilities and services is most likely to occur when

    a. a metropolitan area encompasses many relatively independent local governments.

    b. there is only one local government in an entire metropolitan area.

    c. local government contracts with private firms to provide services.

    d. a community grows beyond a certain size.

10. Monies made available to cities by the State and Local Fiscal Assistance Act may only be used

    a. when a locality is facing a fiscal crisis.

    b. for specific projects that receive prior federal approval.

    c. if a locality is facing bankruptcy.

    d. for locally determined projects that conform to broad federal guidelines.

APPLICATIONS

1. This news item appeared in the *Wall Street Journal.*

"Federal environmental rulings have forced sharp limits on street parking in midtown New York. Thus, demand has increased for spaces in parking garages, forcing up the rates. Instead of denouncing the government for reducing the supply of parking and raising the price of the remaining spaces, New York's Consumer Affairs Commissioner announced a crackdown on parking garage 'gougers.'"

Assume that you are an economist representing the New York Parking Lot Owners Association and that you must defend the higher parking fees now being charged. Your position is that the lot owners have performed a socially responsible act by raising their prices. Fully explain and support your statement, and in your analysis, consider the market situation prior to enforcement of the environmental rulings.

2. Public transit systems (subways, buses, and trains) are often crowded during rush hours, and underutilized at other times. Typically, transit fares do not vary according to time of day, and regular users are offered a discount.

   a. What modifications in the fare structure specified above could be made to achieve less crowding during rush hours and greater utilization of existing facilities during other times of day?

   b. How would the changes you recommend in Part a influence an individual's decision about whether private auto or public transit should be used for transportation?

   c. How might you respond to criticisms that your recommendations are unfair to some groups in society?

ANSWERS

Fill-in Questions

1. factors of production
2. external diseconomies
3. zoning laws; external diseconomies
4. economic good
5. elasticity of demand
6. social costs
7. managerial skill
8. high taxes
9. revenue sharing
10. tax base
11. free goods
12. social costs
13. user charge

Multiple Choice Questions

1. b
2. d
3. a
4. b
5. b
6. a
7. c
8. d
9. a
10. d

APPLICATIONS

1. The environmental rulings reduced the supply of on-street parking spaces in New York City, and thus created a shortage of on-street parking at the prevailing price. Consequently, the price of on-street parking must rise. As the price of on-street parking goes up, demand for the substitute good, parking lots, will increase and so too will the parking-lot prices if the market is to reach equilibrium.

    The central issue here is one of allocating a scarce resource, a basic problem in any economic system. As long as the price system is used to allocate parking spaces, prices will increase until the market reaches equilibrium. By raising their prices, lot owners have performed the socially necessary and responsible act of allocating a limited number of parking spaces among those who need a space.

2. a. Higher fares during rush hours and lower fares during slack times will promote a more even utilization of existing facilities. If the goal is even utilization of the transit system, discounts should be avoided *except* at slack times.

    b. This scheme will, of course, make use of private automobiles more attractive during rush hours and less attractive at other times. Reducing the overall congestion of transit facilities and surface streets is a complicated allocation problem that would require more than a modified transit-fare structure.

    c. Any allocation scheme, whether for space on public transit or in parking lots, is bound to be unfair to some people. With excess demand at the prevailing price, it is necessary to discriminate against some potential users in favor of some others.

Chapter 34

The Economics of Poverty and Discrimination

LEARNING OBJECTIVES

The economic basis of poverty in the United States and possible solutions to that problem are described in this chapter. In addition, the economic effects of discrimination and possible remedies for it are presented. This chapter represents an extension of the discussion in Chapters 28 and 29 of the functioning of resource markets.

After reading this chapter, you should be able to:

1. list several criteria for identifying poverty, and evaluate the merits and short-comings of each;

2. describe current and historical explanations of the causes of poverty, and the policies to remedy poverty that are implied by these alternative explanations;

3. explain what is meant by discrimination, specify the economic consequences of discrimination, and describe strategies to eliminate that problem;

4. explain how the labor force participation rate of women has changed since World War II, and the implications of that change for the economy;

5. summarize the central features of the dual labor market theory of poverty and discrimination;

6. identify contemporary government policies and programs that attempt to combat discrimination and to alleviate poverty.

CHAPTER OUTLINE

I. Poverty may be defined in several ways. Regardless of how it is defined, many people in the United States are poor.
    A. A family is defined as poor in *absolute* terms when it cannot afford to purchase basic necessities. Alternatively, *relative* poverty is defined by a ranking of individuals or families according to income. The poor are those in the lowest portion of that ranking.

1. Other definitions of poverty are difficult to make operational because they involve value judgments about what constitutes an adequate or comfortable standard of living.

C. Short-run income inequality may prove to be beneficial to the economy because it provides productivity incentives.

D. The government uses net family income data to determine poverty. In 1977, nearly 12 percent of the population, or roughly 25 million Americans, had incomes below the poverty level.

1. Blacks, households headed by a woman, the young and the elderly, and those living in rural areas are more prone to poverty than are urban whites and families headed by a male.

E. There is a significant degree of income inequality in the United States. In 1967, the wealthiest third of all families received nearly two-thirds of all personal income while the poorest sixth of households received less than 4 percent of total personal income.

1. Analysis of the distribution of income in the United States shows a majority of families in the middle income group and a minority of families at the extremes.

2. Income inequality may be plotted on a Lorenz curve which shows the differences between an equal distribution of income and the actual income distribution.

II. Historically, poverty was thought to be caused by personal inadequacy. Currently, poverty is believed to result from a variety of causes, many of which are beyond an individual's control.

A. The greatest cause of poverty seems to be low worker productivity resulting from insufficient investment in human capital.

1. Government programs to increase human capital include expenditures for health, education, and training.

B. Other government activities aimed at alleviating poverty in America involve increasing worker mobility, providing information about the job market, and promoting competition among employers.

III. A major cause of poverty is discrimination which exists when, between two workers with the same skills and training, one worker is preferred over the other on the basis of some criterion that is not directly related to the worker's ability to perform the job.

A. Studies show that blacks, persons of Spanish origin, and women, among others, are subject to labor-market discrimination which results in costs to society in the form of reduced output and higher prices.

1. Some of the differences in wages paid to women and minorities may be due to differences in the amount of human capital possessed by individuals in these groups and to differences in their productivity.

IV. Since World War II, women have entered the labor market in increasing numbers in order to maintain and increase standards of living, and to pursue career goals.

A. The discrepancy between incomes of males and females who work full time cannot, in general, be accounted for by differences in education. It may be explained by differences in labor-market experiences.
 1. Because of their child-bearing role, women tend to have fewer years of work experience than men.
 2. Many women are employed in occupations (such as secretaries) where pay scales are typically lower than in occupations which are predominately filled by men.
B. Public financing of day-care centers would enhance the ability of women (particularly poor women) to enter the labor market, to seek full-time employment, and to pursue higher-level employment opportunities. Such a program would help remedy the problem of poverty, particularly in households headed by a female.

V. The dual labor market theory of poverty and discrimination suggests there are two separate labor markets in the United States: a primary market of high wages and desirable employments, and a secondary market characterized by undesirable jobs which pay low wages. In the secondary market, carelessness on the job, high turnover rates, and casual attitudes toward work are common. The theory assumes that the poor are confined to the secondary market.
A. Since a worker's skills and habits are reinforced by the labor market in which he or she works, unfavorable work habits and attitudes which are common in the secondary market may prevent many workers from moving to primary markets, even if they obtain additional human capital.
 1. The model of the dual labor market indicates that a partial solution to the poverty problem might involve changing the characteristics of secondary jobs.

VI. There are no easy solutions to poverty and discrimination because of the complex nature of these problems. While additional investments in health, education, and training will remedy some of the poverty in the United States, other approaches are also required.
A. The incomes of those in poverty are supplemented by several income-transfer programs including OASDHI, SSI, AFDC, Food Stamps, Medicare and Medicaid, and Unemployment Compensation. A negative income tax has been proposed to replace many welfare programs which are thought to be inefficient and degrading to those receiving assistance.
B. More vigorous enforcement of legislation to prevent discrimination and stiffer penalties for noncompliance will make new job opportunities available to the poor.
 1. Several laws and Executive Orders prohibit discrimination against minorities, women, and older workers.
  a. Quotas have been used to force employers to end discriminatory hiring programs. These sometimes lead to reverse discrimination where the most qualified applicants must be rejected in favor of minority workers.

KEY TERMS

You should be familiar with the meaning of the terms listed below. For definition of these terms, please refer to the glossary at the end of your textbook and to the appropriate section in this chapter.

Lorenz curve   discrimination
human capital   negative income tax

CONCEPTS AND DEFINITIONS

Fill-in Questions

Complete each sentence by writing in the blank the most appropriate word or words from the terms listed below or by circling the word in parentheses that is correct.

absolute poverty   net income
Lorenz curve   negative income tax
area of inequality   opportunity cost
middle-income   discrimination
earnings   relative poverty
human capital

1. Unless incomes are made exactly equal, it will never be possible to eliminate _____ although _____ could be eradicated.

2. The federal government determines eligibility for antipoverty aid in the United States by measuring _____ according to family size.

3. Differences in average salaries between black and white male workers may be attributed to _____ and to differences in _____.

4. Antipoverty programs that only fund direct training expenses may fail if participation entails an unacceptably high _____ to participants.

5. There is a strong, positive correlation between the amount of human capital possessed by an individual and the individual's _____.

6. The area between the income-distribution curve and the 45-degree line on a Lorenz curve constitutes the _____.

7. The well-known court case *Bakke* v. *The University of California* alleged a form of _____ in a University's policy of admissions to medical school.

8. A graph that compares an actual distribution of income to an equal distribution is known as a _____.

9. Low worker productivity is often attributed to poor health and little education, or a lack of _____.

10. A _____ has been proposed as an alternative to specific welfare programs in the United States.

11. Income is distributed in such a way in the United States that most households fall in the _____ range.

Multiple Choice Questions

Circle the correct answer.

1. One purpose of a negative income tax is to

    a. encourage investment in human capital.

    b. reduce the need for secondary jobs.

    c. correct for differences in accumulated wealth.

    d. provide work incentives.

2. Suppose that 10 percent of the households in the United States in 1915 had incomes of less than $1000 and in 1980, only 3 percent had incomes below $1000. What conclusions could you draw from these data?

    a. Incomes were more equally distributed in 1915 than in 1980.

    b. Incomes were less equally distributed in 1915 than in 1980.

    c. There are fewer very poor households in 1980 than in 1915.

    d. These figures do not reveal anything about poverty or the distribution of income in either 1915 or 1980.

3. The present system of transfer payments to the poor

    a. is free of abuses by program administrators and recipients.

    b. is operated by the Internal Revenue Service.

    c. requires extensive and expensive administrative machinery.

    d. provides funds automatically to those whose incomes drop below a certain level.

4. A preference by employers for white male employees is likely to cause

    a. an optimal allocation of resources.

    b. a larger quantity of output.

    c. a higher price for final products.

    d. output and price to remain constant.

5. A worker is likely to receive a wage that is lower than marginal revenue product if he or she is employed

    a. by a competitive firm.

    b. by a monopsonist.

    c. in a dual labor market.

    d. by either a competitive or a monopsonistic firm.

6. A government free clinic providing preventive medical care is most appropriately regarded as an investment in

    a. human capital.

    b. physical capital.

    c. social overhead capital.

    d. the economic infrastructure.

7. According to the text, more and more people today accept the idea that poverty

    a. is a reflection of personal inadequacy.

    b. is a sign of insufficient aggregate demand.

    c. is an interruption of the circular flow.

    d. results from complex causes including discrimination.

8. Is it possible to be poor in relative terms without also being poor in absolute terms?

    a. Yes, if your income is large enough.

    b. Yes, if your income is small enough.

    c. Impossible to determine without specific figures.

    d. No, regardless of the size of your income.

9. It is suggested in the text that income inequality is important in order to

    a. provide short-run benefits to the poor.

    b. allow the poor to provide savings which may be borrowed for investment purposes.

    c. provide disincentives for workers on the job.

    d. provide jobs for social workers and program administrators.

10. By defining poverty on a net income basis, government

    a. ignores the differences between money income and real income.

    b. takes account of regional differences in the cost of living.

    c. is using a comprehensive definition of poverty.

    d. is using the New School definition of poverty.

11. In 1977, what fraction of the United States population had incomes below the poverty level?

    a. 8 percent.

    b. 12 percent.

    c. 20 percent.

    d. 25 percent.

12. The purpose of a Lorenz curve is to show

    a. the degree of inequality in the distribution of income.

    b. income differences between blacks and whites.

    c. the distribution of wealth in the United States.

    d. the social impact of an equal distribution of income.

13. According to the text, Calvinists believed that poverty

    a. could be alleviated if government issued bootstraps to the poor.

    b. was a manifestation of God's displeasure with man.

    c. was largely a problem beyond an individual's control.

    d. was caused by insufficient investment in human capital.

14. Investment in human capital will help to eliminate poverty by

    a. increasing the expectations of workers.

    b. forcing workers to save (since savings must equal investment).

    c. eliminating discrimination against women and minorities.

    d. increasing worker productivity.

15. The argument that the increased number of women in the labor force has reduced employment opportunities for men and raised their unemployment

    a. tends to be supported by available evidence.

    b. is false, because women are employed in women's jobs such as librarians, nurses, and secretaries.

    c. is unlikely to be true since the amount of work to be done in an economy is not a fixed total.

    d. is likely to be true since women are attempting to move into positions traditionally held by men.

16. According to the dual labor market theory,

    a. workers in secondary markets are often perceived as unable to perform the kinds of work available in primary markets.

    b. full-time workers are employed in primary markets while part-time workers are employed in secondary markets.

    c. workers may move from the secondary to the primary market, but not vice versa.

    d. increasing aggregate demand will not materially change the economic circumstances of those in primary markets.

17. Government determines who is eligible for antipoverty aid by evaluating

    a. net income according to family size.

    b. gross income according to family size.

c. real income according to family size.

d. per capita income according to family size.

18. In the United States, there has been

a. no change in the relative distribution of income.

b. a move toward greater equality of income distribution.

c. a move toward greater inequality of income distribution.

APPLICATIONS

1. Consider the Lorenz curve shown below.

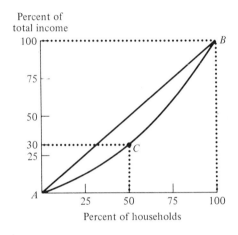

a. What is indicated by the line segment *AB* (the 45-degree line)?

b. According to this curve, approximately what fraction of income is received by the lowest fourth of households in the economy? the lowest half? the upper fourth of households?

c. If the curved line *ACB* were to sag more toward the lower right corner of the diagram, what would that represent?

d. What would line *ACB* look like if incomes were distributed in an absolutely equal fashion?

ANSWERS

Fill-in Questions

1. relative poverty;
   absolute poverty
2. net income

6. area of inequality
7. discrimination
8. Lorenz curve

3. discrimination;
    human capital
4. opportunity cost
5. earnings

9. human capital
10. negative income tax
11. middle-income

Multiple Choice Questions

1.	d	10.	a
2.	d	11.	b
3.	c	12.	a
4.	c	13.	b
5.	b	14.	d
6.	a	15.	c
7.	d	16.	d
8.	a	17.	a
9.	b	18.	b

APPLICATIONS

1. a. Line segment *AB* depicts an absolutely equal distribution of income.

    b. 10 percent; 30 percent; 40 percent

    c. A more unequal distribution of income would be depicted.

    d. If incomes were equally distributed, line *ACB* would lie on top of line *AB*.

Chapter 35

The Economics of Energy

LEARNING OBJECTIVES

This chapter describes energy markets in the United States. The role of government in these markets is examined as is the impact of OPEC on energy supplies and energy prices during the 1970s. United States energy policy for the 1980s is discussed and the model of demand and supply is used to gain insight into the short- and long-term effects of government regulation and to evaluate long-run strategies for assuring adequate energy supplies.

After reading this chapter, you should be able to:

1. identify key events in the 1970s that were responsible for worldwide attention on energy and energy markets;

2. describe the causes of the 1973 energy crisis and the events which led to a second crisis in 1979;

3. trace the history of government regulation and control in the markets for oil, natural gas, coal, and nuclear power;

4. specify the impact of environmental restrictions on the demand for and supply of energy;

5. assess arguments for relying on the free market and on government to meet future energy needs, and speculate about the way in which those needs will be met in the United States.

CHAPTER OUTLINE

I. Although energy problems had been predicted well before October 1973, the American public remained unconcerned until gasoline shortages appeared in the last quarter of 1973 when a selective embargo and a general production cutback by members of the Organization of Petroleum Exporting Countries, OPEC, triggered the 1973 crisis.

    A. The embargo and the increased price of crude oil led to worldwide shortages of gasoline and products derived from petroleum, to worldwide recession and, simultaneously, to worldwide inflation.

    B. By mid-1974, most of the short-term effects of the 1973 crisis had disappeared and the longer-term effects of inflation and recession diverted attention from the source of the problem.

    C. A second crisis in 1979 resulted from government control of the domestic oil and energy-producing industries and from an interrupted flow of Iranian oil to world markets.

II.   Government intervention and control in energy-producing industries has protected and enhanced the position of some energy suppliers, inhibited domestic energy production, and served to increase the quantity of energy demanded by consumers.

    A. Prior to 1973, oil-import quotas served to increase the price of domestically produced oil. Since that time, domestic price controls on oil seem to have inhibited the search for additional oil.

    B. Since the 1920s government has regulated levels of production, the price of natural gas transported across state lines, and the distribution of natural gas to consumers (a natural monopoly). The historically low regulated price of natural gas has encouraged demand for this fuel.

       1. Attempts to augment dwindling domestic supplies of natural gas from foreign sources have been frustrated by technological problems, diplomatic difficulties, and a lack of pipeline facilities.

    C. Coal mining and marketing operations remained free of government control until the 1960s when a growing concern with the environment prompted restrictions on strip mining and on the use of coal with a high sulfur content.

       1. Since the United States has vast coal reserves, coal will play an increasingly important role in meeting United States energy needs as the prices of other sources of energy continue to increase.

    D. Nuclear fuel has been used by private firms to generate electricity since the 1950s. Because of the potential danger from nuclear radiation, government control in this industry has been substantial.

III. Since 1900, the long-term trend in energy use in the United States has been upward, generally following the growth of domestic output and incomes.

    A. Long-term reductions in energy demand will depend upon the strength of government policy in the 1980s, and upon the effect of higher prices on quantity demanded.

IV. While many alternatives have been proposed, two distinct methods are available for dealing with the energy problems confronted by the United States and other Western industrial countries.

    A. The market approach to the energy problem relies on price and profit signals to restrain consumption and spur production until quantity demanded is equal to quantity supplied.

       1. The advantage of using price as a mechanism for rationing scarce re-

sources, as well as for increasing supply, is that prices provide necessary information for decision making by both consumers and producers in an economic and political environment in which free choice is emphasized.

    2. Several objections have been raised regarding the use of markets for dealing with the energy situation.

        a. Higher energy prices impose a special burden on individuals with low income.

        b. Higher prices add to produce profits which may not be used for increasing supply but, rather, for corporate expansion in new areas.

        c. Higher energy prices contribute to domestic inflation and a continuing inflationary spiral.

B. A second method for dealing with energy problems involves a more active government role in assuring adequate supplies of energy as well as in allocating existing supplies.

    1. Government could expand its role in energy markets by directing and funding research and development activities, and by promoting the national interest by its policy decisions.

        a. Government has taken steps to reduce long-term energy demand by establishing minimum standards for energy use that auto and appliance manufacturers and producers of other products must meet.

        b. Another way government has influenced long-term energy demand is by providing tax incentives for efficient energy use.

        c. Government may also direct how resources are used. In gasoline markets, for example, government may restrain consumption through programs of coupon rationing.

C. Current federal energy policy, embodied in both old and new legislation, has been shaped by diverse goals and by political pressures exerted by competing groups in the economy.

    1. Federal energy policy stresses conservation and controls the price of domestically produced oil and refined petroleum products.

    2. To inhibit demand, President Carter decontrolled domestic crude oil prices in 1979 according to a gradual timetable. It was hoped that this action would encourage additional production and curb energy demand. It might also aggravate inflation.

        a. Domestic price controls and allocation schemes have usually caused production bottlenecks and shortages of some products.

V. As supplies of easily accessible oil and natural gas have dwindled in the United States and as dependence on foreign sources to meet demand for these fuels has grown, the need to develop alternative sources of supply has increased.

A. Although many alternative energy sources exist, none are currently capable of providing substantial amounts of heat or electricity at a cost that is competitive with fuels currently available. While higher prices of conventional energy sources will spur development of alternatives, government support of research and development programs is likely to be essential if new sources of energy are to be developed quickly.

KEY TERMS

Although there are no new terms introduced in this chapter, you should be familiar with the meaning of the terms listed below which are used in this chapter.

alternative sources	governmental action
coal	interstate commerce
embargo	intrastate commerce
rationing	natural gas
enhanced recovery	oil
free-market approach	solar energy
geothermal power	uranium

CONCEPTS AND DEFINITIONS

Fill-in Questions

Complete each sentence by writing in the blank the most appropriate word or words from the terms listed above or by circling the word in parentheses that is correct.

1. As the supplies of easily accessible oil and natural gas in the United States dwindle, it is anticipated that _____ of energy will be used to meet demand.

2. _____ is generated by trapping steam from underground hot springs.

3. At present, the United States obtains nearly all of its energy from the following four fuels: _____ _____ _____ _____.

4. Because natural gas in _____ was not subject to federal controls, it commanded a higher price than natural gas transported in _____.

5. The least regulated of the four major sources of energy currently used in the United States is_____.

6. Among the most promising alternative fuel sources is _____ which has the long-term potential of yielding unlimited quantities of non-polluting energy.

7. The two distinct ways of dealing with energy problems in the United States are the _____ and _____.

8. _____ involves injecting water, steam, or chemicals into an old oil reservoir to increase the flow of more viscous oil or oil trapped in geological formations.

9. A(n) _____ is a situation in which one country refuses to sell a commodity to another.

10. The gasoline shortages in 1973 and 1979 may be attributed to the fact that _____ rather than the _____ was the cornerstone of federal energy policy during those years.

11. Some measures undertaken in the interest of American energy independence have served to make fuel (more/less) expensive.

12. A free-market solution to the energy crisis would allow energy prices to (fall/rise).

13. An allocation of fuel based on some criterion other than price is known as _____.

Multiple Choice Questions

Circle the correct answer.

1. The federal government has taken active steps to restrain energy demand by
   a. dictating specific product goals for energy consumption.
   b. initiating coupon rationing programs.
   c. imposing odd-even gasoline buying programs.
   d. vigorous enforcement of antitrust laws to promote competition in energy production and distribution.

2. If the federal government provided funds and incentives for a maximum effort to develop alternative energy sources, such a program would be expected to
   a. encourage additional current production by OPEC nations.
   b. reduce current production by OPEC nations.
   c. have no effect on current production by OPEC nations.
   d. drive the price of OPEC oil higher in the short run.

3. A principal objection to the free-market approach for dealing with energy problems is that
   a. firms will not follow self-interest in making production decisions.
   b. higher prices for energy from traditional sources will inhibit the development of new alternative energy sources.
   c. higher prices will force greater reliance on foreign sources of supply.
   d. profits obtained from higher prices may be used for corporate expansion in fields other than energy.

4. The fuel shortages that closed schools and factories during the winter of 1974 have been directly attributed to

a. an OPEC embargo.

b. a strike of refinery workers.

c. domestic price controls.

d. environmental restrictions.

5. From 1900 to 1979, energy use in the United States

a. has grown at an average annual rate of between 5 and 6 percent.

b. has generally followed the growth of domestic output and incomes.

c. tended to drop on a per-capita basis because more efficient appliances and automobiles have been developed each year.

d. grew more slowly than it did during the nineteenth century, as more efficient fuels were discovered during the later period.

6. Approximately what fraction of energy currently used in the United States comes from coal?

a. 20 percent.

b. 35 percent.

c. 50 percent.

d. 65 percent.

7. Natural gas is supplied to most consumers by natural monopolies

a. in order to take advantage of diseconomies of scale.

b. since artificial monopolies would violate provisions of the Sherman Act.

c. in order to provide consumers with a lower price than would be possible with competition.

d. in order to avoid federal price ceilings on supplies moving through interstate pipelines.

8. Government intervention and control in energy-producing industries

a. is a recent development in response to the actions of OPEC.

b. is necessary since in many of these markets, quantity demanded is greater than quantity supplied.

c. is for the sole purpose of helping consumers obtain adequate supplies of fuel and energy.

d. has been responsible, at times, for inhibiting domestic energy production and also for increasing energy use by consumers.

9. In the United States, coal, natural gas, oil, and uranium

a. are priced according to regulations established by the United States Department of Energy.

b. are produced and distributed by natural monopolies.

c. have been used since the Depression as commercial sources of fuel or electricity.

d. are used to produce nearly all of the energy consumed domestically.

10. An embargo such as that imposed by OPEC on the United States and the Netherlands is a situation in which one country

a. raises the price that other countries must pay for imports.

b. refuses to sell goods to another.

c. relies on absolute rather than comparative advantage in trade.

d. changes the terms of trade with its trading partners.

11. Low energy prices may discourage

a. consumption.

b. production.

c. allocation.

d. distribution.

APPLICATION

1. One component of President Carter's energy program involved a substantial increase in the federal excise tax on gasoline. This tax would have the effect of increasing gasoline prices above current levels. The goal of this action is to reduce energy consumption, and the Federal Energy Administration has determined that every 10 percent increase in price will result in a 1 percent decrease in fuel consumption in the short run, and an even larger decrease in the long run.

a. Assuming the government's figures are accurate, is the demand for gasoline elastic, inelastic, or unit elastic? How do you know?

b. If the oil companies decided to raise the price of gasoline (over and above any energy tax), what impact would that have on their revenues?

c. It has been suggested by federal officials that the long-run response to increased gasoline prices would be greater than the short-run response. What economic justification could be offered to support this assertion?

ANSWERS

Fill-in Questions

1. alternative sources
2. geothermal power
3. oil; natural gas; coal; uranium (in any order)

7. free-market approach; governmental action (or vice versa)
8. enhanced recovery
9. embargo

4. intrastate commerce;
    interstate commerce
5. coal
6. solar energy

10. governmental action;
    free-market approach
11. more
12. rise
13. rationing

Multiple Choice Questions

1.	a	5.	b	9.	d
2.	a	6.	a	10.	b
3.	d	7.	c	11.	b
4.	a	8.	d		

APPLICATIONS

1. a. Demand is inelastic since the percentage change in quantity demanded (1 percent) is smaller than the percentage change in price (10 percent).

    b. Any price increase in a product for which the demand is inelastic will cause company revenues to increase

    c. In the short-run, comparatively few substitutes for gasoline are available to consumers. Consequently, consumption is relatively insensitive to price hikes (demand is inelastic). Over time, in response to higher prices, consumers will make adjustment to lessen their dependence on and use of gasoline. The elasticity of demand will thus increase over time in response to the short-run adjustments that are made.

Chapter 36

Comparative Advantage and International Trade

LEARNING OBJECTIVES

The earlier chapters of the text are primarily concerned with the microeconomic and macroeconomic activities of households, businesses, and government *within* an economy. Since relationships *between* economies are also important, we now investigate the economics of international trade. The reasons for trade and the benefits that it offers are explored and the impact of trade on output and prices is discussed.

After reading this chapter, you should be able to:

1. identify the conditions under which specialization makes trade beneficial for all participants;

2. demonstrate the relevance of the principle of comparative advantage for international trade;

3. explain how the terms of trade between nations are established;

4. show how trade affects world output, national income, and the prices of output and inputs.

CHAPTER OUTLINE

I. Trade between nations occurs because it permits a more efficient use of resources and a larger total output than would otherwise be possible.
    A. This larger output is produced when trade takes place according to the principle of comparative advantage, which states that if one country can produce each of two goods at a lower opportunity cost than another country and can produce one of these goods at a lower opportunity cost than the other, it should specialize in the production of the good with the lower opportunity cost and should trade with another country to obtain the other good.

1. For example, if we consider two economies that each produce just two goods, steel and cloth, the opportunity cost of producing one ton of steel is the amount of cloth forgone. The nation that sacrifices the least amount of cloth in producing one ton of steel should specialize in steel production. Similarly, the nation that sacrifices the least amount of steel to produce one unit of cloth should specialize in cloth production.
   a. A nation's opportunity cost of producing one good in terms of the forgone production of another good is its domestic exchange ratio.
      (1) If, for example, the United States gives up 10 units of cloth (C) for every 30 units of steel (S) it produces, its domestic exchange ratio is 3S:1C. That is, the opportunity cost of producing 3 units of steel is 1 unit of cloth.
      (2) Domestic exchange ratios differ among nations because the resource endowments of nations vary and because the efficient production of various goods requires different technologies or combinations of resources.
         (a) This means, for example, that a nation well endowed in capital will be able to produce steel, a good whose production process is capital-intensive, at a lower cost in terms of cloth than a nation with relatively little capital at its disposal.

II. Negotiation is necessary to determine the terms at which one country trades with another.
   A. The terms of trade (international exchange ratio) indicate the number of units of one good that must be given in exchange for another. This ratio will lie somewhere between the domestic exchange ratios of the two nations.
      1. For example, with exchange ratios of 3S:1C in the United States and 1S:1C in the United Kingdom, the United States can exchange 1 unit of steel for 1/3 unit of cloth without trade, while the United Kingdom can exchange 1 unit of cloth for 1 unit of steel without trade. Trade will occur, therefore, only if the United States can exchange 1 unit of steel for more than 1/3 unit of cloth, and the United Kingdom can exchange 1 unit of cloth for more than 1 unit of steel.
         a. The United States might settle for 1/2 unit of cloth in exchange for a unit of steel, which implies an *international* exchange ratio of 2S:1C. These terms may also be acceptable to the United Kingdom since this would permit the purchase of 2 units of steel for each unit of cloth, as opposed to the United Kingdom's *domestic* exchange ratio of 1S:1C. Thus, the terms of trade will lie between the two domestic exchange ratios, with the exact ratio being determined by the relative bargaining strength of the two nations.
      2. The possible combinations of goods available to each nation upon establishment of the terms of trade are shown by a terms-of-trade line.
         a. The gains from trade are calculated by subtracting the pretrade levels of production and consumption of each good by each nation from the post-trade levels.

III. The economic impact of trade may be measured in terms of its effect on world output, output and input prices, and national income.
   A. World output increases because trade results in a more efficient use of resources.
   B. International differences in the price of a good tend to be eliminated as a result of changes in demand and supply caused by trade.
      1. For example, cloth was relatively cheap in the United Kingdom prior to trade and relatively expensive in the United States. With trade, the demand for United Kingdom cloth increases as does its price. In addition, United Kingdom exports of cloth increase the supply of cloth in the United States, thereby reducing the price of cloth in the United States. Consequently, the international difference in the price of cloth is eliminated over time.
   C. International differences in the price of an input tend to be eliminated through trade in a manner similar to that of the output price equalization process described above.
      1. Capital, the relatively cheap and abundant factor in the United States, becomes less abundant and more expensive as trade increases the production of steel. Labor, the scarce factor in the United States has become less scarce and cheaper because the import of cloth from the United Kingdom has caused the cloth industry to contract, freeing up labor resources.
      2. In the United Kingdom, the demand for labor (abundant and cheap) will increase and cause its price to rise. At the same time, the demand for capital (scarce and expensive) will fall as the steel industry contracts, and the price will fall too.
   D. The introduction of international trade means that NNP (national income) becomes the sum of consumption, investment, government spending, *and* net exports (the value of exports minus the value of imports): NNP $= C + I + G + (X - M)$.
      1. If the level of exports exceeds that of imports, aggregate demand rises and NNP increases by some multiple of the change in aggregate demand. When imports exceed exports, aggregate demand is reduced and national income declines by some multiple of the change in aggregate demand.
         a. Changes in net exports significantly affect the economies of nations in which international transactions represent a sizable portion of NNP.

KEY TERMS

You should be familiar with the meaning of the terms listed below. For definition of these terms, please refer to the glossary at the end of your textbook and to the appropriate section in this chapter.

absolute advantage   terms of trade
comparative advantage   terms-of-trade line
domestic exchange ratio   theory of factor endowments

CONCEPTS AND DEFINITIONS

Fill-in Questions

Complete each sentence by writing in the blank the most appropriate word or words from the terms listed below or by circling the word in parentheses that is correct.

absolute advantage   exports
net exports   comparative advantage
specialization   theory of factor endowments
opportunity cost   terms of trade
production possibilities   domestic exchange ratio
consumption possibilities   terms-of-trade line

1. The _____ provides one explanation for differences in domestic exchange ratios between nations.

2. When _____ are negative, United States purchases of foreign goods and services are (greater/smaller) than foreign purchases of American goods and services.

3. Trade between nations may be mutually beneficial even if one country possesses a(n) _____ in the production of all goods.

4. Mutually beneficial trade does not alter the _____ of a nation, but does increase its _____.

5. If the domestic exchange ratios for wheat (W) and corn (C) in the United States and Canada are 4W:1C and 2W:1C, respectively, the _____ may turn out to be 3W:1C.

6. In reference to the above question, Canada's 2W:1C domestic exchange ratio indicates that the _____ of producing 1 unit of corn is 2 units of wheat.

7. _____ in production and trade is appropriate when the opportunity cost of producing goods differs among nations.

8. The slope of the _____ reflects the international exchange ratio.

9. A nation may have a _____ in the production of a good even if it does not possess an absolute advantage.

10. If the _____ is the same in nation A as it is in nation B, neither country possesses a comparative advantage in the production of any good.

11. According to the theory of comparative advantage, it would be advantageous for countries to trade with one another if their domestic exchange ratios were (equal/unequal).

12. The ratio at which goods are traded in the international market is known as the
    _____.

13. The amount of one good that must be sacrificed in order to obtain more of another good, or the opportunity cost of the good, is also known as the
    _____.

14. There will be an expansionary effect on national income if there is a surplus of
    _____.

Multiple Choice Questions

Circle the correct answer.

1. For mutually beneficial trade to occur, each nation must possess

    a. a comparative advantage in the production of one of the traded goods.

    b. an absolute advantage in the production of one of the traded goods.

    c. the ability to produce the traded goods with equal efficiency.

    d. identical resource endowments.

2. If the domestic exchange ratios for frisbees (F) and rum (R) in the United States and Puerto Rico are 5F:1R and 2F:1R, respectively, mutually beneficial trade

    a. requires that the United States specialize in rum production.

    b. requires that Puerto Rico specialize in frisbee production.

    c. cannot occur under these circumstances.

    d. could occur if the international exchange ratio is 3F:1R.

3. Assuming that the domestic exchange ratios for diamonds (D) and coffee (C) in South Africa and Brazil are 4D:1C and 1D:1C, respectively, trade between these two nations would be mutually beneficial if the international exchange ratio is

    a. 6D:1C.

    b. 3D:2C.

    c. 4D:1C.

    d. 1D:1C.

4. If its net exports equal zero in a particular year,

    a. aggregate demand in the United States is unaffected by international trade.

    b. the United States is not involved in international trade.

   c. the United States is importing goods, but foreign countries are not purchasing goods produced in the United States.

   d. the United States is not exporting any nets.

5. If, in the absence of trade, 3 pounds of bacon (B) can be exchanged for 6 pounds of potatoes (P)

   a. the international exchange ratio is 3B:6P.

   b. mutually beneficial trade may occur with a nation whose domestic exchange ratio is 1B:2P.

   c. the opportunity cost of producing one pound of potatoes is 1/2 pound of bacon.

   d. this nation should specialize in bacon production.

6. Specialization in production

   a. reduces the degree of interdependence between nations.

   b. may be appropriate if two nations produce commodities with varying degrees of efficiency.

   c. is always inappropriate if a nation has an absolute advantage in the production of all goods.

   d. promotes economic self-sufficiency.

7. The terms-of-trade line

   a. depicts the various combinations of output which a nation can produce when its resources are fully utilized.

   b. lies inside the production possibilities curve when mutually beneficial trade is possible.

   c. has a negative slope because the per unit cost of production and the level of production of any good are inversely related.

   d. shows the various combinations of output which are available for consumption as a result of trade.

8. A nation that specializes in the production of a labor-intensive commodity is likely to be

   a. capital-abundant.

   b. labor-abundant.

   c. technologically advanced.

   d. land-abundant.

9. The process of international trade

   a. reduces national income by encouraging imports.

   b. lowers the price of products that can be produced relatively cheaply.

   c. reduces the price of scarce, relatively expensive resources.

d. results in an outward shift of the production-possibilities curve of all trading nations.

10. International trade necessarily causes inflation whenever

a. net exports increase.

b. net exports decrease and the economy is already operating at full employment.

c. net exports decrease.

d. net exports increase and the economy is already operating at full employment.

APPLICATIONS

1. Assume that the annual production possibilities schedules (PPSs) for steak (S) and beer (B) in the United States and West Germany are as follows:

	United States			West Germany	
	Steak (units produced)	Beer (units produced)		Steak (units produced)	Beer (units produced)
A	0	30	A	0	90
B	5	20	B	10	60
C	10	10	C	20	30
D	15	0	D	30	0

a. Which country has the absolute advantage in the production of steak? Explain your answer.

b. Which country has the absolute advantage in the production of beer? Explain.

c. Which country has the comparative advantage in the production of steak? Explain.

d. Which country has the comparative advantage in the production of beer? Explain.

e. Assuming that the terms of trade are 2S:5B, plot both the production-possibilities curves (PPCs) and the terms-of-trade lines (TTLs) for the United States and West Germany. Measure steak on the vertical axis and beer on the horizontal axis. (Note: For each country, plot the PPC and the TTL on the *same* graph as is done in *Fig. 36.3* in the text.)

f. Assume that, prior to trade, the United States chooses to operate at point *B* on its PPS (5 units of steak, 20 units of beer), while West Germany chooses to operate at point *B* on its PPS (10 units of steak, 60 units of beer).

(1) By how much will total output increase as a result of trade?

(2) If the terms of trade are 2S:5B, and both the United States and West Germany desire exactly the same amount of steak after trade as they did before trade, show how the increased output resulting from trade is distriubted between the two nations.

ANSWERS

Fill-in Questions

1. theory of factor endowments
2. net exports; greater
3. absolute advantage
4. production possibilities; consumption possibilities
5. terms of trade
6. opportunity cost
7. specialization
8. terms-of-trade line

9. comparative advantage
10. domestic exchange ratio
11. unequal
12. terms of trade
13. domestic exchange ratio
14. exports

Multiple Choice Questions

1. a
2. d
3. b
4. a
5. c

6. b
7. d
8. b
9. c
10. d

APPLICATIONS

1. a. West Germany has an absolute advantage in the production of steak. If it specialized in steak production it could produce 30 units of steak, whereas the United States is capable of producing just 15 units.

    b. West Germany has an absolute advantage in beer production. It can produce 90 units of beer through specialization in beer production, while the United States could produce only 30 units.

    c. The United States has a comparative advantage in steak production. Its domestic exchange ratio is 1S:2B, which means it sacrifices 2 units of beer for every unit of steak produced. West Germany's domestic exchange ratio, on the other hand, is 1S:3B, so that it forgoes 3 units of beer for every unit of steak it produces. Since the opportunity cost of steak production is lower in the United States than in West Germany, the United States has a comparative advantage in the production of steak.

d. West Germany has a comparative advantage in beer production. Its domestic exchange ratio of 1S:3B means that it can produce 3 units of beer while giving up just 1 unit of steak. The United States domestic exchange ratio indicates that it could produce only 2 units of beer in exchange for a unit of steak. Consequently, the comparative advantage in beer production lies with West Germany.

e. The PPCs are constructed by plotting the combinations of steak and beer in the respective PPSs. The TTLs are constructed on the basis of the international exchange ratio (terms of trade) of 2S:5B.

In the case of West Germany, the TTL intersects the x-axis at 90 units of beer. This indicates that West Germany specializes in beer production and thus its production is limited by its production possibilities. The TTL intersects the y-axis at a higher level than does the PPC, which indicates that the international exchange ratio is more favorable than the domestic exchange ratio. With a 2S:5B international exchange ratio, 90 units of beer can be traded for 36 units of steak internationally (2S:5B = 36S:90B). Domestically, the same amount of beer brings only 30 units of steak in exchange because the domestic exchange ratio is 1S:3B.

The United States TTL can be interpreted in a similar way because 15 units of steak bring 37.5 units of beer internationally, but only 30 units of beer in the absence of international trade.

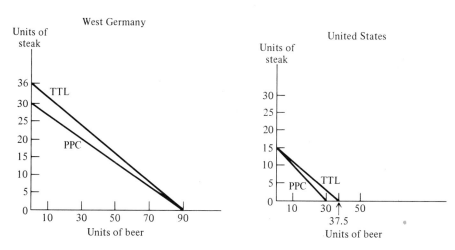

f. (1) 10 units of beer. Explanation: Prior to trade, total steak production is 15 units, while beer output is 80 units. With the United States and West Germany specializing in steak and beer production, respectively, steak output is 15 units and beer output is 90 units. Therefore, as a result of trade, total output increases by 10 units of beer. (2) Beer consumption in each country increases by 5 units. Explanation: The United States produces 15 units of steak, retaining 5 units for domestic consumption and exporting the remaining 10 units. With an international exchange ratio of 2S:5B, the 10 units of steak is exchanged for 25 units of beer. Before trade, the United States produced and consumed 5 units of steak and 20 units of beer. With trade, it consumes the same amount of steak, but 5 additional units of beer.

West Germany, on the other hand, produces 90 units of beer, but wants to import 10 units of steak. With the terms of trade at 2S:5B, it must export 25 units of beer to get the desired amount of steak. Thus, it retains 65 units of beer for domestic consumption and imports 10 units of steak. Before trade, West Germany produced and consumed 10 units of steak and 60 units of beer. With trade, its consumption of steak remains constant, but its beer consumption rises by 5 units.

Chapter 37

Barriers to Free Trade

LEARNING OBJECTIVES

While each participant benefits when nations trade according to the principle of comparative advantage, most countries undertake policies that tend to restrict the international flow of goods and services. In this chapter, several restrictive trade policies are examined, with tariffs receiving special attention. The economic effects of tariffs are discussed, as are the arguments supporting and opposing their use. In addition, the role of politics in tariff policy is considered.

After reading this chapter, you should be:

1. familiar with quotas, tariffs, and other barriers to international trade;

2. aware of the economic impact of a tariff, as it affects both the country that imposes it and the nation against which it is levied;

3. able to explain the basic arguments supporting tariff policy as well as the counterarguments of free-trade advocates;

4. aware that tariffs are often imposed for political, rather than economic, reasons.

CHAPTER OUTLINE

I. There are several types of restrictive trade policies.
    A. A tariff is a tax on imported commodities.
       1. It may be a fixed charge on each unit of an imported commodity (specific tariff) or it may vary according to the value of the imported good (*ad valorem* tariff).
    B. A quota limits the amount of a particular good that may be imported during a specified time period.
    C. Embargoes and licensing requirements are other barriers to trade sometimes utilized by government.

       1. An embargo represents a refusal by one country to trade with another.

       2. Licensing requirements provide a nation with direct control over the number of importers and indirect control over the volume of imports.

II.   The tariff, often employed to protect an inefficient domestic industry, is the most commonly used restrictive trade policy.

   A. Since it increases the costs of foreign producers, a tariff raises the price of an imported good, and thereby reduces domestic consumption. Consumers, then, are adversely affected.

       1. When a tariff is imposed, the price of imported goods increases relative to domestically produced items. Hence, domestic firms experience increased demand.

          a. While domestic industry output and employment increase, the economy as a whole suffers because the tariff causes a relatively inefficient domestic industry to use more of society's scarce resources. The long-run result is a lower level of domestic output than would be possible with free trade.

   B. Despite higher prices and inefficient resource allocation, several arguments are made in favor of tariffs.

       1. Tariffs protect workers and firms in relatively inefficient industries.

       2. Some contend that tariffs stimulate domestic employment in general by increasing demand for relatively cheap domestic goods.

          a. This argument fails to consider the effects of possible retaliatory actions by trading partners.

       3. Tariffs foster the development of infant domestic industries currently unable to compete with mature foreign firms.

       4. Tariffs can be used to sustain domestic industries vital to national defense, such as steel, rubber, and munitions.

       5. The threat of a tariff may persuade a foreign country to reduce the price of its exports. When this occurs, the terms of trade improve for the tariff-threatening nation.

          a. Such action is effective, however, only if the trading partner does not retaliate.

   C. The implementation of a tariff is usually done for political rather than economic reasons.

       1. Labor unions and business associations may lobby for tariff protection when their industries are threatened by foreign competition.

          a. Since most citizens are unaware of the undesirable effects of tariffs, it is apparent to politicians that the welfare of a small, but vocal, group of individuals can be enhanced by restricting trade in this manner, while the burden is borne by an unaware public.

       2. Since it can be instituted by presidential decree, without Congressional approval, a tariff may be considered politically superior to a more efficient program requiring the consent of Congress.

KEY TERMS

You should be familiar with the meaning of the terms listed below. For definition of these terms, please refer to the glossary at the end of your textbook and to the appropriate section in this chapter.

tariff
specific tariff
ad valorem tariff

CONCEPTS AND DEFINITIONS

Fill-in Questions

Complete each sentence by writing in the blank the most appropriate word or words from the terms listed below or by circling the word in parentheses that is correct.

quota
embargo
infant industry
comparative advantage
inefficiency

retaliatory measures
national defense
ad valorem tariff
tariff
specific tariff

1. A 10 percent tax on the total value of all shipments of Russian vodka into the United States is an example of a(n) _____.

2. Since tariffs benefit comparatively disadvantaged industries, they subsidize
_____.

3. A tariff may elicit _____ by adversely affected trading partners.

4. A tariff may be imposed to protect and develop industries considered necessary for _____.

5. A(n) _____ places an absolute limit on the volume of imports, and a(n) _____ simply makes imports more expensive.

6. If the United States desires to eliminate, rather than limit, trade with another country, the appropriate policy is to declare (a)n _____.

7. If Brazil wishes to encourage domestic automobile production, the government may justify a 10 percent tax on all imported automobiles because automobile production is a(n) _____.

8. When restrictive policies are enacted by nations, international trade cannot be conducted solely on the basis of _____.

9. The effectiveness of a(n) _____ in restricting trade is reduced during extended periods of significant inflation.

10. A(n) _____ is preferable to a(n) _____ if a government desires to limit the importation of a good for which the domestic demand is highly price inelastic.

11. Identify each statement as an argument for protectionist policies (P) or an argument for free trade (F).

    a. Some industries may not have a comparative advantage but they are vital to national defense.

    b. Some newly created industries need time to become competitive with the same industries in more advanced countries.

    c. The protection of "disadvantaged" industries results in an allocation of resources to inefficient industries.

    d. A nation that produces only one good will be at the mercy of the world market price for the good and may suffer greatly from world price fluctuations.

    e. In the absence of retaliation, a country will be able to export more than it imports.

    f. Monetary and fiscal policies would have more immediate effects on employment without inefficient resource allocation.

    g. Tariffs may provide badly needed revenues to the government.

    h. Diversification of the economy may not be the best road to economic development.

    i. Wealth is money and there will be more money coming into the country than leaving the country.

Multiple Choice Questions

Circle the correct answer.

1. In today's economy, the primary motive for imposing tariffs on imported goods is

    a. to generate revenue for government.

    b. to protect domestic firms from foreign competition.

    c. the desire to achieve self-sufficiency through the elimination of international trade.

    d. to protect the consumer by preventing an influx of inferior foreign goods.

2. Viewed from a supply and demand perspective, a $25 per ton tax on imported steel would

    a. increase the supply of imported steel, and decrease the demand for domestic steel.

b. decrease the demand for imported steel without affecting the domestic market.

c. increase the demand for domestic steel, and decrease the supply of imported steel.

d. increase the demand for domestic steel without affecting foreign steel producers.

3. If a demand for an imported good is price elastic, the imposition of a tariff will

a. cause the price of the good to increase by the amount of the levy.

b. not alter the amount of the product that is purchased.

c. result in a significant increase in price, but an insignificant reduction in quantity demanded.

d. result in a marked reduction in quantity purchased.

4. Import quotas are sometimes employed when

a. an embargo fails to reduce imports.

b. a price elastic product demand renders a tariff ineffective.

c. a tariff fails to discourage domestic purchases of foreign goods.

d. domestic producers are unable to satisfy increases in demand because they are already operating at full capacity.

5. If comparative advantage dictates that the United States import cabbage from Ireland, but a tariff is subsequently imposed on this product by the United States,

a. cabbage will be produced more efficiently than it had been in the past.

b. the nation possessing an absolute advantage should specialize in cabbage production.

c. Americans will pay a higher price for cabbage than they would have paid if trade was unrestricted.

d. Americans will pay a higher price for cabbage than they would have paid in the absence of trade.

6. The impact of a tariff on overall domestic employment is

a. difficult to predict without more information.

b. positive, because domestic producers of the commodity on which the levy is imposed satisfy increased demand by hiring more labor.

c. positive, even if foreign countries respond by imposing tariffs of their own.

d. negative, because the tariff reduces production thereby causing a decline in employment opportunities.

7. One problem associated with imposing tariffs to protect infant industries is

a. the difficulty of determining how long this protection should be maintained.

b. the inability of recently established firms to meet the increased demand for output generated by the tariff.

c. that such protection retards the industrialization process in less developed countries.

d. the tendency of unprotected industries to experience sharp decreases in demand.

8. The political popularity of tariffs may be accounted for by the fact that

a. they increase the price of imports while domestic prices are unaffected.

b. their adverse economic impact is not well understood by the general public.

c. they definitely increase employment opportunities in the economy as a whole.

d. they restrict the flow of American dollars abroad.

9. A tariff subsidizes protected firms in the sense that

a. these firms experience increased demand as a result of the levy.

b. the revenue generated by the levy is used to provide direct financial assistance to these firms.

c. it reduces their production costs.

d. it reduces their tax burden.

10. A United States embargo on all grain exports to the Soviet Union would likely

a. leave the income of United States wheat farmers unchanged.

b. affect the supply of grain in the United States market, but not its price.

c. decrease the supply of grain in the United States market.

d. decrease the price of grain in the United States market.

APPLICATIONS

1. As a government trade official, you propose to limit automobile imports over the next five years by imposing a tariff. Would a government forecast of 15 percent annual inflation over this time period affect your decision as to the *type* of tariff which should be levied? Explain.

2. a. Demonstrate, through use of the accompanying supply and demand graphs, how the imposition of a $1000 tax on all American imports of Japanese automobiles affects the markets for both American and Japanese produced automobiles.

   b. Explain how the degree of price elasticity of demand for Japanese autos influences the effectiveness of the tariff, assuming that the purpose of the levy is to protect the American auto industry.

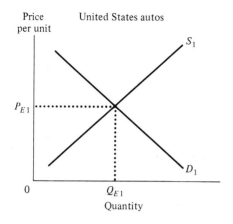

Price per unit   United States autos

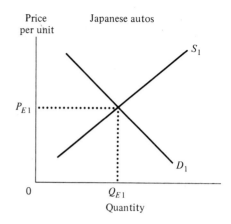

Price per unit   Japanese autos

ANSWERS

Fill-in Questions

1. *ad valorem* tariff
2. inefficiency
3. retaliatory measures
4. national defense
5. quota; tariff
6. embargo
7. infant industry
8. comparative advantage
9. specific tariff
10. quota; tariff

11.
a. P
b. P
c. F
d. P
e. P
f. F
g. P
h. F
i. P

Multiple Choice Questions

1. b
2. c
3. d
4. c
5. c
6. a
7. a
8. b
9. a
10. d

APPLICATIONS

1. If the purpose of the tariff is to protect the domestic automobile industry, an *ad valorem* tax would be preferable to a specific tariff during an extended period of inflation. This is true because the fixed per unit charge associated with the specific tariff is less successful in discouraging imports as continued inflation lessens the severity of the tax bite. An *ad valorem* tariff, on the other

hand, would be a given percentage of the automobile's market value. Therefore, as inflation causes auto prices to rise, the absolute size of the tariff also rises, and the ability of the levy to limit imports is unaffected by the inflationary spiral.

2. a. The tariff causes the price of Japanese autos to increase (to P_{E2}) and the quantity sold to decrease Q_{E2} as the supply curve shifts to the left (from S_1 to S_2). This higher price makes autos produced in the United States appear relatively cheap, so the demand for American autos increases from D_1 to D_2 with a corresponding increase from Q_{E1} to Q_{E2} and from P_{E1} to P_{E2}.

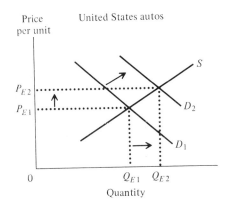 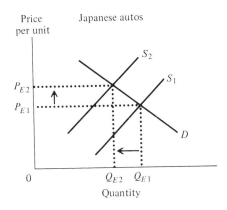

   b. If the demand for Japanese autos in the United States is highly price inelastic, the higher price has little effect on the number of cars sold. If demand is highly elastic, consumers are very responsive to the higher price and reduce their purchases of Japanese autos significantly. In terms of protecting the American auto industry, therefore, the tariff will be more effective if the demand for Japanese autos is price elastic than if it is price inelastic.

Chapter 38

Exchange Rates and the Balance of Payments

LEARNING OBJECTIVES

Having identified the advantages of unrestricted trade between nations in Chapter 36, we now consider the *process* by which trade takes place. When nations trade, money is exchanged for commodities. Since monetary units employed in each trading nation differ, however, currencies must be exchanged so that the seller receives payment in domestic monetary units. In this chapter, we investigate how the rates at which currencies may be exchanged for one another are determined. In addition, the impact of trade on exchange rates is considered, as are the economic implications of both fluctuating exchange rates and imbalances between exports and imports.

After reading this chapter, you should be able to:

1. explain how exchange rates are determined under a gold standard, a gold exchange standard, and a system of floating exchange rates;

2. explain how each of the exchange rate systems eliminates export-import imbalances;

3. cite the advantages and disadvantages of each of the exchange rate systems;

4. identify the components of the balance-of-payments statement;

5. distinguish between a nation's balance of payments and its balance of trade.

CHAPTER OUTLINE

I. Since sellers generally desire payment in domestic currency, international trade requires that buyers convert payments into the monetary unit of the seller's nation. The price at which one currency is converted into another is called the exchange rate. For example, an exchange rate of $2 = 1 £ indicates that two American dollars may be exchanged for one British pound, and vice versa. Three exchange rate systems have been employed during the twentieth century.

A. Under the gold standard, each country agreed both to convert paper money into gold at a set rate and to send gold in the amount by which its imports exceeded its exports to trading partners.
   1. Since the exchange rate was fixed, each buyer knew precisely how much currency would have to be exchanged in order to purchase foreign merchandise.
   2. Under the gold standard, a nation's money supply was directly related to its domestic gold stock.
      a. For example, if imports exceeded exports, gold would flow out of a country, thereby reducing its money supply. This contraction in the money supply, in turn, reduced aggregate demand, which ultimately resulted in production cutbacks and increased unemployment. The lower level of spending also exerted downward pressure on prices or, at least, diminished inflationary pressures in the economy.
         (1) The moderation in the rate of inflation made domestic goods relatively cheap in comparison to foreign goods. The relatively cheap domestic goods made a nation's exports attractive to foreign countries, while imports appeared more costly to domestic consumers. Consequently exports increased and imports decreased, so that the original trade imbalance was eliminated over time.
B. At the end of World War II, many nations adopted a modified version of the gold standard called the gold-exchange standard. Under this scheme, the exchange value of each currency was fixed in terms of gold and American dollars.
   1. In an attempt to alleviate the unemployment problem resulting from large gold outflows under the gold standard, the new system allowed a nation with a *temporary* export-import imbalance to borrow needed funds from the International Monetary Fund (IMF). Repayment was expected as soon as the unusual circumstances causing the imbalance were rectified.
C. In 1971, the United States announced that a system of floating exchange rates would replace the gold-exchange standard. The change occurred because a long-term balance-of-payments deficit had both increased the stock of foreign dollars in the United States and shrunk the domestic gold supply, thereby leading the United States to cease conversion of foreign-held dollars into gold.
   1. Exchange rates are presently determined by the forces of supply and demand, as importers and exporters purchase the currencies they need to conduct trade.
   2. The undesirable side effects of eliminating a trade imbalance under floating exchange rates are not as serious as those associated with the gold standard.
      a. If, for example, American imports from West Germany exceed its exports, the demand for marks increases as does the value of German currency relative to the American dollar. Each mark, therefore, is

worth more American dollars than previously, while each dollar exchanges for fewer marks.

(1) As a result, German products, priced in terms of marks, cost more dollars than before. American goods priced in dollars, on the other hand, require fewer marks in exchange. Consequently, American exports appear more attractive to West Germans, while West German products (American imports) are less attractive to Americans. This change in relative export and import prices caused by the fluctuating exchange rate ultimately eliminates the trade imbalance.

(2) While prices and employment conditions in industries heavily involved in international trade are affected by this adjustment process, there are no gold inflows or outflows which cause significant changes in the overall domestic rates of inflation and unemployment.

b. The main disadvantage of this system is that fluctuating exchange rates create uncertainty for parties involved in international transactions. Foreign trade and long-term capital investments abroad, therefore, may be inhibited.

(1) Fluctuating rates created a problem for exporters and importers because the precise costs and revenues associated with *future* transactions cannot be predicted with certainty.

(a) In light of this situation, trading parties often sign a futures contract that specifies the exchange rate at which a future transaction will take place.

(2) Long-term capital investments in foreign countries are perceived as being more risky under a system of fluctuating, as opposed to fixed, exchange rates.

II. As opposed to considering only *merchandise* exports and imports, the entire range of a nation's international transactions is considered in calculating a nation's balance-of-payments position.

A. A balance-of-payments statement reflects all transactions involving funds flowing into and out of a country during a given time period. The statement is divided into three parts: the goods-and-services account; the unilateral-transfers account; and the capital account.

1. The goods-and-services account consists of merchandise transactions, military transactions, and invisible transactions.

a. If a nation's merchandise exports exceed its imports, it has a balance-of-trade surplus. When imports exceed exports, a trade deficit results.

b. Invisible transactions are transactions that do not involve the exchange of tangible goods. Investment income and transactions involving services are important items in this category.

2. The unilateral-transfers account records international transfers of resources involving no exchange or return.

a. Examples of such transfers are gifts from residents of the United States to relatives living abroad, government pension and Social

Security payments to individuals living abroad, and grants from the United States government, to foreign countries.

b. The unilateral-transfers balance is usually negative in economically advanced nations.

3. The capital account records private capital flows resulting from loans and investments that individuals and businesses make abroad. These transactions are divided into long-term and short-term capital flows.

a. A transaction generates a long-term capital flow when the funds involved are expected to remain outside of the country from which they originate for more than one year.

b. Short-term capital flows are expected to remain in a foreign country for less than one year.

B. If the outflow of dollars from the United States in these three accounts is greater than the corresponding dollar inflow, the United States experiences a balance-of-payments deficit. When inflows exceed outflows, a balance-of-payments surplus exists.

KEY TERMS

You should be familiar with the meaning of the terms listed below. For definition of these terms, please refer to the glossary at the end of your textbook and to the appropriate section in this chapter.

exchange rate	International Monetary Fund (IMF)
gold standard	floating exchange rates
gold points	futures contract
arbitrage	balance-of-payments statement
gold-exchange standard	balance of trade

CONCEPTS AND DEFINITIONS

Fill-in Questions

Complete each sentence by writing in the blank the most appropriate word or words from the terms listed below or by circling the word in parentheses that is correct.

gold-exchange standard	unilateral-transfers account
International Monetary Fund	floating exchange rates
invisible transactions	balance-of-payments statement
exchange rate	balance-of-trade deficit
gold points	capital account
goods-and-services account	gold standard
arbitrage	futures contract
balance of trade	

1. All of a nation's annual monetary transactions with the rest of the world are recorded in its _____.

2. The _____ was established to provide funds to nations with temporary export-import imbalance problems.

3. The purpose of establishing _____ around a basically fixed exchange rate was to allow the exchange rate to reflect changes in the cost of shipping gold between nations.

4. An American importer of German beer might purchase a(n) _____ _____ for an impending shipment of Beck's beer if the value of the dollar is expected to fall relative to the mark.

5. If the price of a particular product differs in different nations, the price differentials will eventually be eliminated through the process of _____ _____.

6. Under the _____, exchange rates for currencies were defined not only in terms of gold, but also in terms of United States dollars.

7. A fixed _____ provides trading partners with certainty regarding the costs and revenues associated with an anticipated transaction.

8. When a nation's merchandise imports exceed its exports in a given year, a(n) _____ results.

9. Under the _____, changes in a nation's stock of gold directly affected the size of its money supply.

10. In comparison to the gold standard, the adjustment process to trade imbalances under a system of _____ is largely confined to exporting and importing industries, while relatively minor impact is exerted on the economy as a whole.

11. The account of exports and imports of merchandise is also called the _____.

12. Payments such as interest on foreign investments that do not involve an exchange of tangible goods are often called _____.

13. The *basic* balance of payments is made up of the balances on three accounts caled the _____ _____ accounts.

Multiple Choice Questions

Circle the correct answer.

1. If a nation's exports exceed its imports under the gold standard, the international adjustment process to this imbalance will cause its

   a. price level to decrease.

   b. money supply to decrease.

    c. exchange rate to increase.

    d. stock of gold to increase.

2. The adoption of the gold-exchange standard by most important trading nations at the end of World War II

    a. caused significant uncertainty for importers and exporters since exchange rates were no longer fixed.

    b. meant that the exchange value of each currency was no longer fixed in terms of gold.

    c. increased the prominence of the American dollar in international trade.

    d. strengthened the link between a nation's gold stock and its money supply.

3. As a result of the role played by the International Monetary Fund (IMF) under the gold-exchange standard

    a. nations with temporary trade deficits could ship borrowed funds, rather than gold, to their trading partners.

    b. the inflows and outflows of gold previously associated with trade imbalances were completely eliminated.

    c. the plight of nations with long-term trade deficits was greatly improved.

    d. the domestic impact of trade deficit was softened as nations were permitted to ship dollars, rather than gold, to trading partners.

4. Under a system of floating exchange rates, a nation with a balance-of-trade surplus ultimately finds that

    a. each unit of its currency can be exchanged for fewer units of foreign currency.

    b. the prices of the goods that it imports increase.

    c. its stock of gold is increased.

    d. its exports appear relatively expensive to citizens of foreign countries.

5. The gold-exchange standard ceased to operate because

    a. the IMF declared bankruptcy.

    b. the United States stopped converting foreign-held dollars into gold.

    c. foreign countries refused to accept American dollars, the value of which was declining, as payment in international trade transactions.

    d. widely fluctuating exchange rates were disrupting international trade.

6. Assuming all other factors constant, if American demand for Mexican oil increases under a system of floating exchange rates

    a. each dollar will exchange for more pesos than previously.

    b. the cost of oil to American consumers will increase, but the prices of other items imported from Mexico will be unchanged.

   c. the cost to American consumers of all goods imported from Mexico will increase.

   d. each peso will exchange for fewer dollars than previously.

7. A gold standard is superior to a system of floating exchange rates in that it

   a. renders inflows and outflows of gold, in response to trade imbalances, unnecessary.

   b. provides importers and exporters with reliable information regarding the costs and revenues involved in future transactions.

   c. minimizes the effect of eliminating trade imbalances on the price and output levels of trading nations.

   d. provides a self-adjusting mechanism through which export-import balances may be corrected.

8. Under a system of floating exchange rates, an American citizen considering the purchase of a Sony color television set from a Japanese manufacturer next year would desire a futures contract if she expects

   a. That American imports from Japan will far exceed American exports to Japan during the current year.

   b. the exchange rate to remain constant.

   c. that the exchange rate will change from its current level of $1 = 250 yen to $1 = 300 yen next year.

   d. that each dollar will buy more yen next year than it buys this year.

9. If, in a given year, merchandise exports are $85 billion while imports are $82 billion, the United States shows

   a. $3 billion balance-of-payments surplus.

   b. $3 billion balance-of-payments deficit.

   c. $3 billion balance-of-trade deficit.

   d. $3 billion balance-of-trade surplus.

10. A credit entry in the United States' balance-of-payments statement results when

   a. a United States resident receives interest income from a business investment in Brazil.

   b. the United States government sends free food to countries experiencing famine.

   c. a United States citizen deposits dollars in a Swiss bank account.

   d. the United States imports perfume from France.

11. If the United States' balance-of-payments statement shows a surplus for a given year

a. its exports necessarily exceed its imports.

b. its imports necessarily exceed its exports.

c. more dollars flowed into the United States than flowed out.

d. more dollars flowed out of the United States than flowed in.

APPLICATIONS

1. The Cardoza family wishes to purchase a BMW automobile. What is its price in American dollars, if its British price is £ 12,000 and

   a. the exchange rate is 1 £ = $2.30? _____.

   b. the exchange rate is 1 £ = $2.50? _____.

2. Given your understanding of the concept of price elasticity of demand, how would you expect the dramatic increase in oil prices charged by OPEC nations to affect the balance of trade in the U.S.? Explain.

ANSWERS

Fill-in Questions

1. balance-of-payments statement
2. International Monetary Fund
3. gold points
4. futures contract
5. arbitrage
6. gold-exchange standard
7. exchange rate

8. balance-of-trade deficit
9. gold standard
10. floating exchange rates
11. balance of trade
12. invisible transactions
13. goods-and-services, capital, and unilateral-transfers

Mutliple Choice Questions

1. d
2. c
3. a
4. d
5. b
6. c

7. b
8. a
9. d
10. a
11. c

APPLICATIONS

1. a. $27,600 (2.30 × 12,000)

   b. $30,000 (2.50 × 12,000) (NOTE: When the value of the dollar declines relative to other currencies, the price of American imports increases.)

2. Since the demand for oil is price inelastic, American imports of this product have not declined significantly, despite drastic price increases in recent years. Consequently, the value of oil imports has skyrocketed, contributing greatly to persistent American balance-of-trade deficits.

Chapter 39

Current Problems in International Economics

LEARNING OBJECTIVES

Having studied the basic theoretical aspects of international trade and finance in Chapters 36 through 38, we now examine the international sector from an historical perspective. In this chapter, events that significantly affected world trade from 1914 to the present are discussed. Furthermore, several factors which may influence the course of activity in the world economy during the 1980s are considered.

After reading this chapter, you should be able to:

1. explain how and why tariff policy in the United States has changed since World War I;

2. explain how balance-of-trade disequilibria have been eliminated under the gold standard, gold-exchange standard, and floating exchange-rate system;

3. cite the factors which have contributed to the decline of the American dollar in recent years.

CHAPTER OUTLINE

I.   World Wars I and II, the Great Depression, and changing attitudes regarding protectionism greatly influenced international trade over the past 60 years.
    A. Balance-of-trade surpluses and gold inflows characterized American foreign trade activity during World War I as European nations depended heavily on the United States for supplies.
    B. World trade was vigorous during the 1920s, but declined drastically during the thirties.
       1. Worldwide depression reduced income significantly, thereby decreasing the demand for American exports.
       2. Many nations imposed import tariffs in an attempt to stimulate demand for domestic products. These measures discouraged world trade.
    C. During World War II, worldwide demand for goods increased spectacularly, and the volume of trade escalated.

   1. Since production in the United States was not interrupted by enemy attacks, demand for American exports was healthy, and gold flowed into the country throughout the war.
   D. In the early post-World War II period, the General Agreement on Tariffs and Trade (GATT) significantly reduced tariffs in most major trading nations. As a result, international trade expanded.
   1. The Trade Expansion Act, passed by Congress in 1962, led to further tariff reductions.
   2. During the 1970s, however, trade restrictions have been adopted in the United States to protect industries that are experiencing stiff foreign competition.
   E. Formation of the European Economic Community, or Common Market, has liberalized trade between member nations. Whether or not the world, as a whole, will benefit from this arrangement is, as yet, uncertain.
II.   In the area of international finance, the methods of dealing with balance-of-trade disequilibria have changed significantly over time.
   A. Under the gold standard, trade imbalances were rectified by gold transfers between trading nations.
   1. Gold outflows, however, ultimately resulted in significant unemployment in trade-deficit nations.
   B. Partially as a response to the unemployment caused by gold outflows, a gold-exchange standard replaced the strict gold standard in 1944. Under this arrangement, American dollars, as well as gold, could be used to erase trade deficits.
   1. To ease the impact of eliminating a long-term trade deficit, a nation was permitted to devalue its currency by 10 percent.
   2. Temporary imbalances could be remedied by borrowing the necessary funds from the IMF.
   C. Despite an attempt to stabilize government gold holdings through the adoption of a two-tier gold system, international reserves were insufficient to settle routine trade imbalances. Consequently, the Jamaica Agreement of 1976 established a system of freely fluctuating exchange rates to correct trade imbalances.
   1. Special Drawing Rights (SDRs), a type of international reserve, replaced gold and dollar reserves as the medium for settling international trade imbalances.
      a. If one nation's balance-of-payments deficits resulted in an undesirably large accumulation of its currency in a foreign country's central bank, SDRs could be used by the nation with the deficit to purchase its currency.
      b. As long as central banks are willing to accept SDRs in settlement of international debts, the trade liquidity problem will be solved.
III.   Over the last 20 years, the value of the American dollar has generally declined.
   A. Since the gold-exchange standard allowed trade imbalances to be rectified with either gold or dollar reserves, and since the United States has generally

experienced balance-of-payments deficits over the past two decades, the amount of American dollars in foreign central banks has skyrocketed.

1. Since the demand for American dollars abroad has not kept pace with the rapidly growing supply, the value of the dollar has declined.

   a. Dollar devaluations in 1971 and 1973, while helpful, have not eliminated American balance-of-payments deficits. Therefore, foreign central banks continue to view their holdings of American dollars as excessive.

   b. The events contributing most significantly to the decline of the dollar are the increase in American dollars overseas caused by both the Marshall Plan and the Vietnam War, the tendency of highly industrialized economies, like the United States, to import more than they export, and the growing dependence of the United States on increasingly expensive imported oil.

      (1) Speculation regarding the ability of the United States to maintain the value of the dollar has sometimes led to waves of selling. Under these circumstances, the dollar's decline accelerates.

IV. International trade in the 1980s will be greatly influenced by the ultimate disposition of petrodollars by OPEC nations, by the tenor of East-West relations, by the as yet uncertain role to be played by less developed countries, and by the degree of success of the world community in managing the liquidity problems associated with trade imbalances.

KEY TERMS

You should be familiar with the meaning of the terms listed below. For definition of these terms, please refer to the glossary at the end of your textbook and to the appropriate section in this chapter.

"most favored nation" clause	parity value
European Economic Community	Special Drawing Rights (SDRs)
devaluation	petrodollars

CONCEPTS AND DEFINITIONS

Fill-in Questions

Complete each sentence by writing in the blank the most appropriate word or words from the terms listed below or by circling the word in parentheses that is correct.

devaluation	parity value
dumping	"most-favored-nation" clause
trade-adjustment assistance	petrodollars
two-tier gold system	European Economic Community
tariff reductions	Special Drawing Rights (SDRs)

1. Under the floating exchange-rate system, _____ are used to settle international trade imbalances.

2. _____ attempts to minimize the adverse impact of tariff reductions on relatively inefficient domestic industries.

3. As a signatory of GATT, France benefits under the _____ from a tariff-reduction agreement between the United States, a GATT signatory, and China, a nonsignatory.

4. A currency's _____ stipulated the rate at which it could be exchanged for dollars under the gold-exchange standard.

5. Increasing American imports of OPEC oil have resulted in large sums of _____ in Middle Eastern nations.

6. An agreement specifying a general round of _____ ultimately results in increased international trade.

7. With establishment of the _____ in 1968, the price of privately held gold became subject to the market forces of supply and demand.

8. _____ of the American dollar makes American exports relatively cheap in the world market, while American imports become more expensive.

9. The purpose of the _____ is to increase trade among its members through the gradual elimination of tariffs and quotas.

10. While _____ of foreign goods on the market in the United States adversely affects domestic employment, it benefits the American consumer.

Multiple Choice Questions

Circle the correct answer.

1. The "dollar shortage" in the early World War II period was partially the result of

    a. a dramatic decrease in the American money supply.

    b. hoarding.

    c. persistent American balance-of-payments deficits.

    d. the inability of many foreign nations to produce goods for export to the United States.

2. When a group of nations agrees to general tariff reductions

    a. trade increases, but domestic production in each nation is reduced.

    b. trade occurs on the basis of absolute, as opposed to comparative, advantage.

c. consumers in all nations involved pay lower prices for imported goods.

d. all industries in all nations involved benefit from the agreement.

3. When a nation devalues its currency

   a. it may be attempting to remedy a persistent balance-of-trade deficit.

   b. the price of its export goods to foreign nations increases, while the price of the goods it imports declines.

   c. its rate of unemployment eventually increases.

   d. each unit of its currency exchanges for a greater number of units of foreign currencies.

4. The two-tier gold system was introduced in order to

   a. stem the gold inflows and outflows associated with correcting balance-of-trade disequilibria.

   b. stabilize the stock of government gold reserves.

   c. eliminate gold transactions between private (nongovernmental) parties.

   d. tie the private sector price of gold to the parity value established by government.

5. Under the current system of floating exchange rates, trade imbalances may be settled by the transfer of

   a. gold between nations.

   b. dollars between nations.

   c. either gold or dollars between nations.

   d. Special Drawing Rights between nations.

6. The declining value of the American dollar

   a. only serves to worsen our balance-of-trade situation.

   b. makes European vacations more costly for American tourists.

   c. increases the price of domestically produced goods to American consumers.

   d. could be reversed if American imports exceeded exports.

7. Over the past 20 years, the United States has generally settled its balance-of-payments deficits by

   a. persuading foreign governments to hold their surplus dollars.

   b. shipping gold to its trading partners.

   c. generating balance-of-payments surpluses to offset the deficits.

   d. imposing tariffs so as to reduce imports.

8. In attempting to defend the value of the dollar in recent years, the American government has occasionally

a. sold dollars to foreign buyers on the world market.

b. undertaken policies that lowered domestic interest rates, and thereby attracted foreign capital to the United States.

c. sold gold to foreign buyers on the world market.

d. increased the rate of growth of the money supply as a sign to the world community of the American commitment to eliminating domestic inflation.

9. The decline of the American dollar during the 1970s can be partially attributed to

a. an influx of foreign currencies into the United States.

b. a lack of economic growth that accelerated American demand for imported goods.

c. the massive outflow of petrodollars to the OPEC nations.

d. waves of speculative dollar buying in the private sector.

10. The American government objects to the "dumping" of foreign goods in American markets because this practice

a. helps reduce inflationary pressures in the economy.

b. ultimately reduces employment opportunities in certain domestic industries.

c. results in import prices that exceed production costs.

d. results in an influx of low-quality consumer goods.

ANSWERS

Fill-in Questions

1. Special Drawing Rights (SDRs)
2. trade-adjustment assistance
3. "most-favored-nation" clause
4. parity value
5. petrodollars

6. tariff reductions
7. two-tier system
8. devaluation
9. European Economic Community
10. dumping

Multiple Choice Questions

1. d
2. c
3. a
4. b
5. d

6. b
7. a
8. c
9. c
10. b

Chapter 40

Alternative Economic Systems

LEARNING OBJECTIVES

The capitalist market economy described in this text is just one of the many ways of organizing and utilizing resources to meet human needs. In this chapter, some alternatives to capitalism are described, and these alternatives and capitalism are then compared and evaluated according to several criteria. The purpose of these comparisons is not to determine which system is best, but rather, to provide insight into the ways that each system attempts to answer the basic economic questions confronting society.

After reading this chapter, you should be able to:

1. identify the criteria that are commonly used in comparing the performance of alternative economic systems;

2. describe the characteristics of a capitalist or market economy and a socialist or command economy, and assess the performance of each;

3. identify the ways in which the American economy differs from the model of a capitalist economy, and how the Soviet economy differs from the socialist model;

4. describe the characteristics of other economic systems that contain features of both capitalism and socialism, and identify some of the strengths and short-comings of those systems.

CHAPTER OUTLINE

I. Although exact comparisons are not possible because of measurement difficulties, there are several criteria that are commonly used in comparing different economic systems: size of real per-capita GNP; rate of economic growth; stability of prices and output; the extent of individual economic security; how efficiently resources are used; the degree of equity in the distribution of income and wealth; and the extent to which economic freedoms are available to the population.

A. Economic systems are often classified according to the way in which activities of various sectors of the economy are organized and directed or according to ownership of productive resources.
  1. A decentralized system of decision making is the foundation of a market economy. Large numbers of individuals act independently to determine what will be produced, how, and the distribution of output.
  2. A centralized or command economy relies on agencies of the central government to decide what and how much to produce and, at times, how output is distributed.
  3. Economic systems in which most resources are privately owned are identified as capitalist, and systems in which most productive resources are publicly owned are called socialist.
II.   Central to the economic model of capitalism is a price system that coordinates the independent activities of households and firms. Capitalism also is characterized by consumer sovereignty.
A. The capitalist model is effective in achieving a high degree of efficiency in resource allocation, in producing a large real per-capita GNP, and in providing economic freedom.
B. As judged by other critieria, the capitalist model is less successful. There are no mechanisms to promote equality in the distribution of income or to provide individual economic security; consequently, these goals must be pursued by government policies or other means. The market mechanism also receives low marks when judged according to the criteria of economic stability and growth.
  1. The failure to achieve and maintain full employment and price stability is accounted for by the decentralized and uncoordinated decisions of individuals rather than from private ownership of the means of production.
  2. A market economy does not automatically promote economic growth because individual decisions tend to ignore long-term social benefits from savings and investment.
C. When the economy of the United States is compared to the model of a market economy, the following differences are observed.
  1. Resource allocation is not optimal because competition is absent in many markets and because the price system fails to reflect social costs.
  2. Some economic freedoms are limited by government intervention in the marketplace. This has, however, resulted in improvements in equity, economic security, stability, and growth beyond what is predicted by the capitalist model.
III. In a socialist or command economy, there is collective ownership of the means of production and decision making is centralized. Answers to the questions of what, how, and how much to produce are determined by a central planning board, with necessities receiving high priority.
A. The model of a command economy is successful in providing economic stability and security. Since the government employs all workers and controls prices, there is no unemployment and prices rarely change in response to

conditions of shortage or surplus, and they fail to reveal any inflationary pressures that may exist.

    1. Government may take steps to regulate demand by increasing taxes levied on items in short supply.

B. Income differences arise in socialist economies because compensation often is tied to the productivity of individual workers. The resulting degree of income inequality is less, however, than in most market economies.

C. In a command economy, individual freedoms may be limited in order to achieve collective goals. Consumers are free to determine their own consumption patterns, however, based on their incomes and the range of goods that are available.

D. The economy of the USSR differs from the model of the socialist state in that decisions made by central planners often fail to be fully or accurately implemented because of the extensive Soviet bureaucracy. Production decisions may also be subverted by the incentive systems used to reward managers in production facilities.

IV. Most modern economies have adopted features of both the capitalist and the socialist models.

A. In Yugoslavia, public ownership of resources is combined with a system of worker management where production and pricing decisions are made by workers at the factory level. Supply and demand influence what to produce and the profitability of specific operations. Since wages are partly tied to profitability of indiviudal firms, efficiency in production and market expansion are encouraged.

    1. Under market socialism, the central government is responsible for the overall allocation of resources in the economy.

    2. While the Yugoslav economy boasts a high rate of economic growth, it cannot provide the consistent full employment that a pure socialist economy might.

B. Since World War II, Britain has pursued a goal of greater equity through income redistribution. In this basically capitalist economy, high income taxes have been used to finance extensive social-welfare programs. The British government has also nationalized key industries that were unprofitable when privately owned and has subsidized others in order to preserve jobs in certain industries for British workers.

    1. Recent political changes in Britain indicate the possibility of lower taxes in the future and potentially less government involvement in the economy.

C. From 1949 to the mid-1970s, the economy of China under communist rule emphasized rural over urban development and equity over economic growth. Since the death of Mao Tse tung, however, Chinese leadership has stressed economic growth which has required greater emphasis on industrial production, material incentives, increased trade, and modernization of the economy than when the goal was agricultural development.

KEY TERMS

You should be familiar with the meaning of the terms listed below. For definition of these terms, please refer to the glossary at the end of your textbook and to the appropriate section in this chapter.

capitalist economies   socialist economies
collectivization   turnover tax
communism   command economies
consumer sovereignty

CONCEPTS AND DEFINITIONS

Fill-in Questions

Complete each sentence by writing in the blank the most appropriate word or words from the terms listed below or by circling the word in parentheses that is correct.

socialist economies   market economy
centralized economy   communism
command economies   real GNP
democratic socialism   turnover tax
collectivization   value judgments
economic freedom   capitalist economies
consumer sovereignty

1. _____ in Great Britain relied on heavy taxation to support generous spending programs.

2. In his model of _____, Marx envisioned a system based upon collective owernship of the means of production and centralized decision making.

3. As an abstract ideal, _____ is a classless society where goods are abundant and there is no need for government.

4. In 1929 under Stalin, peasant lands in Russia were confiscated and assembled into large farms through a process of _____.

5. A levy applied by government to every transaction in an economy is known as a(n) _____.

6. A central feature of a capitalist or market economy is _____.

7. A(n) _____ is said to use its productive resources efficiently when no reallocation can bring about an increase in production.

8. _____ are characterized by private ownership of most productive resources, while in _____, resources are owned by the public.

9. A(n) _____ is one in which key economic decisions are made by government.

10. A(n) _____ is characterized by decentralized decision making in which large numbers of individuals act independently.

11. _____ is judged by breadth of choice in selecting consumer goods, in choosing an occupation, and in determining what to produce.

12. _____ is never a fully accurate measure of economic well-being since many kinds of nonmarket activities are not recorded in these figures.

13. It is impossible to determine which economic system is best because any evaluation involves _____ as well as rational appraisal.

14. Another name for centralized economies is _____.

15. For each model or example of an economic system, select the areas in which the system is generally successful or ranks relatively high.

   (a) *Model of the capitalistic market system*

a. plenty	e. equity
b. growth	f. efficiency
c. stability	g. economic freedom
d. security	

   (b) *Model of the socialist command system*

a. plenty	e. equity
b. growth	f. efficiency
c. stability	g. economic freedom
d. security	

16. For each of the criteria below, indicate whether conditions in the United States economy are above or below those of the ideal capitalist market economy.

   a. economic freedom

   b. growth

   c. stability

   d. security

   e. equity

   f. efficiency

Multiple Choice Questions

Circle the correct answer.

1. The term "market socialism" best characterizes the economy of which country?

    a. Britain

    b. Yugoslavia

    c. China

    d. Russia

2. In comparing economic systems, it is impossible to determine which system is best because

    a. there is difficulty in obtaining reliable and complete statistics from all countries.

    b. there are differences among countries in the definition of important variables such as unemployed workers or households in poverty.

    c. there is difficulty in obtaining data from countries that are hostile to the United States and other Western nations.

    d. there are philosophical issues and subjective dimensions for evaluation on which reasonable individuals will always disagree.

3. After World War II, the British government pursued a goal of greater income equality through a program in which

    a. all industry was nationalized.

    b. public-service jobs were given to all workers.

    c. the rich were heavily taxes to finance extensive social programs.

    d. taxes were reduced in order to stimulate the economy and provide good jobs for all workers.

4. Most command economies are characterized by

    a. equality in the distribution of income.

    b. equality in the distribution of goods and services.

    c. full employment and price stability.

    d. economic efficiency in resource allocation.

5. In a socialist economy, the most effective way for a central planning authority to manipulate demand in cases of shortage is

    a. to increase the turnover tax rate on commodities in short supply.

    b. to decrease the turnover tax rate on commodities in short supply.

    c. to leave unchanged the turnover tax rate on commodities in short supply.

    d. to lower the turnover tax rate on all commodites including those in short supply.

6. Economic fluctuations in the United States economy are primarily caused by

    a. private ownership of the means of production.

    b. the absence of perfect competition in many markets.

c. decentralized and uncoordinated decision making.

d. an unequal distribution of income and wealth.

7. Which of the following goals could best be achieved under socialism?

a. efficient resource allocation

b. rapid economic growth

c. economic freedom

d. market equilibrium

8. An economy is using its productive resources efficiently when

a. no reallocation can bring about an increase in production.

b. the distribution of income in society is equitable.

c. households have free choice of occupations and consumer goods.

d. there is a mechanism to coordinate the activities of various sectors.

9. Intercountry comparisons which use real GNP per capita are not always accurate because

a. the rate of inflation differs from country to country.

b. the figures do not show how incomes are distributed among the population.

c. in some countries, the national income must be divided among many more people than in other countries.

d. nonmarket transactions may not show up in GNP accounting.

10. Which of the following goals could best be achieved under capitalism?

a. economic stability

b. equity

c. economic security

d. efficiency

ANSWERS

Fill-in Questions

1. democratic socialism
2. socialist economies
3. communism
4. collectivization
5. turnover tax
6. consumer sovereignty
7. market economy
8. capitalist economies; socialist economies

12. real GNP
13. value judgments
14. command economies
15. (a) a, f, g
     (b) b, c, d
16. a. below
     b. above
     c. above
     d. above

9. centralized economy
10. market economy
11. economic freedom

e. above
f. below

Multiple Choice Questions

1.	b	6.	c
2.	d	7.	b
3.	c	8.	a
4.	c	9.	d
5.	a	10.	d

Chapter 41

Radical Economics: The Old and the New Left

LEARNING OBJECTIVES

This chapter presents the basic outlines of an alternative or radical view of economics. It is based on the premise that the theories of mainstream economics, as presented in the text, have failed to offer plausible solutions to long-standing problems found in capitalistic societies such as inflation, recession, discrimination, an unequal distribution of income, and exploitation of natural resources at home and abroad.

After reading this chapter, you should be able to:

1. describe the fundamental concepts and principles of Marxist theory and the Marxian critique of capitalism;

2. identify the key elements in the radical critique of capitalism;

3. describe the response of traditional economists to radical criticisms of the existing capitalist system.

CHAPTER OUTLINE

I.   The foundation of radical economists is in the works of Karl Marx. Five concepts and principles of Marxist theory are at the center of the radical critique of capitalism.

   A. Capitalism is characterized by the existence of two opposing social classes: the bourgeoisie or capitalists, who own the means of production (factories, equipment, and other forms of capital) and the proletariat, or workers, who are employed by capitalists to produce goods and who, according to Marx, have no chance to own any part of the means of production.

   B. According to the labor theory of value, the exchange value of a commodity (the ratio at which one commodity will exchange for another) is regulated by the amount of labor time necessary for production. That is, the amount of time a worker devotes to the production of a particular product determines its exchange value.

1. In a capitalist economy, capitalists purchase labor power and sell the commodities that labor has produced. Since the working class receives only subsistence wages and since the work day exceeds the time required for a worker to produce the value equivalent of his or her subsistence, the capitalist is able to earn a profit as a result of the efforts of labor. This profit, which originates in the production of surplus value, arises because workers are exploited.

C. Capitalists must constantly acquire new and better capital or they will fall behind in the competitive struggle and be taken over by those who can compete more effectively.

1. The process of capital expansion would normally increase the demand for labor. If that were to happen, however, wages would be driven up and profits would fall. Consequently, the emphasis is on labor-saving investment and on acquiring more and more capital.

2. Investment in labor-saving machinery permits output to expand without an increase in the wages paid to workers. A pool of unemployed workers, the industrial reserve army, exerts downward pressure on wages and keeps them at a subsistence level.

3. Although more goods are now available, workers lack the purchasing power to buy them. As a result of chronic overproduction, the demand for labor is further reduced as individuals are laid off, particularly in capital goods industries. Wages and incomes fall and the misery of the proletariat worsens.

D. To counteract a falling rate of profit, capitalists seek additional outlets for their production. Through imperialism, capitalists are able to expand their markets and to achieve political and economic domination of Third World countries.

E. A proletariat revolution ultimately follows when capitalism becomes intolerable.

II. Marx's analysis predicting the demise of capitalism has had great appeal to the New Left who see features in contemporary society that seem to confirm Marx's observations.

A. The emergence of monopoly and the formation of conglomerates and multinational firms are considered indicative of the advanced stages of capitalism described by Marx.

B. In general, government is regarded to act in ways (primarily by enforcing property rights) that promote the interest of the capitalists at the expense of workers.

III. Radical economists view extant social problems not as random occurrences but as by-products of the capitalist system.

A. The combination of competition, free markets, and private property lead inexorably to inequality, discrimination, irrational behavior, and alienation in capitalist systems.

1. Discrimination as well as inequalities in income and education are encouraged by capitalists for the purpose of diverting hostility away from capitalism and keeping workers subjugated.

2. Irrational abuse of natural resources and excessive expenditures on weapons and nonessential consumer goods results from capitalist society's constant need to expand.

3. Decisions about working conditions are determined by capitalist profit calculations, without any regard for workers as individuals. This leads workers to feel alienated: divorced from their work, from other institutions in their environment, and from other individuals.

B. As an alternative to capitalism, most radical or New Left economists argue that a socialist or communist society and economy should be established in which all forms of private property are abolished. Such a society would be characterized by absolute equality in the distribution of income and wealth, in the social decision-making process, and in opportunities to fully realize one's potential.

IV. While recognizing the contributions of the New Left in emphasizing social problems that must be remedied, traditional economists respond to the radical criticisms of capitalism by attacking the theory that all value is created by labor. They also point out that while most socialist or communist societies share many of the same flaws as do capitalist societies, there is a notable loss of freedoms when an economy is organized under socialist or communist principles.

KEY TERMS

Although there are no new terms introduced in this chapter, you should be familiar with the terms listed below that are used in this chapter.

alienate	labor theory of value
bourgeoisie	liberal
conglomerates	multinationals
exchange value	New Left
falling rate of profit	private property
free markets	proletarian revolution
imperialism	proletariat
industrial reserve army	labor theory of value
inequality	radical
iron law of wages	surplus value
irrational	

CONCEPTS AND DEFINITIONS

Fill-in Questions

Complete each sentence by writing in the blank the most appropriate word or words from the terms listed above or by circling the word in parentheses that is correct.

1. Only through the process of _____ are capitalists able to find markets for ever-increasing levels of output.

2. The increasing misery of the working class under capitalism ultimately leads to a(n) _____.

3. _____ economists see little or no relationship between social and economic problems while _____ or _____ _____economists see social and economic forces as inexorably linked.

4. According to the _____, a commodity's _____ _____ is determined by the amount of labor required to produce it.

5. According to the _____ a worker's income will always remain at a subsistence level.

6. The difference between the value of production and wages paid to workers is called _____ by New Left economists.

7. Marx maintained that a(n) _____ forces investment in more efficient machinery and other forms of capital.

8. Workers who are displaced when capitalists invest in more efficient technology become part of the _____.

9. According to Marx, capitalism is characterized by two distinct social classes, the _____ and the _____.

10. According to New Left economists, the foundations of capitalism, which include _____ and _____, must be eliminated before significant social reform can occur.

11. Firms that operate in many industries are known as _____ while those that operate in many countries are _____.

12. _____ is a process by which a capitalist economy seeks global influence and authority in order to secure raw materials and access to markets.

13. Under capitalism, the actions of the bourgeoisie serve to _____ workers who lose control over their destinies.

14. According to the New Left, the most pervasive of the social problems inherent in capitalism is _____.

15. A society that turns out TVs, stereos, and cigarettes, and that spends billions on advertising these products while some people go without adequate housing and medical care would be regarded as _____ by radical economists.

16. The _____, or unemployed workers, in a capitalist nation keep wages from rising.

17. The _____ own the means of production and employ the _____ in order to produce output.

Multiple Choice Questions

Circle the correct answer.

1. A characteristic of capitalism, according to Marx, is
   a. social equality.
   b. a class structure.
   c. mainstream and radical economics.
   d. long-run competition.

2. The owners of productive assets in a capitalist economy are known as the
   a. proletariat.
   b. radicals.
   c. bourgeoisie.
   d. socialists.

3. Lack of control over one's life and a tendency to see existence as meaningless characterize
   a. alienation.
   b. inequality.
   c. irrationality.
   d. imperialism.

4. Capitalists are able to expand the market for their goods through the process of
   a. alienation.
   b. inequality.
   c. irrationality.
   d. imperialism.

5. Marx refers to the working class in a capitalist society as the
   a. proletariat.
   b. bourgeoisie.
   c. radicals.
   d. imperialists.

6. According to the labor theory of value, two commodities should exchange for one another if they both
   a. contain the same amount of surplus value.
   b. sell for the same price as determined by competitive forces of demand and supply.
   c. contain the same amount of socially necessary labor time.
   d. yield equal utility on the margin to final consumers.

7. Marx argued that capitalists need to accumulate surplus value

   a. in order to compete with other capitalists.

   b. to enable them to maintain their luxurious standard of living.

   c. to avoid overproduction of commodities.

   d. in order to keep the wages of workers at a subsistence level.

8. Surplus value arises in production

   a. because the amount of socially necessary labor to produce a commodity is reduced with mass production.

   b. in order to permit the capitalist to pay for other productive resources.

   c. because workers cannot afford to purchase all of the goods produced by capitalists.

   d. because labor never receives a wage equal to the value of the commodity it produces.

9. The names liberal, New Left, and radical refer to

   a. the same group of economists.

   b. three separate groups of economists.

   c. two groups of economists.

   d. a political party composed of economists.

10. A central belief of radical economics is that

    a. social and economic problems are unrelated but both are caused by the capitalist system.

    b. social and economic problems are related and are caused by the capitalist system.

    c. social and economic problems are related but are not caused by the capitalist system.

    d. social and economic problems are unrelated and neither is caused by the capitalist system.

11. A typical liberal economist would argue that

    a. there is a strong relationship between social and economic problems.

    b. economic problems result from past mistakes or miscalculations.

    c. government is controlled by big business and, thus, will not carry out social reform.

    d. political, sociological, and technological factors interact to form an economic system.

12. According to the New Left, the purpose of discrimination is to

    a. direct worker hostility away from capitalists.

b. ensure that the industrial reserve army can fill its manpower requirements without resorting to the draft.

c. keep women and minorities from competing for jobs for which they are un-qualified.

d. increase the amount of surplus value from the commodities produced by women and minorities.

13. After the revolution, New Left economists envision a society in which

a. the profits from production are used to satisfy human needs.

b. the central government will determine what goods should be produced to yield the greatest social happiness.

c. there is further division of labor in manufacturing so as to increase produc-tion for the good of mankind.

d. all forms of private property are abolished.

ANSWERS

Fill-in Questions

1. imperialism
2. proletarian revolution
3. liberal; New Left (or radical); radical (or New Left)
4. labor theory of value; exchange value
5. iron law of wages
6. surplus value
7. falling rate of profit
8. industrial reserve army
9. bourgeoisie; proletariat (in any order)
10. private property; free markets (in any order)
11. conglomerates; multinationals
12. imperialism
13. alienate
14. inequality
15. irrational
16. industrial reserve army
17. bourgeoisie; proletariat

Multiple Choice Questions

1. b
2. c
3. a
4. d
5. a
6. c
7. a
8. d
9. c
10. b
11. b
12. a
13. d